Worship and Wilderness

Worship and Wilderness

*Culture, Religion, and Law
in the Management of
Public Lands and Resources*

Lloyd Burton

THE UNIVERSITY OF WISCONSIN PRESS

The University of Wisconsin Press
1930 Monroe Street
Madison, Wisconsin 53711

www.wisc.edu/wisconsinpress/

3 Henrietta Street
London WC2E 8LU, England

5   4   3   2   1

Printed in the United States of America

Library of Congress Cataloging-in-Publication Data
Burton, Lloyd.
Worship and wilderness: culture, religion, and law in
the management of public lands and resources / Lloyd Burton.
p. cm.
Includes index.
ISBN 0-299-18080-8 (cloth: acid-free paper)
ISBN 0-299-18084-0 (pbk.: acid-free paper)
1. Nature—Religious aspects. 2. Public lands—Management. I. Title.

BL435 .B87 2002
291.1′78362′0973—dc21
2002003309

Contents

Acknowledgments

Many years ago in imperial Russia, a village rabbi set out on his morning walk to the synagogue to pray, just as he had at the same time every morning for the past thirty years. The town Cossack, in an especially bad mood that day, accosted him and rudely asked, "Where do you think you're going?" "You never know," the rabbi replied. Aware of the rabbi's routines and infuriated at what he considered a disingenuous response, the Cossack marched him straight to the town jail. As he was thrown into his cell, the rabbi turned and repeated, "See? You never know . . ."

The journey ending in production of this book (happily not including a visit to jail) began several years ago, with my having no idea at the time what would be its final destination. A mutual student introduced me to Dave Ruppert, a National Park Service anthropologist and adjunct professor at the University of Colorado campus where we both teach. What grew out of that meeting—and a considerable amount of collaborative research to follow—was a coauthored law review article on the management of sacred sites on public lands, featuring a case study on an intercultural consultation he had facilitated at Devils Tower National Monument. (See Lloyd Burton and Dave Ruppert, "Bear's Lodge or Devils Tower: Inter-Cultural Relations, Legal Pluralism, and the Management of Sacred Sites on Public Lands," *Cornell Journal of Law and Public Policy* 8, no. 2 [1999], 201. Permission to include major portions of that text in chapter 6 and small portions of chapter 12 in this manuscript is hereby gratefully acknowledged.) Dave's firsthand experience and reflective wisdom in advising such consultations gave our work a freshness and depth it would otherwise have lacked.

I thought the journey had come to an end, until senior editor Rosalie Robertson, then at the University of Wisconsin Press, encouraged me to use the article as the basis for a book proposal. She was just as instrumental in getting this project under way as was UWP associate director Steve Salemson in bringing it to completion. My deep appreciation to them both. And in the finishing touches department, thanks to my old friend, mentor, and indexer *extraordinaire* Blair Boyd, former editor and publisher of *Landscape* magazine.

Several scholars with substantial knowledge and experience in the study of culture, religion, and the environment generously advised me in the preparation of this manuscript and critiqued its findings. Among those who most freely shared their own wisdom on these matters were Ronald Trosper, director of the Native American Forestry Program at Northern Arizona University, and Vine Deloria Jr., professor emeritus of history, University of Colorado at Boulder. But for their strong support and encouragement, this book might never have come into being. And since they were equally generous in pointing out areas in which their thinking diverged from my own, I naturally bear sole responsibility for what appears here.

Several of the people acknowledged here helped me understand that for most indigenous peoples, the sacred inheres every bit as much in wildlife as it does in places. Among them, Steve Torbit, staff scientist with the National Wildlife Federation's Rocky Mountain Natural Resource Center, provided me with research and advice on these matters that contributed significantly to the preparation of chapter 8, an earlier version of which also appeared as a journal article. (See Lloyd Burton, "Wild Sacred Icon or Woolly Cow? Culture and the Legal Reconstruction of the American Bison," *Political and Legal Anthropology Review* 23, no. 2 [2000], 21. Permission to include major portions of that text in this manuscript is hereby gratefully acknowledged.)

Over the years a number of wise people from various indigenous culture groups have kindly instructed me in some of the teachings on nature and spirituality that their own elders have authorized them to share with outsiders. At the same time, they all made it clear to me that they were describing their own understanding rather than presuming to speak on behalf of their entire tribe or culture group. In this regard, a heartfelt *mahalo* to Ed Stevens and my *(kama aina)* brother Scott for re-introducing me to the Big Island, and to my sister Barbara for reminding me just how essential to our well-being a personal connection to place can be.

Dozens of federal land management agency employees in the National Park Service, the U.S. Forest Service, and the Bureau of Land Management have expressed to me their own experience-based perspectives on the themes raised in this book. And as with tribal peoples, while these public servants provided me with in-depth background on the challenging management situations they face, they also made it clear to me that they were speaking for themselves, rather than on behalf of the agencies where they are employed.

Regarding rediscovery of the sacred in nature among various Euro-American religious organizations, it was Mirabai Bush, director of the Center for Contemplative Mind in Society, who first introduced me to Paul Gorman and thereby to the National Religious Partnership for the Environment, which he heads. Exposure to this group and to the movement it represents greatly expanded my understanding of the emergence of environmental stewardship as a mainstream Euro-American religious cause, which, in turn, considerably expanded the scope and perspective of this book.

Over the last quarter-century, my own contemplative rediscovery of the natural world has been measurably aided by Buddhist teacher–friends Joseph Goldstein, Sharon Salzberg, and Jack Kornfield. Nature (including humans) as a seamless web of sentient beings who inevitably harm themselves whenever they systematically harm each other is as much a teaching of the Buddhist and Taoist traditions as it is any of those indigenous to the Americas. However, it took these skilled teachers to help me develop an internalized experience of that perspective. The work of Joanna Macy has also been invaluable in this regard.

Not surprisingly, for me such nature-based rediscovery and renewal often happens in the company of family and close friends of many years. For these times together in outdoor re-creation, my enduring thanks go to my wife, Abby, and daughters, Robin and Ginger; to Aidan, Dan, Djuna, Mudita, Robert, Rose, Terry, and Wes; and to fellow Prescotteer Tom Robinson. May all beings be as fortunate as we have been, to see this beautiful world together, and through each other's eyes.

PART ONE
Culture and Spirituality

1

Full Circle

Return to the Source

In the Beginning

In the beginning was ... what? the Big Bang (Western science)? the Word (Judaism, Christianity)? the Tao (Taoism)? Earth Mother and Sky Father (the Zuni tradition)? some combination (or none) of the above?

How you answer that question is important, since it affects how you will understand and react to what you read here. For even though this work addresses broad questions of public policy and law, it is also concerns inner matters: the spiritual dimensions of the personal relationship that we each have with the lands we hold in common. On these issues, we may have deep feelings and strongly held views, and a basis for agreement among us may not always be apparent.

This volume is a study of how culture, spirituality, and law have combined to affect the management of public lands within the United States and how they may also affect the future. The closing decades of the twentieth century witnessed a steady rise in discussions, debates, and sometimes rancorous disputes over the use of public lands and resources for spiritual purposes, especially in the federally held lands in the western states. Many of these cases involved the cultural and spiritual interests of American Indian tribes on the one hand and the recreational, scientific, or resource-extractive interests of the dominant culture on the other; a closer look usually shows the real situation to be far more complex and multidimensional, however.

This book had its genesis in some earlier research on one such case, which concerned the management of a national monument on public lands in northeastern Wyoming.[1] Most of the American public knows the site as Devils Tower National Monument, and experienced rock climbers throughout the world know it as one of the premier vertical crack-climbing structures in the Western Hemisphere. But to many of the Plains Indian tribes in the area, it is the Bear's Lodge, a sacred site where from pre-Columbian times to the present these sometimes warring groups have gathered late every spring to make peace, to trade, and to perform the ritual observances on which their individual spiritual well-being and the cultural survival of their tribes are thought to depend.

Beginning in the early 1990s, several months of discussions, negotiations, and intercultural learning produced a consensus-based climbing management plan for this site that included a moratorium on climbing during June—the month of the summer solstice. But no sooner had the ink dried on the document than a group of commercial climbing guides (whose incomes would be negatively affected) challenged it in federal court, on the argument that for the National Park Service to disallow commercial climbing during the solstice represented a federal government establishment of Indian religion, in violation of the First Amendment to the U.S. Constitution.

A federal trial judge initially agreed in part, ruling that the National Park Service could *ask* climbers not to ascend the six-hundred-foot vertical rock faces during the designated period, but it could not *forbid* them from doing so. In the wake of this ruling, in June of 1998 some 85 percent of the climbers who would otherwise have climbed then agreed not to, while a defiant minority chose the summer solstice of that year to climb directly in the view of a Sun Dance being hosted near the site by a Lakota spiritual leader.

As I watched those climbers inching their way up the west wall on that solstice day, two aspects of this story struck me with particular force. The first was the power of the intercultural learning and healing that had happened near that site over the previous three years, with the climbing management plan being its principal manifestation. Plains tribal representatives had conveyed the understanding that, unlike the nonindigenous peoples of the United States, tribal members who follow traditional ways have little or no choice over where they worship. While some sacred sites are on reservation lands that are controlled by tribal governments, many of the most important ones (like Bear's Lodge/Devils Tower) became federal property during the course of westward expansion in the nineteenth century, and they are now managed for outdoor recreation and conservation purposes by the National Park Service and for a broader array of "multiple uses" by the U.S. Forest Service and the Bureau of Land Management.

Tribal representatives in these negotiations emphasized that their own spiritual renewal and their tribes' cultural survival are directly linked to the performance of specific rituals at specific places—that it is the *place* (in combination with ritual regard for it) that constitutes the religious observance. For their part, recreational climbing group representatives articulated the view that for many of them, there can sometimes be a spiritual dimension to rock climbing as well: the personally transforming, even transcendent, effect of being in such focused contact with so majestic a natural formation.

Although neither side may have fully accepted the other's position on this issue, each communicated a deeply felt, nonmaterial attachment to and respect for the site. Having a shared sense of respect and personal connection with this site was one basis on which the consensus-based plan was founded. Participants in the process were to some extent changed by their participation, and out of this mutually educative process, agreement grew.

The other lesson for me in this story was how the radically different framing of the issues in the adversarial, either/or context of constitutional litigation led to the kind of reinflammation of intercultural relations that I witnessed that day at Bear's Lodge/Devils Tower. The trial judge in that case had several options before him—other paths to a just end that could have been more supportive of the Park Service's efforts at cultural reconciliation than the one he chose.

So the end of the Bear's Lodge/Devils Tower case study was merely the beginning of a much longer quest. The focus of this earlier research was largely on intercultural dispute resolution and constitutional law, which was also the original plan for this book. But as I began to delve more deeply into the subject—and to do more reading, more interviewing, and thus more careful listening—I found that framing the issues according to these conventional categories not only would construct an inappropriately narrow view but also might perpetuate some of the very problems I was hoping to help solve.

As the work progressed, the picture began to appear as far richer, far more subtle, and more deeply interconnected than that reflected in the reductionist categories of "culture," "religion," "negotiation," and "First Amendment jurisprudence" into which I had been trying to organize the material. Something more and perhaps a little different from either a standard legal or an anthropological treatment was being called for so that I might adequately understand and describe what I was seeing.

What I have discovered over the course of this research is cultural *coevolution.* Cultures—including the dominant and indigenous ones of the United States—are not static, nor can they be if they are to survive. In changing times they must continually reweave themselves, in an ongoing process of judging what from the past should be brought forward to meet current and foreseeable future needs and what (at least for a time) should be set aside. In doing this work, I have repeatedly heard tribal spiritual and government leaders say that in facing the unprecedented social and economic problems now threatening their survival, the single most valuable asset they have is the present-day practice of their most carefully preserved spiritual traditions. And at the same time, several Euro-American religious and environmental leaders are beginning to affirm that their rediscovery of the sacred in nature has been and continues to be informed by their growing regard for indigenous American spiritual teachings.

For changes are assuredly underway in the dominant culture on questions of spirituality and the natural environment. The first is the "greening of faith," as Christian and Judaic scholars discover within the histories of their respective traditions more "environment-friendly" teachings than have previously been emphasized in the institutional transmission of their beliefs.[2] The second is the rapidly growing revival of the pre-Christian nature-based spiritual traditions of northern and western Europe, which bear more than a passing resemblance to the teachings and practices of some of the indigenous peoples of the American West.[3] Third, closely related to this pre-Christian revival and to some extent arising directly from it is yet another dynamic, which is the call from many American feminist scholars and leaders for our society to adopt a more caring and life-affirming approach to its relationship to the environment, an area of thought and action commonly referred to as "eco-feminism."[4] Fourth, American society is also experiencing a growing interest in and active practice of the teachings of several non-Western spiritual traditions, which place a central emphasis on reverence for life and oneness with nature, especially Taoism and Buddhism. Fifth, based on mistrust of too much tradition, a fair amount of spiritual ferment is going on within an array of activities apparently aimed at creating entirely new forms of worship, loosely bounded and collectively known as "New Age" spiritualism, which also tends to be heavily nature-based. The sixth and last is the example of the climbing organization representatives in the Bear's Lodge/Devils Tower case. Like those involved in similar negotiations elsewhere in the West—and like American nature writers going back at least to Thoreau—they affirmed a direct, personal, spiritual connection to natural landscape without reference to any organized religious tradition or even to a monotheistic deity.

Cultural critics of these developments see them as self-indulgent at best and dangerously corrosive of Western civilization at worst. But others (like me) see them to be as much about the viable future of Western civilization as are the concerns expressed by indigenous elders at sites like Bear's Lodge/Devils Tower for the future of their own peoples. For the dominant culture, this rediscovery of the divine in nature is an effort to reweave and deliberately diversify cultural identity as a largely instinctive effort to assure physical survival. The understanding here is that a thoroughly respectful and personal relationship with nature is necessary for members of any society who are seeking to sustain the environment on which all life depends.

From this perspective, Western civilization is not corroding but is coming full circle. It is returning to retrieve something it discarded along the way, at about the same time that Enlightenment-era scientism began its march toward dominance of European thought, and

European immigrants began their march toward dominance of the North American landscape and its indigenous peoples. Western civilization is perhaps beginning to relearn lessons from its own history that surviving tribal peoples have managed never to forget. Essayist Barry Lopez suggests that among the most important of these ancient lessons is that "it may be more important now to enter into an ethical and reciprocal relationship with everything around us than to continue to work toward the sort of control of the physical world that, until recently, we have aspired to."[5]

That is why this study begins with the suggestion that our personal perspective on these matters is important. In a democratic society, the collective power of our individual views can have great influence over how gracefully and sustainably (or not) we will go about managing our public lands. The personal and the political are related within the realms of spirituality and the environment to fully the same extent that they are on questions of gender and sexuality, ethnicity, and the control of human procreation.

Is it possible that different understandings of the same phenomenon can simultaneously exist within the mind of the same person or members of the same culture group? Consider these two different creation stories of Bear's Lodge/Devils Tower:

THE KIOWA VERSION

Seven young girls strayed from camp and were chased by bears. As the bears were about to catch them, the girls sought refuge on a low rock about three feet in height. One girl prayed for the rock to take pity on them. As a result the rock began to grow skyward pushing the girls out of reach of the bears. The bears jumped and scratched at the rock [giving it its present columnar character]. The young girls are said to be still in the sky [and became the seven stars of the Pleiades].[6]

THE WESTERN SCIENTIFIC VERSION

Some 60 million years ago, great Earth stresses began to deform the crust of the continent, resulting in the uplifting of the Rocky Mountains and Great Plains region. As the surface rock layers began to crumple and fault, magma from deep inside the Earth welled up into resulting gaps and fissures. . . . The Missouri Buttes and Devils Tower . . . are believed to be necks of extinct volcanoes. Geologic evidence indicates the Missouri Buttes formed first in two separate eruptions. The magma hardened plugging the plumbing underneath. A third eruption to the southeast resulted in Devils Tower.[7]

One way to comparatively understand these two accounts is from the perspective of logical positivism. The two different tales both describe the materialization of the same natural phenomenon; they are mutually exclusive in all their particulars, and an analysis of the available evidence will determine which one is true or correct. But there are other ways to view this apparent conflict. An alternative is to perceive them as simultaneously occurring differences in realms of knowing. Yet another is to acknowledge that each story reflects each culture's attempt to ascribe meaning to and better understand the significance of this unique monolith. The one is dispassionate, removed, and analytical; the other is intimate, personal, and intuitive. Thus the two cultures perceptually construct this landmark in two very different ways: as a geologic curiosity and rock climber's playground through one cultural lens, and as a natural cathedral through the other. This is not to say that the scientific accounting is not an accurate one within its own frame of reference—only that it is but one among several frames.

Historically, these different cultural perspectives also influenced the naming of the place. In accordance with the first of the creation stories, to the Kiowa, Crow, and some other nearby tribes this was "Bear's Lodge," the site at which to save them in a contest with a natural foe, Earth's children were lifted into the heavens. It is a portal of entry into a welcoming universe (presaging movie director Steven Spielberg's casting of the butte as a place of peaceable intergalactic "close encounters"). But to the Euro-American settler culture, which at mid-nineteenth century still tended to fear natural forces and to see wilderness as an ungodly chaotic domain to be tamed and subdued, a more fitting designation was an imprecise translation of another Indian name as "Bad God's Tower," or the "Devils Tower."[8]

Consider also the possibility that these two stories emanate from two different modes of thought. The philosopher Martin Heidegger distinguishes the first as *contemplative* thought, a reflection on meaning, from *calculative* thought, a linear process directed toward the achievement of an action-oriented end result. In many non-Western traditions, contemplative thought and knowledge are based largely on the direct sensory experience of oneself and the environment. In the words of the Keres Indian Larry Bird, "You watch, and wait, and listen and the answer will come to you. It's *yours* then, not like in school." Dennis and Barbara Tedlock, who recorded this observation, go on to comment, "What we learn in school is never ours; lectures by experts can never produce the light in us which comes when, suddenly and all at once, we *know*."[9] Stories from both the contemplative and calculative realms of thought and knowing appear frequently in this study, because as much as anything else this book is about the relationship between the two—in society and in ourselves.

Even on the social science side, there are some interesting divergences. Just as this research was getting under way, I attended a professional conference that included a panel discussion on doing legal ethnography. From the discussion grew agreement that to do this work well requires a certain level of trust between the researchers and the people who are our sources of cultural information, which, in turn, requires that interviewers be open and honest about their intentions.

What we concluded was that it is important to be able to continually, internally ask and answer four questions:

Why am I doing this research?
What are my own views on the questions I am asking?
What do I hope to learn?
How do I intend to share this learning?

The premise underlying this continuing self-examination is that to do this work ethically and to do it well requires some degree of self-awareness—especially the ability to be aware of the culturally shaped lens through which each of us sees the world.

In anthropology's early days, the ethnographer was trained to be sort of an acultural sponge, silently soaking up information about the host group, to be later wrung out into monograph form for other sponges to absorb. By contrast, much current training calls for everyone who is trying to do a proper job of reporting how others are affected by law in culture and society to acknowledge the relevant elements of their own cultural orientation, as well as their purposes in doing their research. The understanding here is that in telling the story of others, we are also inevitably telling a little of the story of ourselves (i.e., the view through our own lens), so we might as well at least be up front about it and try to keep the two as distinguishable as possible.

Over time, then, we have inherited a broad range of writing on law and culture. At one end of the continuum are some early ethnographies in which the observer treated the subject culture like a specimen under a methodological microscope, describing appearances, artifacts, behaviors, and respondent speech in an abstract, distant, formulaic mode of discourse intended to at least suppress if not eliminate the cultural voice of the author. In this positivist tradition, the actions of legal institutions are also described in terms referential to their own internal logic, curiously detached from the cultural and economic forces that constitute their sources of power. But at the other, post-positivist pole is a literature in which some authors tend to be so self-conscious of, so obsessed with, and so mistrustful of their own conditioning that everything they write is in some way both hyperautobiographical and relentlessly hypercritical.

In doing this research and writing up the results, I have tried to steer a middle course between these two extremes. The voice, the approach, and the method vary from chapter to chapter and within each chapter, depending on the subject matter and the nature of received knowledge of the subject. These first two chapters emphasize personal experience more than the rest, by way of setting context.

So here in the beginning it seems important to share some experiences that, over time, have contributed to my own views on these matters, since some level of trust between writers and readers is just as important as that between researchers and respondents if communication is to be meaningful and effective. These short personal stories may help explain why I undertook this study and what I hope to contribute by having done it. Each of these events in some way stimulated contemplative thought, and each has a corollary in our more calculative external knowledge of land use policy.

- The time is nearly a half-century ago, in the bitterly cold pre-dawn hour of Easter Sunday morning, and the place is South Rim of the Grand Canyon. I am a small child sitting outdoors with my family as we watch the sunrise transform the canyon from dark void to softly lit chasm. The minister leading the interfaith Christian service we are attending intones the psalm: "I shall lift up mine eyes unto the hills, from whence cometh my help. My help cometh from the Lord, who made both heaven and earth."

- The time is the fall of 1967, and the place is the Sonora Desert on the western outskirts of Tucson, Arizona. A son in a Yaqui family my family has befriended was in Vietnam at the same time I was. His mother lit a candle for him every day he was there, vowing that if he returned safely, she would walk the nine miles from Pascua Village (then out northwest of town) along desert back roads to San Xavier del Bac Mission *on her knees*. He does make it home alive, and every weekend for the next several months her family drives her out to the place where her progress ended the weekend before. She straps on her kneepads, lowers herself to the ground, and resumes her journey. She completes the pilgrimage and fulfills her *manda* (promise to God).

- The time is a few years later, and the place is a remote Redwood forest in the mountains of northern California. On a long-term silent Buddhist meditation retreat, I am having a rough time of it: horrific wartime flashbacks superimposed over the fog-shrouded forest during sitting and walking meditations. Visions of decomposing bodies, burned villages, and the graveyard outside Danang uncontrollably flow forth. Eventually the mind releases them, and the ageless wooded landscape absorbs them. Eight years of war-induced nightmares finally come to an end.

- The time is the summer of 1970, and the place is the foot of a canyon in the northern shadow of Navajo Mountain. On a backpacking/mountaineering expedition as part of a college orientation program, we have been alone in the field a long time and are nearly out of water. As we descend toward recently drowned stretches of the Colorado and San Juan Rivers, we encounter the astonishing natural sandstone arch that Congress named Rainbow Bridge. It looks like Chartres, like a huge gateway to another universe, and it inspires silent awe. Then through the arch on the other side we see and hear a group of day-hiking tourists approaching with beer, snack food, and a boombox. Lake Powell is rising behind the just-completed Glen Canyon Dam, and this previously remote holy site is now accessible to any power boater who wants to drop anchor a few hundred yards to the north. I am aware that although neither we nor the boaters fully understand what it means to be in this place, as the waters rise and the spirits of the Ancient Ones are slowly, irretrievably entombed, something very tragic is transpiring.

- The time is the late 1990s, and the place is a camp in the San Juan Mountains of southwestern Colorado. On an inward journey, a Tibetan lama leads us in meditation on sunsets and sunrises as a way to more deeply understand impermanence and insubstantiality, and to help dissolve the boundaries between see-er and seen.
- The time is the summer solstice of 1998, and the place is a public campground in the eastern shadow of Bear's Lodge/Devils Tower. I am interviewing a rock climber who has been scaling its vertical faces in defiance of requests from both the Park Service and several Plains tribes, who are there to perform a Sun Dance ceremony. As I proceed through my questions, he asks, "Why are you doing this research? What do you think you'll find out? How would you answer these questions?"

You, the reader, deserve those answers just as much as he did. A first purpose in doing this work is to develop a better understanding of the spiritual dimensions of the relationship that the indigenous and dominant culture groups in the United States have with their environment. A second is to learn what role in these matters has been played by the public law of the dominant culture (especially judicial interpretations of treaties, constitutional amendments, acts of Congress, and agency regulations) in managing disputes between these sometimes conflicting perspectives. And a third is to learn how managers of public lands have tried to achieve mutual accommodation and cultural reconciliation among various groups that are contesting the uses of these public lands and resources for spiritual purposes.

Out of this learning from the experiences of those who have actually had to work through these complex and difficult situations, I do indeed have some possible answers, or at least some suggested ways for us all to think about and deal with these issues in the future. In proposing these answers, I have tried to be thorough enough and balanced enough in telling these stories that even those who do not agree with the conclusions may yet find something of value in the scholarship.

The Personal and the Public

Events such as those portrayed in these personal vignettes are not altogether unique to my own experience. Anyone growing up and living in an area as geographically and culturally diverse as the American West, and who has explored that diversity, will have similar tales to tell. These are but individualized examples of some common characteristics at the confluence of culture and spirituality in the public open spaces of the West. Following are a few of these characteristics or themes:

- *Spiritual differentiation of common landscapes.* In the nearly half-century scope of my own experience, the Baptist preacher at one end and the Tibetan lama at the other both used the landscapes and skyscapes of the Colorado Plateau as object lessons in widely differing religious teachings. Across the multimillennial human habitation of the same area, dozens of different indigenous and immigrant culture groups have invested commonly occupied lands with quite disparate senses of spiritual meaning and significance.
- *Religious uses of public lands.* The traditional and long-standing Easter Sunrise Service at Grand Canyon National Park bespeaks the fact that Anglo-American religious groups have enjoyed time and location-bounded exclusive use of national parks and forests for nearly as long as the federal government has controlled them. But the same has not been consistently true for indigenous peoples wanting the same access.
- *The restorative and healing powers of natural landscapes.* Whether the event is a meditation retreat, church camp, Sun Dance, sweat ceremony, or an Outward Bound expedition, the literature of

every major religious tradition and the oral teachings of most indigenous elders all affirm the ability of direct and intimate contacts with natural environments to restore a lost sense of connection to sources of spiritual sustenance. The contemporary connotation of "outdoor recreation" as a form of exercise and amusement bespeaks an emphasis different from its original meaning: the outdoor experience as a process of recurring "re-creation."

- *Spirituality and place.* The one feature of traditional spiritual practices among tribes of the American West most clearly distinguishing them from the multitude of religions imported by immigrants from other continents is the primacy of place. The creation stories, moral lessons, and seasonal rituals of specific indigenous culture groups are cast in specific geographic contexts. A mythic Eden is not the source of human creation for traditionalist members of the Taos Pueblo; it is Blue Lake, an actual body of water in the nearby Sangre de Cristo Mountains that feeds the stream flowing through their village. If a tribe's sacred sites are mostly on public lands outside their jurisdiction, and the agency controlling them decides that one of them would be a perfect spot for an observatory (Mt. Graham), a ski lift (the San Francisco Peaks), or a reservoir (Rainbow Bridge), there is little if anything a tribe can do about it. In allowing the U.S. Forest Service to build an access road through an Indian cemetery on public lands in 1988, the Supreme Court ruled that federal land management agencies have the power to physically destroy a site even if it means literally destroying a tribe's religion. Interestingly, the same decision also held that an agency can manage a site specifically for tribal religious preservation if it chooses to do so.
- *Spiritual pluralism within culture groups.* Largely for historical reasons explored later in this writing, in most Euro-American religious organizations, institutional affiliation is an either/or affair; one cannot simultaneously ascribe to more than one set of beliefs or doctrines. But in many indigenous culture groups, such mutual exclusivity either does not exist or is at least much less pronounced. Some members of a given culture may adhere mostly to the "old ways," others to teachings imported by the missionaries, while over time many (like the Yaqui) have evolved numerous

artful ways of combining the two (if only to appease colonizing forces). Also as reflected in the Yaqui example, dramatic and powerful acts of spiritual reaffirmation ostensibly emanating from one religious tradition can take on a broader meaning when enacted in an equally dramatic and powerful landscape. Walking nine miles in any desert can arouse one's survival instincts and instill some degree of humility; imagine doing it on your knees.

Organizing Thoughts and the Structure of This Work

One lesson learned from interviewing various people involved in intercultural consultations over the spiritual uses of public lands is how important it is to be able to recognize similarities among all the parties when they do exist, while never underestimating or trying to downplay the sources and strengths of their differences. And what one group may see as a similarity offering grounds for agreement, another may see as an equally serious difference impeding consensus.

For example, some tribal representatives hear with extreme suspicion Anglo rhetoric extolling the spiritual virtues of outdoor recreation. To them it cheapens and demeans tribal religion by apparently putting it on a par with the macho antics of some of the "rock jock" thrill-seekers pounding hardware into the heart of their sacred sites. It also sounds to their lawyers like a back doorway to turn the Indians' religious free exercise claims against them.

In the same vein, some climbers and other extreme sports enthusiasts suspect the tribes of using religious rights talk mostly as a tactic for regaining some measure of control over off-reservation lands they lost in wars and one-sided treaties with the U.S. government over a century ago. If mutual suspicion and animosity grow too strong, the sought-after spiritual common ground can turn out to be no more than a political and legal minefield.

But it is also easy to conclude that because apparent cultural differences can be so great and because strong motives can be so diverse, no basis for reconciliation exists when, in fact, it may. If everyone at the table in these cases has a threshold understanding of each other's cultural construction of the landscape in question, and if they truly share a concern for the well-being of the contested place, then whatever common ground is discovered may eventually become a place of peace.

In some respects, this book is about similarities and differences. Divided into four parts, the chapters in parts 1 and 2 focus on the first three themes in its subtitle: the culturally differentiated spiritual aspects of the environmental history of the United States and how these divergent perspectives have found expression as legally contested differences over management of public lands and resources. The chapters in part 3 apply these concepts and principles to actual cases on the public lands of the United States and to some other common law countries (i.e., other former British colonies with indigenous populations) around the Pacific Rim. Finally, the chapters in part 4 look to the future of cultural coevolution and its possible effect on managing the spiritual uses of these commonly held places.

Language and Understanding

"Words are in the saddle, and ride mankind." A writer friend made that remark about a generation ago (paraphrasing Ralph Waldo Emerson), but his observation rings even truer today than it did then. For like it or not, we think in words. Our calculative thoughts in particular take form and meaning through the words we use to express them. To use an information age metaphor, language is a culture's operating system. It functions mostly in the background and at a barely conscious level; it is so much a part of how we construct reality that we seldom realize how profoundly what we know is conditioned by how we hear and how we speak.

Nowhere is the power of language more evident than in our conversations about the environment. To listen carefully to terms used to describe it is to learn as much about the speaker as about what is being said, since every community of interest has its own private terminology. Looking at the same national forest, a wildlife biologist sees "habitat" and a logger sees future "forest products," while to a miner everything between him and a sought-after subsurface mineral is "overburden." But the most central concern is what we would like to think of as our common language of cultural, spiritual, and environmental description—the words and phrases we all use and tend to assume have the same meaning among all users. When they do not, or when they imply underlying premises we do not actually share, communication can get seriously distorted.

The problem is compounded when the subject of speaking or writing is intercultural relations. Since members of cultures with altogether different root languages think and perceptually construct the world in different terms, there is actually no such thing as a "common language." If everybody is speaking English—usually the only language understood by all parties to multitribal, intercultural consultations—that very fact strongly conditions any effort at common construction of the problem being discussed. The same, of course, is true of this book.

And even within English, we have less agreement than we might hope for on some of the central concepts that are the subject of this book. Given the diverse array of meanings and connotations associated with terms like "culture," "religion," "spirituality," and the "sacred," effective communication with the people interviewed in this work has sometimes required first being clear about what is meant when I use those terms. Before going any further into the substance of the subject, it is equally important to get clear about the conceptual "operating system" used here as well.

The Many Meanings of "Culture"

Like all the other key terms here, the meaning of this one has changed and become much more diffuse during the life of its use. From the Latin *cultura* (to cultivate), "culture" originally alluded to the cultivation of personhood: the development of the mentally unformed newborn into an embodiment of received learning; the inscription of societal values, mental habits, and aesthetics onto the "blank slate" of those born into a given social group.

To be "cultured" meant to have been formally trained in the reception and replication of this learning. From this evolved the class-oriented notions of "high" and "low" (or "popular") culture—the former being the institutional conservation of those qualities of cultivation deemed valuable by societal elites (who controlled the conserving institutions), and the latter being the learned lifeways of "commoners" without access to or influence over those institutions that had assumed authority over cultural conservation.

The meaning changed again with emergence of the social science of anthropology, toward an emphasis on the study of the worldviews and lifeways of what were then called "savage" or "primitive" societies. The perspective of the discipline then was still developmental: a primitive group was one that (according to nineteenth-century federal Indian law) had not yet developed the capability of practicing the "arts of civilization." Only in the latter half of the twentieth century did cultural anthropologists start devoting as much energy and attention to studying their own cultures and microcultures as they previously did to methodically examining the exotic "other."

The contemporary literature offers many different definitions of culture, along with one critical perspective asserting that the very term is anachronistic and misleading—a fruitless effort to describe something that does not exist. My view is that it is a concept that does have value and meaning, but that it is also necessary to be clear about what is meant when using it.

Contemporary definitions tend to fall into one of two categories: the first, a great long checklist of specific behaviors and mental constructs; the other, short, cryptic, generalized phrases. The variance in definitions seems to depend largely on the purpose for which its author is using the concept. Readers familiar with this array of definitions will recognize, first, that the definition I offer below falls more into the latter category than the former and, second, that it integrates key elements of some of the better-known contemporary uses of the term.

As used here, *culture* means a network of learned patterns of thought and behavior among members of a social group by which they understand and relate to themselves, each other, other groups, and their environment. Within this definition, *network* has both ancient and modern connotations: from preindustrial times, it is a woven web or net used to encompass, contain, and carry some things while leaving other things out; in modern times, it is an interactive and at least partly self-contained system of linkages between information points or nodes. The phrase *learned patterns of thought and behavior* emphasizes that culture is intergenerationally and interpersonally communicated through formal and informal learning processes, as distinguished from genetic information transmitted through procreation.

Social groups are those whose members share a common environment (whether geographical or virtual or both) and bear some degree of interdependent relationship with each other, whether by reason of kinship or other institutionally defined behavioral obligations. How the members of this group *understand and relate to themselves, each other, other groups, and their environment* reflects the view that it is through the medium of culture, in combination with sensory input, that they construct the reality they perceive and ascribe meaning to it. In sum, this definition was devised from existing ones[10] in order to be able to describe the interaction of the culturally constructed phenomena of spirituality, law, and environment-related behavior which, along with culture itself, comprise the subject of this book.

The Spiritual, the Religious, and the Sacred

Despite widely differing approaches and methods, all the natural and social scientists studying human behavior evidently agree that the human mind has an innate tendency to organize sensory information into recognizable patterns and categories. Our ancient, evolving power to discern those plants that are nourishing from those that are deadly, and those animals we should run toward to kill and consume from those we should run away from because they want to kill and consume us—in a word, our instinct for survival is one of the principal reasons we are here today. If we did not have this ability (in combination with the ability to act on our judgments), we would not have survived and thrived as a species. But a related skill that may prove to be nearly as important is our ability to make judgments about our judgments; that is, to discern whether our ways of organizing and categorizing reality are actually contributing to our continued survivability.

One reason the study of the history of Western thought usually begins with the ancient Greeks is that (in addition to writing down their thoughts) they were among the first to develop an understanding of their environment based more on direct sensory observation in combination with logical reasoning than on received religious teachings. And one of the earliest and most fundamental distinctions the residents of the groves of academe made in culturally constructing their world was between the "material" and the "spiritual." The material was that which everyone with the same sensory apparatus could see, hear, smell, and touch. By contrast, the spiritual was the unseen, unmeasurable energy that animated life. The Romans later made the same distinction: the word *spirit* is from the Latin verb *spirare*—to breathe. It was the unseen that animates the seen, the rationally unknowable that animates the known.

Over the two millennia since then, our machine-assisted powers of observation and measurement have grown considerably. Electron microscopes and orbiting telescopes have extended our range of vision—or at least mechanical perception—both inward and outward, while other instruments have taught us more than we have ever known before about the mechanics of life itself. And over this time the meaning of spirituality has changed as well. Its connotation now is more toward that which cannot be known by simple physical measurement and calculative thought.

As used here, *spirituality* refers to that realm of human experience characterized by varying mixtures of three qualities. First, spiritual experience is either *nonrational* or *extrarational* in nature; it is a way of knowing that is not accessible exclusively through calculative thought—although the rational process may well bring one to its doorway. Second, such experience is *transcendent*: it involves a sense of moving beyond the rationally constructed boundaries of the self. Third, such experience is *unitive,* involving a sense of unity with existence and forces underlying its continuing creation. This admittedly open-textured definition is grounded in factors of direct human experience because it is based on the understanding that there is a spiritual dimension common to the experience of all human beings, regardless of culture (I am aware that I have just made something of a culture-bound statement) and that we share an interactive relationship between the ascription of meaning to spiritual experience and the continuing construction of culture.

Religion has two Latin roots, one meaning "to bind" and the other "to read over and over." In this study the word is taken to mean an organizationally established and maintained agreement on the nature, significance, meaning, and expression of spirituality. Thus religion is a function of human social organization, and inasmuch as it also involves the intergenerational transmission of patterns of thought and behavior, it is also a function of culture.

Religion and culture cannot exist apart from each other; the former is nested in the latter. From this perspective, the great "world religions" are less monolithic than they might at first appear to be, since the dissemination of religious beliefs operates through a cultural filtration process in which the receiving group first determines whether a nonindigenous set of religious beliefs will be accepted at all, and if they are, in what form. Historically, how successful a given group has been in making such cultural preservation and innovation decisions has depended on factors such as how cohesive and stable the culture group was to begin with, along with its relative ability to repel unwanted external influences.

The Latin and old French origins of "sacred" are derived from the verb to *consecrate,* or set aside, for a spiritual or religious purpose. Thus an artifact, object, geographical site, plant or animal species, or other natural resource becomes sacred because members of a religion or spiritual affinity group agree that it is.

Natives, Anglos, and Americans

In the first volume of his study of British influences in early American cultural history, David Hackett Fischer makes two interesting observations. The first is that demographically, Anglo-Americans (that is, American citizens of English ancestry) currently comprise fewer than 20 percent of the nation's population, and that figure is expected to continue to diminish, relative to other ethnic groups.[11] The second is that British ideas and institutional design principles nonetheless represent the single most pervasive immigrant cultural influence in the development of American society, especially in the realms of government and law.

The British common law of property—perhaps the most individualized and reified in the Western world—had and continues to have a profound influence over environmental management in the United States, in combination with the equally powerful declarations of individual substantive and procedural rights in early amendments to the national constitution. Therefore, "Anglo-American society" and "Anglos" as used here refer not to the dwindling minority of Americans with traceable British ancestry but, instead, to the organizing principles concerning government and law that play so determinative a role over how different culture groups in the United States relate to each other and to the lands we hold in common. When not specifying government principles and institutions, "Anglo-American" and "Euro-American" are used here interchangeably.

If how we name things conditions how we perceive them, the different names we have for ourselves and for each other is perhaps an even more crucial issue than the different place names we might have for common landscapes. Social scientists studying this naming process distinguish between *self*-ascription (what we call ourselves) and *social* ascription (what others call us and what we call others). To name something is not only to mentally create it; it is to invest it with culturally conditioned meaning as well. And in the realm of intercultural relations, it is likewise an inherently political act.

Consider as an example the fifteenth-century European explorers' collective naming of the indigenous peoples of what the conquerors called the Americas. Based on an incomplete and incorrect understanding of world geography, the indigenes became "Indians." The initial error might be understandable, but reasons for the persistent use of the term down to the present day are less clear. One possible explanation is that what successive waves of European immigrants arriving on the Americas' Atlantic shores most desperately desired was their own land, which—to their inconvenience and annoyance— they found to be already well settled.

Europeans needed to construct an image of indigenous peoples as somehow not really belonging here; that is, given their coloration and unintelligible languages, they *should* have been in someplace like India, over on the other side of the globe. It was important for the immigrants to see the indigenes not as native, but as foreign. That ascription by the dominant culture was not significantly challenged until the modern civil rights era of the 1970s, when the term "Native American" came into popular use—a popularity it continues to enjoy. It is also more inclusive than "American Indian," since it includes all the indigenous peoples of the United States.

Yet at the same time, a tradition of diversity in self-ascription among indigenous peoples persists. Among the more prominent indigenous lobbying organizations in Washington, D.C., is the National Congress of American Indians, and among the more militant of the modern advocacy groups born of the civil rights era is the American Indian Movement. Use of the term is a continuing reminder of how important it was for the European conquerors to not acknowledge who was really here first. Moreover, some people who served as sources of information and advice or this research also self-identify with pride as American Indians and do not necessarily appreciate having others change the rules as to how they should be called. Finally, many of the people with whom I have spoken are less concerned with how they are called than that whatever term is chosen is used with respect.

Still others connect strongly with the ascription of "Native American" and resent discouragement of its use as a threat to remembrance of their history. A sharply drawn example of this view is by Sioux essayist Elizabeth Cook-Lynn, in her reaction to the work of western environmental writer Wallace Stegner.[12] In *Wolf Willow*, Stegner both affirms his own affinity with the upper Great Plains ("If I am native to anything, I am native to this") and laments the demise of Plains Indian culture, which he sees as basically having being extinguished with the Euro-American conquest of the western frontier in the late nineteenth century.[13] Cook-Lynn sees in Stegner's asserting his own "native-ness" while downplaying the present-day persistence of indigenous Plains culture an effort to do in the modern American mind what the Seventh Cavalry tried to do to the Sioux and neighboring tribes over a century ago—simply wipe them off the national map. Her bitterness and anger at Stegner and writers like him, seeking to articulate their own native-born affinity with American landscapes, rise from the pages of her writing like steam from a Yellowstone geyser, and her feelings are understandable. In her view, there cannot be two native populations. There are natives and there are immigrants; that is how it was, is, and always will be. From this understanding, to construe history otherwise is to deny her people the respect due an ancestry and an intimate knowledge of place that dates back thousands of years.

Yet this organization of America's cultural history into sharply separated and mutually exclusive categories has its own destructive power. As early as 1830 Alexis de Tocqueville identified a malady of the spirit among Euro-American settlers that, unchecked, would eventually cause untold environmental destruction: "Those Americans who go out far away from the Atlantic Ocean, plunging into the West, are adventurers impatient of any sort of yoke, greedy for wealth.... An American will build a house in which to pass his old age and sell it before the roof is on; he will plant a garden and rent it just as the trees come into bearing; he will clear a field and leave others to reap the harvest; he will take up a profession and leave it, settle in one place and soon go off elsewhere with his changing desires."[14] He was describing a transient, restless, rootless population who saw in their surroundings only a commodity, something not to be cherished but simply consumed before moving westward to repeat the "settlement" process once again. This is a sad legacy, of a people without the capacity to genuinely care for the land because they had no intimate personal connection with it. And as long as their descendants in the dominant culture of the United States are continuously reminded that they are but relative newcomers without legitimate personal bonds to place, the ethic of care so much a part of tribal cultures (even if not always observed in practice) will be most difficult to instill in the population most in need of it.

The root of the Latin *nativus* means "to be born" or "to be born of." One way to read Stegner's passage is as an effort by this preeminent American nature writer to declare that much-needed connection—to underscore the importance of place and of *knowing* where one comes from as essential to curing the destructive, dissociative condition that de Tocqueville so poignantly diagnosed. But in Cook-Lynn's view, Stegner has done this at the expense of her own culture's rightful place in American environmental history, replacing her native-ness with his own.

Dominant immigrant cultures have an inevitable tendency toward displacement—the physical displacement or absorption of the host culture groups they are overtaking, and a reconstruction of history that tends to displace original peoples in the memories of generations to come. What Cook-Lynn and indigenous writers like her compel us all to remember is that the Europeans continuously *invaded* the Americas over a period of several centuries. They were not invited and generally were not welcome. They came and simply took what they wanted because they had the power to do so. This is awkward, unflattering, ignoble history that many if not most members of the dominant culture for the most part would just as soon forget.

But as with the legacy of the importation of African slaves, continuing efforts to "put this all behind us" has just the opposite effect. Just as all Americans share the history of enslavement, we all share the history of invasion and conquest. Remembrance and respect go hand in hand. To ignore, downplay, or deny events such as slavery and the attempted extermination of America's indigenous peoples is to turn a blind eye to the capacity for dominant culture groups to inflict terrible suffering on subordinate groups over whom they have control. And to be blind to that capacity only increases the possibility of such a destructive, wounding history repeating itself.

For indigenous peoples throughout this country, this is not simply archival knowledge in the yellowing pages of dusty books. It is living history, passed down in spoken stories from generation to generation. When they look to the hills around them, they see the sights and hear the sounds of battles fought for control of this land and for their peoples' very survival many, many years ago.

The problem with the archetypical views of Cook-Lynn on the one hand and western environmental writers like Stegner on the other is that they imply a mutual exclusivity. If members of the dominant culture cannot develop their own sense of *nativity*—of being born of this Earth—there is little chance they will ever be capable of developing the capacity to care for it in a genuinely sustainable way. But if in the process of development the dominant culture denies the legacy and the continuing cultural vitality of this continent's founding peoples, it will indeed be contributing to the reconstruction of history in a way that commits a genocide of the collective national memory and which is analogous to the actual attempted wiping out of these cultures in the nineteenth century.

There is a middle path between these two uses of "native," which neither denies the respect due this continent's original peoples nor precludes others from acknowledging that they too are born of this land. Throughout this text, "First Natives" appears interchangeably with "indigenous peoples" and, occasionally, "American Indians" (this also parallels use of the Canadian term "First Nations"). "First Native" acknowledges primacy of historical place and a living continuity with ancient origins for those whose land this was, while also recognizing a sense of *nativity* as instrumental to the dominant culture's evolving efforts to life in a more sustainable relationship with our environment.

The naming of each other can be a contested activity in contemporary American society. Names are more than words. They can express underlying tensions in worldview, in aspiration, and in intention toward the other. Suggesting and using the term "First Natives" in this narrative is a self-conscious attempt to find a linguistic middle ground between the mutually exclusive positions implied in the literatures described above. I hope that most readers will find it a useful contribution to the process of depolarizing intercultural discourse, although I know some others may resent it.

My own view is that the mutual exclusivity implied in Cook-Lynn's writing on the one hand and Stegner's on the other reflects a worldview that is insufficiently broad to encompass the needs of our times. Two metaphors—one from the indigenous cultures of the Americas and the other from the humanism of the Europeans—may combine to form a perspective broad enough to meet the needs of both groups. The first is that of the Earth and heavens as parents of us all, as those dimensions of creation to whom filial respect is due if we are to live in harmony rather than continuous conflict with them; the second is that of all culture groups as offspring of this environmental parentage. In this family of humankind (in an earlier age, the "family of man"), the indigenous peoples of this continent are the elder siblings who carry within their cultures a wisdom born of experience of thousands of years of inhabiting this environment, which the dominant culture simply does not possess because it does not share that experience.

That wisdom is as much a treasure as the natural landscapes we all share. However, it cannot forcibly be obtained, as the land was. The "scientific" study of indigenous cultures will not yield it, and the analysis of captured artifacts locked away in museums will not yield it, either. The only way it can be transmitted intact is by voluntary teaching and voluntary learning. If the dominant culture of North America can develop a regard for the indigenous cultures in its midst akin to that of a younger sibling for an elder one, we may yet discover a way to share "native-ness" that does no violence to the deeply felt needs of either group.

2

Contemplation and Connection

Indigenous Spirituality
and the Environment

The place is a remote, tribal Pueblo in the mountains of northern New Mexico, far from any city or town, and the winter morning is cold, calm, and clear. Wood fires heat the homes of community members, as they prepare for the ceremonial dance being held that day and start cooking up a big feast to serve beforehand.

A tribal official had invited me (as well as other indigenous and Anglo guests) to come see the dance and share a meal. There was a genuine feeling of welcoming and acceptance in the home. His extended family's pride in their culture and the significance of this ceremony for its preservation were evident in everyone's activities leading up to the event. Yet it was a pride not born of exclusivity or superiority. All they wished of their guests was that we exhibit the same respect for this ceremony as we would toward a ritual in our own faiths.

During the meal I said that I was studying how all the peoples who share public lands see them and relate to them—especially for spiritual or religious purposes. I also said that one of the reasons I was doing this work was to try to make better known within Euro-American culture the importance of connection to place and to nature in tribal spiritual practices. I wanted the people hosting me to know this, so they could let me know if any aspect of what I saw that day should not be shared with a wider world.

Although this seemed to be well understood and well received by the host family that had invited me, I soon learned that not everyone there shared these sentiments. Later that day a visiting member of a non-Puebloan tribe from another state confronted me, visibly angry. "Leave the Indian alone," he told me. "No good ever came of a white man writing about the Indian. Whatever you write is for your benefit, not ours."

He then let me know that, in his view, white culture was like a disease infecting Indian people, that white religion was destroying Indian religion, and that history has shown that—say what they might—the actions of white people have always ultimately been aimed at eliminating Indians from the face of the Earth. My only response to him at the time was that if he was looking for someone to defend how European invaders have treated indigenous peoples over the last four hundred years, he was talking to the wrong person and that I thought my culture would pose less of a threat to his culture if my people had a better understanding of and therefore perhaps more respect for his people and their ways.

Later he approached me again. "I'm sorry," he said. "Sometimes the anger just wells up in me so strong that if I don't get it out, it feels like it will burn me up. I know it wasn't you who did these things to try to destroy us, but your people did." He also emphasized that he was apologizing for his rudeness, but not for his views about Euro-Americans or for the depth of feeling in his heart.

Soon after my host provided some context for this hostility. We were standing on a bluff in the forest-rimmed basin where the pueblo is situated. He gestured toward the mountains forming one boundary of the little valley. "That's where the old pueblo stood, eight storeys high, built into the hillside. And over there [indicating the rise on the opposite side of the basin] is where the Spanish Army set up their cannons. We hadn't been part of the revolt [an effort by some Pueblo Indian tribes to drive off the Spanish conquistadors in 1680], but they destroyed our pueblo and everybody in it anyway, just because we are Indians."

He told this story as if it had happened yesterday. He told it calmly, gently, and matter-of-factly—but with an equally calm and gentle insistence that it be remembered: that the story be heard once more. Thus, he brought the past into the present in the context of a specific place and a specific cultural understanding, acting in a capacity similar to what is known to the Western Apache as a "place-maker." The place-maker storyteller's "main objective is to summon [place-based living history] with words and give it dramatic form, to produce experience by forging ancestral worlds."[1] As Keith Basso explained this role in his study of the centrality of place in Western Apache culture and consciousness, "the placemaker often speaks as a witness on the scene, describing ancestral events 'as they are occurring' and creating in the process a vivid sense that what happened long ago—right here, on this very spot—could be happening *now*."[2]

My host, his family, and his people still live at the very site where the massacre of most of their lineage tribe took place, over three hundred years ago. For members of that tribal community, to simply look around the valley is to remember the devastation they suffered at the hands of the dominant culture of the time. And a memory still so powerful, still so fresh, and still so alive inevitably suggests the possibility that, under certain circumstances, such things could happen again.

Well into the early twentieth century, Anglo government and religious leaders were still doing everything in their power to keep Pueblo peoples from preserving their traditional ceremonies.[3] At that same time, at least one well-known anthropologist was alternately deceiving, bribing, and coercing members of some Puebloan communities into disclosing the most closely held secret knowledge of their religious societies, defending such tactics on the rationale that, since these cultures were being wiped out anyway, descriptions of their sacred teachings should be preserved "in the name of science."[4]

To those groups whose secrets had been disclosed, this was the spiritual equivalent of grave-robbing, if not worse. Stolen artifacts and remains can at least be repatriated and reinterred, while stolen knowledge (or more precisely, a description of it) cannot. Little wonder, then, at the hostility and the suspicion that my presence and the sharing of my intentions aroused in my critic. Until recently and with some notable exceptions, the historical track record of my own subcultural group (*academicus publishus*) has not been a great deal better than the U.S. Army's, the bureaucracies', or the missionaries' when it comes to treating tribal members and tribal institutions with genuine respect.

The events of that cold, clear winter day seemed to exemplify the full range of indigenous views about the sharing of knowledge concerning their spiritual traditions that I had encountered up to that time. Pueblo members invited some outsiders to come witness their ceremonies, both because it was an auspicious event they wanted to share with friends of their tribe and because they wanted to demonstrate to all present the importance of seasonal rhythms of life to their spiritual traditions, and thus to their cultural survival. At the same time, my critic on that January day is by no means alone in his view that non-Indians cannot describe tribal cultures without to some degree manipulating and distorting their image. And his sentiments echo more than just a postmodern critique of the social construction of the "other" by a colonizing culture. It was over twenty-five hundred years ago that the authors of the Talmud observed, "We see things not as *they* are, but as *we* are."

Moreover, one of the most sensitive areas for a scholar not of these cultures to depict is that of American Indian spiritual practices. According to some critics, one of the most egregious examples of such manipulation happened during the 1960s and 1970s when environmental groups first began to offer up romanticized, reified versions of nature-based tribal religious teachings as a rationale for advocating changes in public land use policies. This later formed a basis for some environmentalists to criticize tribal leaders for not honoring their own spiritual teachings whenever a tribe undertook a resource-development project of which an environmental group disapproved.[5] In short, this is a touchy subject for an Anglo to talk or write about.

Given this situation, writing this chapter necessitated a renewed focus on my intentions in its preparation. There are three. The first is to provide a knowledge base for comparison with the following chapter on nature and immigrant religions. The second is to provide a means for recognizing the spiritual roots of the case studies and legal disputes described in the chapters in part 3. And the third is to provide readers concerned with the future management of public lands and resources for spiritual and religious purposes (the subject of the two closing chapters in part 4) with descriptions of these teachings and some guidance as to how we might better achieve genuine cross-cultural accommodation.

Crucial to this effort was the need to pay careful attention to the choice of information sources and the portrayal of that knowledge. The sources on which this chapter is based include:

1. Direct observation of ceremonies to which I was invited, in combination with interviews with hosts and participants
2. Literature in which tribal elders and practitioners describe teachings, rituals, and their significance in their own words
3. Writings on tribal religious and spiritual practices by American Indian authors
4. Writings by non-Indian authors who regard their First Native respondents as teachers rather than simply as ethnographic information sources.

I have also used only that information which to the best of my knowledge was not obtained through bribery, coercion, or deceit.

Some Organizing Principles

Any well-stocked university or public library has shelves full of books on American Indian spiritual traditions. With over five hundred different federally recognized groups, bands, tribes, and "nations within," some organizing principles are necessary for determining what within this wealth and diversity of cultural knowledge should be selected for the purposes of this study. To start with, there are no depictions of First Native spirituality as a unified body of belief or practice. As one authority on the subject has observed: "It is evident that in the Americas generally, and in North America specifically, there is neither *an* American Indian tradition nor *a* spiritual legacy, but a rich variety of both. To ignore such a diversity of origin, place, language, and resulting cultural forms, as is so often done under a plethora of stereotypes, is to do great disservice to the American Indian peoples and their history."[6]

How the information in this volume is organized relates directly to why it was gathered in the first place (intentions), as just discussed.

A first organizing principle used here is to structure this material in a way that facilitates comparison between tribal teachings and traditions featured in this chapter and the wide variety of both western European and Asian traditions featured in the next. A second principle is to emphasize teachings and practices that have in one way or another been implicated in public land and resource management disputes featured in part 3 of this book. A third principle is to show that since most publicly owned, federally managed lands and resources are in the West, the predominant emphasis is also on the western tribes that hold cultural affiliations with those lands and resources, since that is also where most of the contemporary conflicts are arising.

To provide a thematic framework for organizing the presentation of material from these diverse western tribes, the approach here also emphasizes cycles: origins of tribes and of the persons within them; learning about the world; sustenance; and healing, death, and renewal. The discussion of most stages in this cycle includes a combination of information sources: usually a summary of some already published teachings, followed by observations based on my own work and experience.

As indicated in the chapter title, the two most consistent features I recognized in the gathering knowledge of these traditions were those of *contemplation* and *connection*. Amid this wide variety of teachings, these two features do serve to most broadly distinguish indigenous spiritual traditions from traditionally received western ones when it comes to relationship to the environment. What is discussed in the rest of this chapter is almost exclusively *contemplative* knowledge—that which, in keeping with the definitions in the previous chapter, is gained through extrarational ways of knowing rather than through calculative, linear thought alone.

It is also knowledge that it is *relational* and *connective:* it concerns the relationship or connection between the culture group or the individual and the environment. This includes connection either to places or to other entities (animals, plants, or landforms). In fact, to speak (as this chapter's title does) of indigenous spiritual traditions *and* the environment is conceptually awkward, since as scholars such as Joe Brown have repeatedly observed, indigenous spiritual traditions are altogether *of* the environment rather than separable from it: "A presiding characteristic of primal people is a special quality and intensity of interrelationship with the forms and forces of their natural environment. As nomadic hunters or gatherers, or as agriculturists, dependence upon natural resources demanded detailed knowledge of all aspects of their immediate habitat. This accumulated pragmatic lore was, however, always interrelated with a sacred lore; together these could be said to constitute a metaphysic of nature."[7]

Born of the Earth

The connection begins with the act of emergence into being—of both the culture group and the person. Different indigenous culture groups—and different tribes within those groups—all have their own received understandings of how they came into being, where they came from (geographically), and what is their relationship to their place of origin. In many instances, these physical locations do not lie within reservation borders, giving the tribes little or no control over how these sites are treated.

Consider, for instance, Tewa tribal member and anthropologist Alfonzo Ortiz's description of the sacred geography of the birthplace of the peoples of the Tewan pueblos: "Approximately sixty miles to the north of San Juan, New Mexico is *Tse Shu Pin* (Hazy or Shimmering Mountain); *Tsikomo* (Obsidian-covered Mountain) is about fifteen miles to the west: *Oku Pin* (Turtle Mountain) is about eighty miles to the south, and *Ku Sehn Pin* (Stone Man Mountain) is about twenty miles to the east. The northern mountain appears on topographical maps as Conjilon Peak; the second by its Tewa name, the third as Sandia Crest, just northeast of present-day Albuquerque, and the last as Truchas Peak. The point to naming and locating them is to give proof of their objective existence, and to give some indication of the conceptual range of the Tewa world. It is about 140 miles north and south, and thirty-five miles east to west."[8]

On each of these peaks is a shrine at the site of what Ortiz translates as its "Earth navel," or place of emergence, from which Tewan peoples were first led into life above the surface of the Earth. This description casts some light on the nature of the birth relationship between peoples of the Tewan Pueblos and these sites—most of which are on lands not controlled by the Tewan Pueblos.

At the same time, it also brings into better focus a dynamic that public land managers working in consultation with neighboring First Native communities are only now beginning to fully appreciate. It is not simply specific spots at specific locations that are sacred to many First Native groups but the regions defined by the geographic juxtaposition of these sites.[9] A good example of this is the case of the Bighorn Medicine Wheel and its relationship to Medicine Mountain in the national forests of northern Wyoming (discussed in detail in chapter 7). According to Forest Service archeologists and the cultural consultants among the tribes they work with, the entire Medicine Mountain area—not just the rock altars on its southeastern flank—is a traditional place of worship.

At the personal level, this sense of birth connection to specific places can be just as significant. Among some of the tribes of the Sonoran Desert of northern Mexico and southern Arizona—especially the Seri and the O'odham (formerly known as the Papago)—placental burial has been reported as one traditional means of reaffirming and reinforcing a newborn child's reciprocal relationship with his or her surroundings. The Seri bury the placenta at the base of a giant cactus, with the understanding that both child and plant may be nurtured by the connection.[10]

And again, these practices originated on lands these tribes once inhabited but now no longer control. Some of the most biotically rich remnants of the Northern Sonora Desert lie within the boundaries of either Saguaro National Park or the Coronado National Forest surrounding Tucson Arizona, which—but for their federal ownership—would long since have been sacrificed to the land developer's bulldozer, as has most of the rest of Pima County. Thus, many of the places where the O'odham have traditionally gone to gather medicinal plants and otherwise reaffirm their connections to place have either been totally destroyed or are now being managed by other peoples with other mandates.

The birth connection phenomenon is by no means unique to First Natives of the Sonoran Desert. Some native Hawaiians on the Big

Island, whose clan members have a historic relationship with sites within national parks and state science preserves, follow the practice of ceremonially burying the umbilicus of their newborn children in the lava fields on the slopes of Kilauea and Mauna Loa as a means of reaffirming these sacred sites as the birthplace not only of the Earth itself and their culture group but also of the individual children within the group. Other native Hawaiian families plant the umbilicus of their children at what is thought to be the birthplace of the volcano Mauna Kea in the center of the Big Island; both native Hawaiians and archeologists agree that Mauna Kea is the birthplace of the Big Island itself. With this reaffirmation of connection comes responsibility—an obligation to care for the place from which they come just as it cared for them by giving rise to their birth, as a people and as individual persons.

Learning from the World

Rituals for learning life lessons from the environment as described in the following examples take two forms: lessons about relating to all creation, and lessons about oneself (which in these traditions are, of course, not altogether separable). While nearly every indigenous culture group has some form of ritual by which their young pass from childhood to adolescence through solitary and intimate contact with the natural environment, probably the best-known example of this learning ritual is the "vision quest," especially as traditionally practiced among Lakota and Dakota. Vision quests can be undertaken at any time in the life of a woman or man, although the earliest ones seem to have particular importance in revealing the path for one's life to follow. As ethnologist Dorothy Lee put it: "To enhance relatedness, to pierce deeper into the mystery of universal oneness and experience the ultimate unity of all, a Dakota had to go through one or more rites, approaching the ultimate in absolute humility and complete abandonment of self. Men and women would undergo the Rite of Purification 'for all the people of the world that they may see clearly in walking the wakan path . . . to make the four-leggeds, the wingeds, the star peoples of the heavens and all things as relatives.'"[11]

The first vision quest can also be particularly arduous. This was summarized from the writings of Dorothy Lee, Luther Standing Bear, and other sources, for example: "For adolescent Dakota boys, the personal vision quest was a mandatory rite of passage into manhood and environmental consciousness. During this solitary sojourn into the mountains, a boy spent several days naked, vulnerable, and fasting as he awaited the arrival of animal spirit allies who might help him to develop and actualize his understanding of the spiritual and ecological unity of nature. For it is possible that such knowledge is only born of solitude."[12]

Place is likewise significant in the vision quest, since in some important regards it is the setting itself that is the teacher. Solitude, quiet, and an opportunity for direct contact with the natural environment are all essential elements. Additional power may come to the experience if it can be conducted in a place where one's ancestors also received their guiding visions. As among the Western Apaches, "the past lies embedded in features of the earth—in canyons and lakes, mountains and arroyos, rocks and vacant fields—which together endow their lands with multiple forms of significance that reach into their lives and shape the ways they think."[13]

Just as the environment can teach what one's proper relationship to it ought to be if studied carefully and held in proper regard, so, too, can that intensely focused attention on one's surroundings provide insight into one's inner state. The following account is of an episode in the training of a *curandera*—a practitioner of a healing art well known to the rural peoples of Mexico and Central America, as well as in the *barrios* of many towns and cities in the southwestern United States. Although *curanderismo* is a form of folk medicine practiced by many ethnic groups, its transmission down to the present day has traditionally occurred mostly within the cultural context of Mexico's indigenous peoples.

This particular training experience was administered in the Sonoran Desert by a Yaqui *curandero* who was both mentor to and a relative of the storyteller. (As of this writing, the storyteller practices her craft in a community mental health center in Denver, Colorado.) As this episode begins, she and her teacher have gone into the desert to gather healing herbs and to perform a ritual that would indicate to her what path she ought to follow from a particularly painful crossroads in her personal life. The instructions consisted of gathering certain ritual objects and seven pieces of wood of a certain size, which at her teacher's instruction she made into a fire. She was then to search the desert for a branch of a certain shape and flexure with which to tend the fire—all of which needed to be done with intensely focused concentration on the environment and every aspect of the ritual fire-making:

> And he asked me to look for the solution to the problem I had. After sorting through the amber and the ashes, it finally came to me.... "So," he said, "What is the solution to the problem? Did you find the solution in the amber or the fire?" "No," I said. "Was it in the ashes or in the stick?" "No," I said. So I pointed to my head and heart and said, "This is where the answer is at." "Ah," he said. That was his highest compliment. He was teaching me that ... I had to trust what I already knew....
>
> The first thing I learned from Don Chito was how to channel that power for myself. How to inwardly heal myself spiritually.... He taught me how to go off to a mountaintop or to the desert by myself, sweat out a lot of things, and concentrate.[14]

Although in this training the journey was an inward one, it was a focus on the outward environment that made possible the insights crucial to her ability to heal first herself and then others. Furthermore, the kind of attention she learned to focus on the ritual fire-making and tending is just as important in locating and harvesting the herbs that play an important role in this healing art, since it is their function to aid reconnection with the life forces that flow through them, the patient, and all creation.

Sustenance

Especially in functions such as medicinal herb harvesting, Don Chito was training Doña Velasquez to see clearly what in the natural environment was available to help those whose needs they were ministering to. As she was trained, she discovered that how and from where these resources are gathered are nearly as important as how they are used once acquired.

As quoted earlier from Joe Brown's writings, indigenous pragmatic lore in the realm of hunting, gathering, and agriculture is connected with sacred lore, because a tribe's cultural and physical survival are thought to depend on the relationship between them. Loss of respect for and loss of a caring attitude toward the environment and the living things within it begins to degrade the environment's ability to care for and sustain human life.

One example of this reciprocal relationship is that of traditional hunters among the Wintu Indians of northern California, some of whose traditional homelands and burial sites are in the national forests of that state. As characterized by several students of this culture, a Wintu hunter's ability to take a deer depends on two things—his skill at the hunt and the deer's willingness to die: "Should luck shine upon him and a deer—in an expression of nature's grand design—willingly die for him, the hunter accepts this gift with humility, gratitude, and courtesy. He accepts the deer's sacrifice only because he and his people genuinely need it.... By accepting the warm, energy and nutrient-laden carcass as a supreme gift, and by honoring its willing sacrifice by respectfully handling its physical remains, the hunter confirms and revitalizes the sacred contract between human beings and kindred animals."[15]

In the view of many western tribes, this willingness of the deer (or any other game animal) to sacrifice itself to the hunter is also a direct reflection of the overall relationship between the game species and the culture group of which the hunter is a member. The most powerful example of this teaching from my own experience came from an invitation I accepted to watch the Deer Dance held at the Taos Pueblo in January 1999 and later to talk with some of its participants.

One of the men with whom I spoke played the role of a hunter, which in this dance is also the role of the clown. As he explained it to me, once the elders announce what dances are to be performed and when, it is necessary to apply for the role one wants to dance. And in order for him to prove his worthiness to dance the role of hunter–clown, he first had to actually hunt and take a deer in the Sangre de Cristo Mountains above the pueblo. Thus the wildlife in the environment surrounding the pueblo also play a part in determining the makeup of tribal rituals.

This particular dance started in mid-afternoon and ended at sunset. It took place in a clearing in front of the adobe church, across the street from tribal government offices. This was a big event with a great many spectators, from both the pueblo and elsewhere. In the midst of the crowd a space had been created, about fifty yards long and twenty yards wide, oblong in shape, with a narrow opening to the northeast (the direction of Blue Lake, the tribe's place of origin).

Lining and defining the space were the women dancers, dressed to represent the Earth, the forest, and its plant life and holding pine tree boughs. As the hunter-clown dancer explained it to me, they were standing in the shape of a valley, since in an actual group ritual hunt, men from the pueblo fan out around the upper periphery of a canyon or deep valley and herd wildlife down its slopes to its mouth, where armed hunters are waiting. Only later did I realize that the oblong space with the narrow opening at one corner was also in the approximate shape of a uterus.

Once the space had been well defined, the animal dancers began to emerge from the kiva on the far side of the plaza. In a slow and steady procession, they made their way to the mouth of the valley. Leading the group were two sets of especially striking figures. One was the deer dancers, who wore large racks of deer antlers on their heads and danced bent forward, holding long sticks in their hands to simulate front legs. They were led by two tall dancers dressed in light buckskin; one of the participants later described them to me as representing "wardens."

Gradually the valley space created, defined, and held by the women forest dancers began to fill with the male animal dancers, who were wearing the actual heads and skins of deer, elk, bison, and other game animals, moving to the beat of the big ceremonial drum being played by a group of elders. And then came the hunter-clowns in grayface, cavorting and pantomiming the hunt. One by one, each "slayed" an animal by hoisting the animal dancer over his shoulders and dancing toward the narrow opening at the corner of the valley.

But at either side of the opening stood the wardens. As the hunterclowns tried to leave the valley with their prey, the wardens forced them back into the clearing, where the animal dancers were released to take new life and dance within the open space, only to be slain again. This ritual kill-and-release took place over and over, first in the space in front of the church and later at another site in front of the largest, oldest residential structure in the pueblo complex. The dance finally came to an end just as the mountains turned pink and the sun began to go down.

At a meeting about a month after the dance, I had an opportunity to discuss the meaning of this ritual in some detail with two of the dancers, one of whom was also a tribal official. I was especially interested in the kill-and-release interaction between the hunter-clowns and the wardens, as well as why the hunters were also the clowns in the first place.

As they both explained it to me, the hunter-clowns had a lot of energy, a lot of skill, and a lot of knowledge as to how to hunt and how to kill lots of animals. What they lacked was wisdom. They had no understanding of what the effects of all their energy, skill, and cleverly effective hunting methods were on the wildlife, whose populations they were needlessly wasting and depleting. It was the role of the wardens to teach the hunter-clowns over and over what fools they were and how their ignorance was threatening their own sustenance, as well as that of everything else living in the forest.

At that moment I realized perhaps more clearly than ever before why this Tiwan community has been able to sustain itself and its physical and cultural integrity in the same location for more than five hundred years, surviving the onslaughts of first Spanish and then Anglo domination and suppression. Among other things, it is because throughout this period of time they have been continuously, ritually reminding themselves of how important it is to live with respect for and in balance with all the various lifeforms on which their own lives and the survival of their culture depend. Euro-American society has no public national ritual even remotely resembling this teaching; and we are the poorer for it.

A more direct personal experience of this sense of connectedness and a brief glimpse into its meaning to some tribal members occurred when I took part in a convocation hosted by the board of directors of the Inter-Tribal Bison Collective, an assemblage of tribes along the western border of the Great Plains who are devoted to reintroducing the American bison to public lands, as well as to reviving the ritual significance of living bison in their respective spiritual practices. This particular gathering began with a series of testimonials by various tribal herd managers, which was to be followed by a feast with bison as the main course. Although clearly heartfelt, each testimonial was also fairly drawn out—at least by Anglo standards—during which time I got hungrier and hungrier. As moving as some of these testimonials were (recounting the significance of bison to their tribes and the benefits they were experiencing by having herds on their reservations), by the time we finally sat down to eat, I was single-mindedly focused much more on satisfying my carnal appetites than my interest in cultural and spiritual knowledge. But as I wolfed down my dinner and my appetite was partially sated, at some point when the pace of consumption slowed down a strange thing happened. A little like some of the flashbacks to Vietnam I used to undergo (but without the fear), suddenly I experienced "in the mind's eye" a prairie landscape, fresh from a spring rain. There was the sight of rolling grasslands, the smell of wet grass, and a view of the late afternoon sun partially obscured by clouds. Then after what was probably less than a minute, I was back in the dining area staring down at my plate of food— a little moved and a little changed.

Later on during the convocation I told one of the herd managers I had gotten to know about my experience. His response was, "It sounds like when you started paying attention, you actually *ate* some buffalo. That can happen, when you're careful." He eventually explained that when you concentrate carefully enough on what you are eating and the circumstances under which the food came to you, it becomes possible to get some sense of the life experience of that which you are eating. In sum, he pointed out, it only makes sense to treat that which you may someday eat (such as bison and other living things) with respect, since in one way or another your treatment of them will come back to you.

Health and Healing, Death, and Renewal

As exemplified in the work of *curandero/as* and other indigenous healers, connection to things (such as healing herbs) is important to the maintenance of health and the curing of ills, just as connection to places can be. For healers in tribes such as the Yaqui, Hopi, and Navajo, the site from which a medicinal herb is taken can be important in determining how useful it will be in a healing ritual. Hence, both plants and animals have habitats.

From these and similar traditions also comes the understanding that the health of persons and the health of places is interrelated, as in the relationship between the Seri and the cacti where their placentas are buried. For herbal medicines to retain their healing power, so must the place where they grew. This is one reason that tribes such as the Hopi and Navajo have periodically disclosed some elements of their healing rituals that otherwise probably would have remained secret, in legal efforts—usually futile—to protect sacred herb sites from damage or destruction.[16]

"Health and healing" are terms usually applied to the status of an individual person. But what of an individual's relationship to the community, or the status of the community overall? In the view of some who have studied it, maintaining or restoring the health of these connections is one of the functions of the Sun Dance. According to some well-documented accounts, the ceremony probably began as a pre-hunting ritual among the Cheyenne, first witnessed by Europeans at around the beginning of the eighteenth century. After the brutal suppression of the Ghost Dance by the U.S. government after the Plains tribes were conquered near the end of the nineteenth century, the Sun Dance reemerged in the early twentieth century as a ritual focused on the redemption of Indian communities and the reaffirmation of tribal values—a ritual of solidarity in the face of the implacable hostility reservation-bound Plains tribes were encountering in relationship to Euro-American society at the height of the assimilation era.[17]

Now associated to some degree with all the Sioux tribes, as well as with the Ute, Shoshone, and other Plains tribes, in modern times the Sun Dance has also been used as an instrument for the expression of intertribal unity as well. A common feature across its observance in all these cultures seems to be that participants vow to undertake the rigors of the ceremony in order to "live in this world and struggle for the good of all, rather than withdrawing from it. Proper life in this world requires keeping a 'good heart,' sacrificing for others, and behaving selflessly toward family, the wider network of kin and friends, and ultimately, the entire Sundance community."[18] Depending on who is conducting the ritual and for what purpose, the Sun Dance can generally last anywhere from one to several days. Especially in the longer ceremonies, participants may have a vision that lends specific guidance in understanding and living their lives after the ceremony has ended. Additionally, some dancers report being cured of physical ailments by reason of participation in the ceremony.[19]

Since this rite is about the renewal and reaffirmation of connection, where it is held is also important. Particularly auspicious is a place where it has been held traditionally, as a way of maintaining continuity with one's ancestry. For this reason, the more sacred a site to a given tribe, the more important it is that access be allowed for this ceremony, especially if it is a place where such rituals have been conducted historically.

Teachings on death and the afterlife vary widely from tribe to tribe, but one commonality is again the primacy of place, whether it be the place where bodies of the deceased are buried (for those tribes that bury their dead) or where spirits are thought to reside once they have left the body. The Zuni understanding of these matters is that if the deceased had been initiated into a kachina society, upon death the spirit usually goes to reside at the underwater kachina village, from which they can return to visit the living, "to give the living the kind of good fortune that it is particularly theirs to give: *ky'ashima,* all kinds of life-giving moisture" (including not just rain but also fecundity and beauty, as expressed in nature and in the art of the Zuni people).[20] One of the many life-links the kachinas share with living persons is to be united with them during ceremonial dances: "The kachinas who owned their own masks in life may return among the living in spirit form, entering the masks of the living dancers. Anyone at Kachina Village may return among the living as a cloud, most happily in a whole group of rainclouds."[21]

Unfortunately for some other Puebloan cultures, such as the Hopi, the place where their kachina spirits reside is not a mythic lake on their own reservation but one of the major geographic landmarks of northern Arizona—the San Francisco Peaks in the Coconino National Forest, near Flagstaff. In the Hopi understanding, their kachinas inhabit the peaks from mid-summer to mid-winter (from which they govern natural events such as rainfall). The other half of the year they live among the living Hopi, entering the bodies of masked performers during kachina dances.[22]

When the Forest Service decided to allow a concessionaire to expand a ski resort at the peaks, the Hopi mounted an ultimately unsuccessful effort to stop it. Tribal Chairman Abbott Sekaquaptewa testified at trial: "It is my opinion that in the long run if the expansion is permitted, we will not be able successfully to teach our people that this is a sacred place. If the ski resort remains or is expanded, our people will not accept the view that this is the sacred Home of the Kachinas. The basis of our existence as a society will become a mere fairy tale to our people. If our people no longer possess this long-held belief and way of life, which will inevitably occur with the continued presence of the ski resort ... a direct and negative impact upon our religious practices [will result]. The destruction of these practices will also destroy our present way of life and culture."[23]

As if to crown the eventual desecration of this site with an additional insult to Hopi spiritual traditions, the expanded resort development was later renamed the "Kachina Ski Area."

In the updated edition of his widely acclaimed *God Is Red*, Vine Deloria maintains that there are three ways that sites have become sacred, in the histories of both Western civilization and the indigenous peoples of North America:

1. By human acts performed there (such as Gettysburg National Cemetery and Wounded Knee, South Dakota)
2. By transmission of a teaching from a deity to humans (such as St. Paul's conversion on the road to Damascus or the original giving of medicine by the Gaans to the Apache on Mt. Graham in southeastern Arizona)
3. By reason of divine presence (such as Mt. Ararat and the San Francisco Peaks).[24]

Unfortunately, in his view, American society as a whole seems much better at desacralizing existing sites than it is at either maintaining the existing ones or allowing new ones to come into being.

Therefore, he argues, we must remain open to a fourth way, which is the possibility of new revelations at new sites. Neither indigenous nor imported religions can stay static if they are to stay vital and relevant to their practitioners. We must stay open to the possibility that our respective religious and spiritual traditions have not yet taught us all we need to know to live wisely on this Earth.

3

Nature as Haven, Nature as Hades

The Role of Wilderness in Immigrant Religions

Of everything the first permanent European immigrants brought to North America, perhaps the most enduring effect on the environment and its indigenous peoples would not be the colonists' tools and technologies, dress, or diseases but, rather, their ideas and beliefs. For these were the ways they conceptually constructed their "New World": how they determined what was right and wrong behavior, how they were moved to use the environment to meet their needs and desires, and how they sought to order their relations among themselves and with their indigenous neighbors.

The views on nature and religion that the seventeenth-century European colonists brought to bear on their new circumstances had not developed overnight. Although some ideas and beliefs clearly dominated immigrant perceptions and behaviors on and after their arrival, the colonists actually imported their whole history of thought on these matters. Understanding the wide variety of spiritual practices being conducted on the public lands of the United States in the present day means tracing the origins of those practices through an ancient, diverse, and yet thoroughly intertwined historical root system.

Europe's Earthen Religious Heritage

One problem with our knowledge of human prehistory is how changeable it is. Every time we dig a big enough hole in the ground carefully enough, and compare what we've found with existing artifacts, we learn a little more about who we used to be. Sometimes findings confirm existing ideas, but just as often they suggest the need to restructure or at least amend received learning. Constructing the past is a continuous work in progress, and everything written about who we were needs to be understood within that context; it is a still-life, frozen-in-time image of a continuous process and an ever-changing understanding.

That being said, contemporary learning in the area of European archaeology and ancient history portrays a rich heritage of Earthen[1] spiritual traditions, the first evidence of which coincides roughly with the end of the most recent Ice Age. At about the same time the First Native hunting tribes of North America were establishing cultures based on the herds of wild mammals they lived among, the same thing was evidently happening in Europe. Cave paintings in France and Spain dating back at least fifteen thousand years depict many such animals, especially large, horned ungulates such as the aurochs (wild ancestor of the domestic cow). Artifacts suggest that religious ceremonies were conducted in the presence of these frescoes and that participants dressed in the skins of and "became" their quarry, perhaps to maintain a relationship with the species on which the future success of the hunt was thought to depend.[2]

The tradition of deities in nature—either in the specific plants and animals themselves or in mythic figures that combine human and other animal features—seems to have developed continuously since that time. By about eight thousand years ago, the major culture groups of central Europe were all producing images of gods and goddesses, and worship of these images focused on seasonal changes, favorable climatic conditions, fecundity, successful hunts, and (with the development of large-scale agriculture) abundant harvests.

The relationship between modes of sustenance and social organization is a source of active interest among archaeologists and historians alike, particularly the shift from hunting and gathering to well-organized agriculture, the former having been the predominant domain of men and the latter of women in most Neolithic societies. In *The Rise of the West,* William McNeill reports the following:

> A widespread shift in human relations brought about by the transition from hunting to agriculture seems also to have affected Neolithic cults. In proportion as women became the major suppliers of food for the community, their independence and authority in the community probably increased; and various survivals in historic times suggest that matrilineal family systems prevailed in many Neolithic communities. Correspondingly, the spread of agriculture was connected everywhere with the rise of female priestesses and deities to prominence. The earth itself was apparently conceived as a woman—the prototype for the Great Mother of later religions—and the numerous female figurines which have been unearthed from Neolithic sites may have been intended as representations of the fruitful earth goddess.[3]

These traditions seem to have thrived unabated until about 3500 B.C.E., when they began to succumb to the invasive pressures of more warlike, patriarchal, and often monotheistic culture groups from the Near and Middle East and the eastern steppes, as well as from the northerly region the Romans would later name Gaul. Social commentator Riane Eisler refers to these invader groups as all exhibiting the "dominator model of social organization: a social system in which male dominance, male violence, and a generally hierarchic and authoritarian social structure was the norm."[4]

In *The Chalice and the Blade,* Eisler offers a treatment of European social and religious history as one characterized first by the ancient goddess worship McNeill describes above, but later by the desacralization of nature and related social subordination of women in all matters religious (as well as economic and political). More recently, Eisler's and similar writings have stimulated an acrid backlash from a few classical scholars, disputing that there ever was a time in European antiquity during which women and their association with nature enjoyed the kind of respect and adulation authors such as McNeill and Eisler describe.[5]

Regarding the relationship between gender roles in social relations and the centrality of nature in religious observations, however, it is far more difficult to refute the carefully researched and thoroughly documented work of much recent archaeology on the subject. In the second edition of her highly regarded *Gods and Goddesses of Old Europe,* archaeologist Marija Gimbutas makes a convincing case not so much for a bygone golden age of female religious hegemony as for prehistoric societies that are characterized more by relative gender balance and by direct union with nature. Human and nonhuman life forms are blended, and the symbiosis of female and male form and energy (rather than the domination of one by the other) is emphasized, perhaps anticipating the later development of Taoism in the East. As Gimbutas observes:

> Almost all Neolithic [European] goddesses are composite images with an accumulation of traits from the pre-agricultural and agricultural eras. The water bird, deer, bear, fish, snake, toad, turtle, and the notion of hybridization of animal and man, were inherited from the Paleolithic era and continued to serve as avatars of goddesses and gods.... In Old Europe the world of myth was not polarized into female and male as it was among the Indo-European and many other nomadic and pastoral peoples of the steppes. Both principles were manifest side by side. The male divinity in the shape of a young man or a male animal appears to affirm and strengthen the forces of the creative and active female. Neither is subordinate to the other; by complementing one another, their power is doubled.[6]

Further to the north and later on, decidedly more militaristic and patriarchal culture groups such as the Celts came to power, yet maintained religious traditions closely tied to the natural environment. This North European culture group worshiped more than three hundred different gods and goddesses, many being the patron spirits of specific wells, rivers, and sacred groves. Among the most important were the mother goddess Matrona (usually depicted with children or plentiful harvests, and closely associated with the River Marne), and the horned gods Cernunnos (the body of a man with the horns of a stag, who as "lord of the animals" was usually featured in a posture of meditation with other wild animals around him), Taruos

Trigaranus (the bull god), and the white-horned bull from the Táin Bó Cuailnge (a Celtic epic). The Celtic priesthood serving these deities were the Druids, whose name means "knowing the oak tree"; in pre-Roman times, most religious observances were conducted not in temples or other structures, but in forest sanctuaries.[7]

The Mediterranean's patriarchal societies of classical antiquity evidently started out with the worship of human-and-animal-blended deities such as Pan. By the time Homer provided his definitive description of the Greek pantheon, it was one in which the gods and goddesses resided not in nature or among mortals but above them. Each deity had earlier been associated with a natural element or entity, and they occasionally descended to Earth in human form to amuse or avenge themselves. But in the Greek religion of the Homeric age, the gods and goddesses controlled nature but did not permanently embody it, just as they sought to control human behavior while not living permanently in human form themselves. These were deities at a distance.

And this was the pantheon as well as its arm's-length relationship to mortals that the Romans inherited. They changed the names and reputed behaviors of the key figures in this heavenly assemblage, eventually adding a few of their own military and political leaders to the group (which, as it turned out, would cause serious legitimacy problems in trying to secure the sincere spiritual devotion of many Roman citizens). And it was with this attenuated Earthen Roman state religion that Christianity would do battle during the four centuries after Jesus' life and times.

European Christianity and the Reconstruction of Earthen Spirituality

One of the enduring ironies in the history of world religions is the extraordinary disconnect between the actual words of the historical figures in whose name some of them were founded (such as Siddhartha Gautama, Jesus, and Mohammad) and the behaviors of the ethnic groups, religious and political factions, and nations claiming identity as followers of those teachings. Europe's most graphic example of this phenomenon is the actions of its various military and political leaders, taken in the name of the Prince of Peace, to forcibly

Christianize first that continent and then its nation-states' colonies over the last two millennia.

Christianity came to Roman society at a time when the empire was beginning to falter, and its leaders were in search of blameworthy causes for its problems external to their own power structure. Christians made excellent scapegoats, as when Nero persecuted them on the unproven rationale that they were responsible for the burning of the imperial capital. The sect had been imported from a sometimes-rebellious eastern colony, and its earliest adherents in Rome were mostly from the social groups who had the least to lose and the most to gain from the overthrow of the government. In a repressive and hierarchical slave-holding society, a message of salvation and spiritual liberation through a direct personal relationship with a loving deity— who lived in one's heart, as well as the heavens above—had understandable appeal to the enslaved and the downtrodden.[8]

Depending on the personalities of the leadership and the relative level of domestic discord, Roman leaders during this period (about 100 to 300 C.E.) vacillated between accommodating spiritual pluralism and brutally suppressing it. Refusal to publicly practice the state religion and to swear allegiance to its deities (including present and past government leaders) was sometimes seen as tantamount to treason and was punished accordingly. This was a particular problem for Christians, who—unlike the many other religious minorities at that time—refused to practice the state religion along with their own. During periods of official intolerance, it was not only Christians who suffered; just as suspect and just as persecuted were those who practiced any form of magic, whether it was the "white magic" of healing and love or the "black magic" of death and destruction. To practice magic was again to establish a direct personal relationship with the spiritual powers that be and to incline them to one's own will, rather than acknowledging the exclusive power of the state to govern all matters spiritual and material.[9]

As the empire continued to unravel, those who sought the demise of the existing government naturally sought to enlist the support of those who were suffering the most from such oppression. As Christianity began to spread more broadly through Roman society (although still very much as a social phenomenon of urban populations rather than the more socially conservative rural gentry and peasantry), its more politically active adherents began to significantly influence the changing balance of power. Overthrow of Rome's military and political power structure from within the power structure would ultimately come at the hands of Constantine I, who then assumed the emperorship himself, reigning until his death in 337 C.E.

Many historians cite Constantine's conversion to Christianity as one of the single most important events in the religious history of Europe, in part because he continued the tradition of the direct state control of religion. The only difference was that now the state religion was urban-centered Christianity, and now it was the rural gentry and peasantry—the pagans (*paganis* being the Latin term for "country-dweller" or "country-folk")—who were to be the sometimes tolerated and sometimes oppressed religious minority.[10] Constantine organized and thoroughly dominated several conferences and councils for the purpose of establishing orthodox (i.e., state-approved) doctrine and affecting church governance structures. In turn, this bestowed considerable legitimacy on some powerfully anti-pagan doctrines that were being formulated by church leaders. Condemning the disturbingly carnal nature of the pagan tradition, for instance, the influential third-century C.E. Christian theologian Origen wrote that "the world of flesh is the world of demons. Gross matter . . . is the domain of Satan."[11]

Theologians of this era conceived doctrines that included an artful weaving of neo-Platonic cosmology and Christian scripture. The Greeks had already described a vertical Great Chain of Being, with inert matter and plant life at the base, animals above them, humans above the animals, and the heavens above them. Added now were a Christian God above and a church-defined Devil below. Humans were literally suspended between heaven and hell. Their spiritual proclivities made possible ascendancy and perfection, but it was their own flesh—their sensual ties to the natural world—that constantly threatened their spiritual aspirations. The sacred no longer existed in nature alone—not in flowing water, not in groves of trees, and certainly not in animals, either domestic or wild. Earth was no longer a venerable mother, home, or object of worship. It was a spiritual mine-field, with threats to eventual salvation lurking behind every tree, as well as in one's own sensual appreciation of life itself.

In positing a powerful and fearsome icon of evil incarnate—a Devil—early theologians also solved a vexing doctrinal problem. For throughout his teachings, Jesus had stressed the importance of loving and living peacefully with one another (including one's enemies) and of treating others with the same respect and regard as one would wish to be treated. Yet for most of the two millennia following the origins of these teachings, the Christian nations of Europe repeatedly conducted some of the most brutal wars in recorded history. Particularly when it came to either repelling or conquering pagans and infidels, Christian soldiers and their religious advisors—in early Europe, in the Middle East during the Crusades, and later on in the New World—needed a rationale that would allow them to act with moral impunity. And that rationale would be that they were making war not on other humans of equal spiritual standing but on the legions of Satan. Furthermore, if it was to be conflict fueled by religious fervor, what better form could there be for evil incarnate than the ancient gods of conquered Earth-worshiping peoples: especially the horned, hoofed, half-human, half-beast whose particular talent lay in controlling and corrupting humans through manipulation of their own sensuality and of nature itself.[12]

Heaven, Hell, and Enlightenment in a New World

Early Spanish conquests in the Americas coincided roughly with the worst excesses of the Inquisition in the conquistadors' home country. Jews, gypsies, magicians, witches, and others suspected of practicing anything other than the state church–approved religion in the state church–approved way were being persecuted just as mercilessly as had been the first Christians of pagan Rome. It was patently evident to the Spanish conquerors that they had stumbled on new lands that were at once materially rich and spiritually afflicted. In their rituals of nature worship (and in the case of the Aztecs, occasional human sac-rifice), the entire indigenous population was obviously possessed of the Devil, and it was the colonizers' clear moral duty to save their souls while relieving them of their real estate.

Along the northern Atlantic seaboard in the early seventeenth century, the situation was somewhat different. New England's first British colonists had come to the Americas not to establish the Church of England but to escape its control. Their home country was in turmoil; Britain was in the throes of a civil war that would continue off and on for most of the seventeenth century.

One source of terrible social strife during this time was the struggle over the state control of religion. In defying the authority of the pope to dictate either his or his subject's moral behavior, King Henry VIII had gone to the extreme of rejecting the Catholic Church entirely as the primary institution for Christian worship and, instead, had set up his own Protestant state church. Social conflict—periodically manifesting as armed conflict—between Catholics and Protestants ensued and was one of seventeenth-century England's defining historical characteristics. Once the Protestants had gained dominance, conflict resumed over which of its various sects would control the development of doctrine and ritual within the newly established Church of England.

As de Tocqueville would later observe, "It is not the happy and the powerful who go into exile,"[13] and so it was with the Puritan religious dissenters who crossed the Atlantic to establish a "New England" in the Americas in the early 1600s. These were religious refugees, leaving their homeland not gladly and in pursuit of new prospects but sadly and in retreat from persecution by dominant factions within the Anglican Church. They were also close-knit urbanists, not independent explorers. America was not a new Eden into which they were happily moving but a grim and forbidding wilderness to which they felt they were being banished. The idea of living in nature was anathema; in the words of their leader John Winthrop, their intention was rather to transform the forested landscape they confronted into a "city upon a hill."[14]

Their disregard for uncultivated lands and fear of all things wild was itself a product of their religious training. The first appearance of the word "wilderness" in the English language was in the first English translation of the Bible, in the late fourteenth century;[15] and then in association with harsh, bedeviled environments into which God occasionally cast sinful humans as punishment. According to Roderick

Nash: "The Old Testament reveals that the ancient Hebrews regarded the wilderness as a cursed land.... The identification of the arid wasteland with God's curse led to the conviction that wilderness was the environment of evil, a kind of hell.... Like that of other cultures, the Hebraic folk imagination made the wilderness the abode of demons and devils."[16]

Such religious attitudes had dire environmental consequences for medieval Europe: "In early and medieval Christianity, wilderness kept its significance as the earthly realm of the powers of evil that the Church had to overcome. This was literally the case in the missionary efforts to the tribes of northern Europe. Christians judged their work to be successful when they cleared away the wild forests and cut down the sacred groves where the pagans held their rites."[17]

Along with a fear of wilderness itself, the Puritans also mortally feared efforts by anyone trying to personally influence natural forces, especially through witchcraft or the practice of magic in any form (which they viewed as synonymous). In America's seventeenth-century British colonies, over 95 percent of all formal charges of witchcraft (of a total of at least 344) and over 90 percent of executions for this offense (35) happened in Puritan New England.[18]

By contrast, other colonies of the time were much less obsessed with witchcraft (Virginia made false accusation of it a crime) and tolerated or even encouraged the practice of certain kinds of magic and astrology.[19] The Quakers of Pennsylvania did not believe in a Devil ("We have no horns nor hoofs in our religion") and had no laws against witchcraft.[20] And among the early-eighteenth-century Celtic immigrants to the Appalachian backcountry, many forms of magic and witchcraft were actively practiced and to some extent revered, and informal pagan fertility rites were very much a part of spring planting rituals.[21]

But in British colonial society as a whole, such beliefs and behavior were the exception rather than the rule. The Old Testament injunction to "overcome the Earth and subdue it" was the religious text chosen to justify remaking the American environment in the image of European civilization and for banishing wildness in the name of holiness: it was God's commandment that wilderness be tamed and transformed. And in this enterprise, an equally compelling rationale was to be found in new attitudes toward nature being fostered back in the home country, in the "Age of Enlightenment."

In the pre-Christian Earthen religious traditions of Old Europe, nature and divinity were one and the same, and natural environments (especially forests and groves) were a spiritual sanctuary. In later European Christianity, natural environments were chaotic and ungodly. Both visions of nature were spiritually charged, albeit at opposite poles. In contrast, leading thinkers of the scientific revolution such as Francis Bacon, René Descartes, and Isaac Newton posited a world that was essentially devoid of either positive or negative spiritual significance. Instead, nature was likened to monumental and intricate machinery. The challenge to the human mind was to learn first how all its parts worked and then how to better operate them to human advantage.

By the time the British colonies became the United States and the scientific revolution (an improved understanding of how nature works) ushered in the industrial revolution (an improved understanding of how to better manipulate it), the desacralizing of nature fostered by Enlightenment-era thought had come into convenient alliance with the demonizing of nature asserted by earlier Christian theologians. Just as the Devil was the enemy of God and of godly humans, so was scientific ignorance of nature the foe of the rational mind. And just as it was the duty of the faithful to convert heathen wildness (both the wilderness and its indigenous human inhabitants) into tamed and obedient servants of Christian society, so, too, was it the duty of an emerging secular priesthood of scientists and engineers to convert natural forces into expressions of human mastery over nature.

Harnessing such power was more than simply a means to better meet basic human needs. In America's richly endowed natural environment, it would also prove to be a source of incredible material wealth. Humans no longer lived in nature; they inhabited a self-made environment peripherally and abundantly stocked with "natural resources":

In the wake of the Enlightenment, nature became primarily a resource to be exploited in the human quest for progress and the regaining of Adam's dominion over the nonhuman world. The point no longer could be to gain rapport with nature in the hope of gaining wisdom from it or being favored by it. For the most part, in the Enlightenment view of things, nature was passive, dumb, and wild. It begged for development, exploitation, and manipulation by human beings to eradicate a range of evils and to meet perennial needs such as adequate food and shelter. To rest content with the current state of economic, scientific, and technological progress would be irresponsible and an unheroic abdication of human destiny as set forth by God, which was to acquire complete dominion over the earth.[22]

East Meets West in the American Conservation Movement

For most of the nineteenth century, a combination of self-aggrandizing Calvinist theology, unswerving faith in science and technology, and the consumer appetites of a rapidly growing Euro-American population combined to utterly transform most of America's natural environment. But as the country became bigger, wealthier, and more urbanized, concern began to grow that as a nation we were paying too high a price for material gain. A few lonely—if eloquent—voices began to speak out against the environmental despoliation that Americans in their schools, their churches, and their legislatures were being told was the inevitable price of progress.

In the realm of nature and religion, by about mid-century some fresh amendments were being worked into the American cultural soil. To the Earthen traditions of First Natives and the Christian and pagan traditions of European immigrants were added some Asian perspectives, which appeared in the English language for the first time. In 1844 a French scholar named Eugene Burnouf produced the first known Western translation of the classic Mahayana Buddhist text, the *Lotus Sutra,* along with a detailed general introduction to Buddhist philosophy.[23] That same year, the first English translation from Burnouf's French was written and published in a New England literary magazine under the title "The Preachings of the Buddha" by a young essayist named Henry David Thoreau.[24]

In some respects, Thoreau was to the American conservation movement what Martin Luther had been to the Protestant Reformation three hundred years earlier. Thoreau was among the first to articulate a moral vision of the relationship between the human and the divine (regarding attitudes toward nature) that was sharply at odds with the mainstream religious teachings of the time—a vision that provided both inspiration and resolve to those who would follow. And, like Luther, he held in low regard the dominant religious institutions of his time, which he accused of fostering an attitude of "forest-hating" and which he once likened to a "rotten squash"; on another occasion, he analogized "the church [as] a sort of hospital for men's souls, and as full of quackery as the hospital for their bodies."[25] Equally ill-conceived, in Thoreau's view, was the Enlightenment-era construct of nature as a vast, intricate machine, devoid of divinity and knowable to the human mind only through rational analysis and empirical observation (although he himself was also an astute empiricist).

Thoreau and fellow transcendentalists such as Ralph Waldo Emerson undertook a deep investigation of Eastern religions not simply in search of a doctrinal replacement for the prevailing Protestant theology and accompanying scientism of their times. They were not "converts" to Buddhism, Taoism, or Hinduism, nor did they seek to persuade others to follow those paths. Instead, they encouraged inquiry into the underlying unity in all religious teachings (or, in Emerson's case, the overarching presence of the "Over-soul")—a unity that could be accessed only through transcendence of the limited, culturally conditioned understanding of God and nature being taught in the schools and churches of their times. For Thoreau in particular, it was religious institutions and their quest for social control more than the doctrinal distinctions between religious teachings that were the problem; Thoreau believed that the similarities in the underlying values taught in these traditions outweighed their differences for the most part. In *A Week on the Concord and Merrimac Rivers,* Thoreau mused, "I know that some will have hard thoughts on me, when they hear their Christ named beside my Buddha. . . . Yet I am sure that I am willing they should love their Christ more than my Buddha, for the love is the main thing."[26]

The transcendentalists' introduction of orientalism into American religious thought was not by way of proselytizing. Rather, they were using it more as a counterbalance—a means of broadening their own understanding (and that of those who shared their views) beyond the confines of the conceptual constructs of God and nature into which their society had originally enculturated them. Thoreau encountered and extrarationally experienced the divine directly in nature itself. He was not a theist, in either the Christian or the pagan sense of the term, but his assertion of the ability to directly experience divine presence in nature was decidedly Earthen in character and more in keeping with the spiritual traditions of America's indigenous peoples than he was ever to know. What he and other transcendentalists failed to recognize in the creation of their East–West synthesis, especially regarding divinity in nature, was how closely their views paralleled the beliefs and practices many of North America's First Natives had been observing in some form for several thousand years.

Thoreau believed that while the feeling of separation from and impetus to exert dominance over nature may be endemic to industrialized society and may well be our cultural inheritance, it need not dictate our future. More than a century before his words would be embodied in public policy, Thoreau asserted that humankind's survival lay not in the conquest of wilderness by the industrial age but in cherishing the wilderness as a source of spiritual renewal. To destroy that source was to lose the ability to respect and ultimately to sustain all life. "In wildness," he told the Concord Lyceum in 1851, "is the preservation of the world."[27]

The transcendentalists were spiritual explorers and cultural innovators. In keeping with the inventive energy of the times, they exhibited what de Tocqueville had already described as quintessentially Yankee traits: borrowing freely from a wide variety of existing materials to create something both original and newly indigenous to American culture. It had happened in the area of government in the eighteenth century, and it happened with spirituality in the nineteenth. Yet to Thoreau, orientalism was less an introduction of something new and foreign into the cultural mix than it was a rediscovery of something quite basic to the character of all immigrants to the New World. "There is an orientalism in the most restless pioneer," he once observed, "and the farthest west is but the farthest east."[28]

Thoreau may not have known how literally true these words were when he wrote them. For just as East and West were meeting in the transcendentalists' intellectual synthesis in New England, so too were immigrants from "the farthest east" (mostly China, and later Japan) beginning to settle in significant numbers among the "farthest west" Euro-American immigrants (including conquered Mexicans and nearly extinct indigenous peoples of California). Philosophical and religious views toward nature that the transcendentalists were studying in theory were being practiced in fact in most urban centers in the state. By 1860, one in ten Californians was Chinese, and wherever they were gathered in sufficient numbers to create community, one of the first substantial structures to appear was the temple, in which a popularized mixture of Taoism, Confucianism, and Buddhism found continuous and authentic ritual interpretation.[29]

The spiritual inspiration of Thoreau and Emerson's writings began to find significant political expression later in the nineteenth century. It was then that John Muir, a Scottish immigrant who had been reared in a culture of Calvinist disdain for all things wild, emerged from a prolonged solitary existence in California's Sierra Nevada Mountains to become one of the leading conservationists of his generation. In advocating the establishment of Yosemite National Park (1890) and in organizing the Sierra Club (1892), Muir placed consistent emphasis on wilderness as the purest expression of divinity to be found on Earth. Although he was not religious, in terms of institutional affiliation, nearly all of Muir's nature writings were explicitly spiritual in character, in keeping with the style if not precisely the substance of Thoreau (Muir was a theist, seeing in nature the evidence of God's work, whereas Thoreau saw pervasive divinity in all of nature itself).

Among Muir's first published works was an 1876 newspaper editorial, "God's First Temples: How Shall We Preserve our Forests?" The theme of God in nature and wilderness preservation as an Earthen religious endeavor is to be found in nearly every significant publication he produced. According to Nash, "most of Muir's ideas were variations on the transcendentalists' staple theme: natural objects were the 'terrestrial manifestations of God.' At one point he described nature as a 'window opening into heaven, a mirror reflecting the Creator.' Leaves, rocks, and bodies of water became 'sparks of the Divine Soul.'"[30]

With the establishment of the National Forest Service, the National Park Service, and President Roosevelt's protection of millions of acres of federal land from unregulated resource exploitation, in the early days of the twentieth century the American conservation movement began to come of age. While a spiritual motivation for the protection of wild places on public lands was seldom directly acknowledged in acts of Congress and presidential directives, the rhetoric of Muir and his colleagues advocating such public policies was replete with references to America's wild lands as sanctuaries for worship and spiritual renewal—for re-creation in the fullest sense of the word.

There is no small irony in this turn of events, from the standpoint of the American Indian tribes who formerly inhabited the nation's national parks and forests. As chapter 4 demonstrates, westward expansion of the frontier and the confinement of tribes to reservations in many instances meant either restrictions on or a denial of access to some of their most sacred sites, which were seldom within reservation borders. This was to some extent deliberate, inasmuch as one of the policy goals of the federal government during the nineteenth century was to assimilate American Indians into the dominant culture. And this meant converting them to Christianity, which included strongly discouraging or in some cases criminalizing the practice of native religions.

But once the newly acquired public lands had been largely emptied of their indigenous inhabitants, resource exploitation on those lands eventually proved so ruinous that the conservation movement came into being—a movement that emphasized the importance of spiritual connection with nature. Not surprisingly, the first lands in the public domain to be accorded protection as national monuments, parks, and (later) wilderness areas were the ones that contain the most remarkable scenery and unusual geologic features—the very same attributes that had made them sacred sites for indigenous peoples in the first place.

Environmental Legacy of Immigrant Religions

The emphasis in the early days of the conservation movement was primarily on establishing national parks, forests, and recreation areas in the public domain and on preserving them from privatization and plunder. In the latter half of the twentieth century, greater attention was devoted to how these lands and resources—now set aside for public use—ought to be managed. And while the late-twentieth-century language of conservation advocacy may not have been as self-consciously and explicitly spiritual as the words of Emerson, Thoreau, and Muir, nevertheless it has reinforced the sense that the religious and spiritual dimensions are much more important than policy makers and even some environmental advocates are usually comfortable in acknowledging.

Just what is the environmental legacy of the dominant culture's immigrant religions? Is there something inherently antienvironmental about Judeo-Christian teachings? Or, instead, is the problem a historically selective reading of those traditions' texts as a way of morally rationalizing the heedless exploitation of this land's natural riches? That debate has been going on at least since Thoreau's time, but it has taken on an especially keen edge in the closing days of the twentieth century and the early days of the twenty first, with a renewed interest in the relationship between spirituality and the environment.

One of the most influential contributions to the modern dialogue was Lynn White's brief article in a 1967 issue of *Science*, "The Historical Roots of Our Environmental Crisis," which since its publication has spawned literally hundreds of articles and dozens of books reflecting on religion and the environment in contemporary American society.[31] White asserted that the tradition itself is antienvironmental, although at this point in time, the evidence weighs heavily on the side of historical selectivity.

The only language in the Bible that is regularly cited as justification for human domination of nature and that the natural environment exists only to serve human needs consists of two passages in Genesis and one in Psalms. In the words of the Old Testament God to his followers:

> Be fruitful, and multiply, and replenish the earth, and subdue it: and have dominion over the fish of the sea, and over the fowl of the air, and over every living thing that moveth upon the earth. . . . Behold, I have given

you every herb bearing seed, which is upon the face of all the earth, and every tree, in the which is the fruit of a tree yielding seed, to you it shall be for meat. (Gen. 1:27–29)

Be fruitful and multiply, and replenish the earth. And the fear of you and the dread of you shall be upon every beast of the earth, and upon every fowl of the air, upon all that moveth upon the earth, and upon all the fishes of the sea; into your hands they are delivered. Every moving thing that liveth shall be meat for you; even as the green herb have I given you all things. (Gen. 9:1–3)

And in the words of the psalmist to the God of the Old Testament:

What is man that thou art mindful of him? and the son of man, that thou visitest him? For thou hast made him a little lower than the angels, and hast crowned him with glory and honor. Thou hast made him to have dominion over the works of thy hands; thou hast put all things under his feet: all sheep and oxen, yea, and the beasts of the field; the fowl of the air, and the fish of the sea, and whatsoever passeth through the paths of the seas. (Psalm 8:4–8)

Relative to other world religions, these texts and reliance on them as a rationale for Western civilization's subsequent assault on the natural world led Lynn White to observe: "Especially in its western form, Christianity is the most anthropocentric religion the world has seen. . . . Man shares, in great measure, God's transcendence of nature. Christianity, in absolute contrast to ancient paganism and Asia's religions . . . not only established a dualism of man and nature but also insisted that it is God's will that man exploit nature for his proper ends."[32] However, as numerous scholars have since emphasized, in the same texts there is ample evidence of very different views toward nature and humankind's relationship to it. Even within the same collection of Psalms that at one point emphasizes dominion, there is another which—as echoed in the writings of Thoreau and Emerson three thousand years later— speaks instead of seeing in nature itself a reflection of divinity: "I will lift up mine eyes unto the hills, from which cometh my help. My help cometh from the Lord, which made heaven and earth" (Psalm 121:1–2). A few pages later one encounters the *Song of Solomon,* which is one long love poem to the ripeness of life itself. This is a verbal celebration of love in the flesh, replete with nature-based analogies to the delight the poet takes in the lover's physical charms. It reads more like a pagan hymn to all creation than anything else to be found in the literature of this tradition: "The flowers appear on the earth; the time of the singing of birds is come, and the voice of the turtle is heard in our land; The fig tree putteth forth her green figs, and the vines with the tender grape give a good smell. Arise, my love, my fair one, and come away" (Song of Sol. 1:12–13).

As for the New Testament, in the actual teachings of Jesus one searches in vain for the kind of rhetoric that led Lynn White to observe: "To a Christian a tree can be no more than a physical fact. The whole concept of the sacred grove is alien to Christianity and to the ethos of the West. For nearly two millennia Christian missionaries have been chopping down sacred groves which are idolatrous because they assume spirit in nature."[33]

Whatever the actual motives for the medieval missionaries who clear-cut the forests of Europe or the Euro-Americans who have been doing the same thing here for the last four hundred years, it has nothing to do with anything Jesus actually taught. Instead, Jesus repeatedly emphasized an appreciation for nature and frequently used analogies to nature to make a point. In advising his disciples on how to spread his teachings, he recommends, "be ye therefore wise as serpents, and harmless as doves" (Matt. 10:16). And rather than telling his followers that they lived divorced from nature and should therefore have no regard for it, he instead expressed the importance of admiration for the natural beauty around them: "Consider the lilies of the field, how they grow; they toil not, neither do they spin: And yet I say unto you, That even Solomon in all his glory was not arrayed like one of these" (Matt. 6:28–29).

As with the five hundred different cultural groups comprising indigenous America, the true legacy of immigrant religions' perspectives on the natural world is one of incredible diversity. In colonial history, we have New England Puritans burning to death deviant conjurors at one extreme and Appalachian Celts out boogying in the bushes in a planting-time re-creation of their pagan heritage at the other. Faith later turned to science and technology as sources of bounty, only to be countered by an infusion of Eastern thought and a new Euro-American indigenous synthesis proclaiming a rediscovery of the divine in nature, to be apprehended through direct spiritual experience rather than the medium of religious institutions. As a result, in the realm of nature and religion, we now live in the midst of the widest array of spiritual beliefs and related ritual observances in the history of American society.

History is becoming more circular and less linear, as the most ancient becomes the most modern (or perhaps postmodern). Wicca and other forms of neopaganism together constitute one of the fastest-growing forms of spiritual expression and observance in the country today. Whether seen as part of this movement or distinguishable from it, Goddess worship is for its adherents very much a rediscovery of pre-Christian Earthen spiritual traditions, while to critics both Wicca in general and Goddess worship in particular are latter-day fabrications based on shaky historical foundations and undeserving of the status of religion.

In some ways, this controversy may be losing its relevance to the future of Earthen spiritual practices in America. The archaeological and written historical evidence of Wicca and multiple forms of Goddess worship in the pre-Christian West is fairly incontrovertible. And as journalist Margot Adler points out in her comprehensive study of the subject,[34] although there is no way to prove conclusively that the rituals of Wicca and Goddess worship perfectly mirror their ancient genealogies, modern-day devotees of these movements practice their rituals with every bit as much sincere spiritual commitment, devotion, and attention to ritual detail as do the Baptists, the Buddhists, and the Baha'is. There seems to be no doubt in the minds of adherents to these newly formed groups that their beliefs and actions are the embodiment of a living spiritual tradition.

The answer to the question of whether these are religions depends on who is asking the question, and why. The Internal Revenue Service, the Department of Defense, the courts, the phone company, academia, and the plethora of existing religious denominations all have their own criteria for determining what does and does not constitute religious movements and organizations, and for granting or denying status accordingly. In keeping with the definition of religion given in chapter 1 (the institutionalized expression of extrarational, transcendent, unitive human experience), Wicca and Goddess worship as described in the current literature do very much qualify as Earthen religions.

Contemporary conventional religious denominations are all very much in the process of rediscovering nature-appreciating aspects of their own traditions—aspects that critics such as Lynn White had assumed do not exist. And like the controversy over Wicca, there is plenty of debate within many of these "mainstream" denominations over the question of whether contemporary writings on the "greening" of Christianity and Judaism rests on sound theological scholarship emphasizing long-suppressed teachings on benevolence toward nature, or if, instead, this is simply an exercise in "greenwashing" traditions that inherently hold nature in subordinate regard.

For any religious tradition to remain viable, it must continually maintain a balance between faithfully replicating received learning and effectively responding to the needs of the present and the foreseeable future. All the traditions spoken of here—First Native, pre-Christian, Judeo-Christian, and Eastern alike—see themselves as seeking to address a common threat: a growing environmental crisis engendered in no small part by modernism's divorce of the wild from the wise, the scientific from the sacred, and the spirit from the flesh.

Historically Asian spiritual traditions such as Buddhism and Taoism generally receive more favorable treatment in environmentalist critiques of religious thought because transcendence of the self and unity with nature (actually, with all existence) lie at the very core of their teachings. Indeed, figures such as longtime Zen student and poet Gary Snyder have made some of the most significant contributions to the spiritual dimensions of American conservationist literature since Thoreau. However, it also appears that these teachings have historically done little to dissuade their host cultures (e.g., India, China, Japan, and countries in Southeast Asia) from regularly making ruinous environmental decisions. Moreover, while present-day adherents of Buddhism and Taoism (of both Asian and European extraction) may profess reverence for nature, some critics contend that for many if not most of them—just like the rest of American society—an affinity for material acquisition and personal convenience far outweighs genuinely reverential treatment of the environment in their personal lifestyles.

Beyond these tradition-based forms of spiritual expression lie those that, although woven from various strands of old religious yore, acknowledge themselves to be new syntheses, oriented not toward replicating a past age but toward the creation of a "New Age." The term itself covers a diverse group of beliefs and practices incorporating varying mixtures of numerology, astrology, crystal power, sight/sound/aroma therapies, and guided meditations—all emphasizing direct contact with the natural world. For skeptics and cultural conservators, these groups are the easiest to deride, because they readily admit that they are making it up as they go along, just as Thoreau and Emerson did. In terms of extrarationality, transcendence, and unitive experience, they certainly qualify as spiritual; whether they also qualify as religious remains as much an organizational as a theological question. Suffice it to say that American spiritual inventiveness is every bit as vigorous and volatile today as it was in the transcendentalists' time—if not more so.

What are the implications of all the Earthen spiritual and religious ferment for the management of public lands and resources? They are many, and they are multidimensional. To a greater extent than perhaps any other time in our history, indigenous and immigrant-descended Americans of every conceivable spiritual orientation see our public lands—especially our national parks and monuments, forests, and wilderness areas—as places of spiritual sanctuary and worship. And as the following survey of legal doctrines and case studies involving many of these spiritual groups makes clear, issues of culture, spiritual orientation, and constitutional law are likely to play a far more important role in the future management of our commonly held public lands and resources than they have in the past.

PART TWO
Law

4

Culture and Justice

Nature and the Rule of Law in the "New World"

Defining Law

What is law? Who has it, and who does not? Does "law" refer to only the acts of legislatures and edicts of courts, or does the "rule of law" encompass the whole framework of understandings within which members of any society decide questions of right and wrong, resolve disputes, and maintain order?

As with the issue of what is (and is not) religion, much depends on who is asking the question and why. To classical scholars and nineteenth-century social scientists, the existence of written laws and government institutions to enforce them were among the most important hallmarks distinguishing "civilized" from "savage" societies. The former had law, and the latter clearly did not.

The Oxford English Dictionary's first definition of law is "A rule of conduct imposed by authority. . . . The body of rules, whether proceeding from enactments or from custom, which a particular state or community recognizes as binding on its members or subjects," reflecting the view of most Western scholars studying law and society in more recent times. Abandoning the Euro-centric perspective that law could only be found in Western-style institutions, as early as the 1920s anthropologists such as Bronislaw Malinowski found sophisticated, enforceable mechanisms of reciprocal obligation and social ordering in nonliterate cultures that formerly were considered to be devoid of principles of justice.[1]

Later came the 1941 publication of *The Cheyenne Way*, a detailed accounting of dispute resolution among North America's indigenous peoples of the western plains. In this landmark study, Karl Llewellyn and Adamson Hoebel likewise discovered a complex system of norms, principles, and related case law preserved by oral tradition, which tribal elders used to both maintain domestic tranquility and ensure some measure of cultural preservation.[2] Based on this and later studies, Hoebel concluded that most of humankind's culture groups have developed recognizable means of accomplishing four major tasks necessary for social cohesion and cultural continuity, which he referred to as "law jobs": (1) social control, (2) conflict resolution, (3) adaptation and social change, and (4) norm enforcement.[3] Since that time, much of comparative legal anthropology has consisted of seeking to determine how various culture groups go about accomplishing these tasks.

By the late twentieth century, however, a more critical perspective on the study of culture was calling into question the comparative framework method. The core criticism was that to approach the study of any culture with preconceived categories into which social behaviors would be organized and by which they would be named is to intellectually colonize the culture being studied, as well as to so narrowly conceive the subject culture that much of its richness and hidden genius would be inevitably overlooked.[4] The alternative, "grounded theory" approach unquestionably does a better job of describing in respondents' own terms and to some extent through their own eyes what the experience of "living their culture" actually is. Nonetheless, for our purposes here, there are two reasons that a comparative framework such as Hoebel's still has its uses. First, the perspective at this point is historical, and there is no way to go back and interview either the indigenous peoples or the European colonists from the time of first sustained contact nearly four centuries ago. All we have to rely on is the written record generated by the colonists and the oral traditions of the First Native cultures still in existence. Second, a very wide array of cultures occupied the historical field at the time of European colonization, and these cultures continue to exert influence today: about five hundred indigenous ones, as well as English, Spanish, and (to a lesser extent) French imports, all of which have made significant contributions to our contemporary confluence of customs and practices. Some form of comparative framework is needed to make sense of so much diversity.

Understanding the Sources and Evolution of American Law Ways

Just as religious expression is largely a product of the culture within which a religious tradition is maintained, so, too, is the law first and foremost a product of the culture that sustains it. The definition of "culture" in chapter 1 spoke of inherited understandings of how persons in a given society relate to themselves, each other, other groups, and their environment. How did different culture groups cohabiting North America during European colonization relate to each other through the medium of their respective law ways, and how have those relationships changed over time?

To better understand the uses of law to govern these changing relationships over the last two centuries, four different dimensions, or descriptive continua, are worth keeping in mind:

- *Individual/communal.* What were the varying degrees of emphasis that indigenous and immigrant traditions of social ordering and dispute resolution placed on the rights and interests of individuals, relative to the wants and needs of the communities of which they were a part?
- *Lateral/hierarchical.* Especially regarding relationships between communities or between different culture groups, were these characterized more by voluntary associations of coequals or by the superimposition of a hierarchical framework of governance over them both?
- *Cooperative/coercive.* Was the formulation of and adherence to norms of behavior and social ordering accomplished primarily through consensual action, or was resort to either the threat or reality of force necessary to accomplish these objectives?
- *Sacred/secular.* Were law ways and religion ways indistinguishably intertwined, or were they consciously kept separate and distinct?

Throughout the following overview of how the legal doctrines and principles currently governing the spiritual uses of public lands and resources came into being, these four descriptive dimensions provide a common framework for understanding not only how this rich and sometimes confusing tapestry of diverse and divergent doctrines was woven together in the first place, but what form it might take in the future as well.

Indigenous Governance and Early European Contact

It is no easier or more advisable to make generalizations about indigenous law ways than about indigenous forms of religious expression, either historically or in the present moment, and for the same reason: extraordinary diversity. Hundreds of different indigenous linguistic groups lived in North America at the time of European colonization; their forms of social ordering (and thus their law ways) no doubt differed significantly from each other then, just as they do today.

The European colonists knew well only those tribes with whom they had most frequent commercial (and later military) contact, so their observations and generalizations were necessarily based on a somewhat restricted sampling. For the most part, early European and Euro-American students of First Native lifeways seemed most fascinated by the distinctions they saw between European law ways and what they found among the tribes with whom they came in contact. Regarding the cooperative/coercive dimension, some colonial observers remarked at the evident lack of enforcement infrastructure necessary for accomplishment of tribal "law jobs": no courts, no jails, and no police force. Instead, a great deal of time was apparently spent in council, with an emphasis on collective consultation in matters related to social control, conflict resolution, adaptation, and norm enforcement.

In a bagatelle, Benjamin Franklin wrote the following: "Savages we call them because their manners differ from ours, which we think the perfection of civility; they think the same of theirs. The Indian men, when young, are hunters and warriors; when old, councilors; for all their government is by council of the sages; there is no force, there are no prisons, no officers to compel obedience or inflict punishment."[5]

Franklin's words almost perceptibly glow with the romantic sentiments of his times (he was also an aged councilor himself, representing post–Revolutionary American interests in France by the time he
penned these observations). He was writing in an era when radically
different constructions of First Natives were competing for attention
and for claims as a basis for policy making in the Euro-American
mind. Westward expansionists were describing American Indians as
heartless, Godless, bloodthirsty subhumans intent on erasing Western
civilization from North America; alternatively, romanticists saw them
to be morally untainted "Noble Savages" reposing in a North American Eden. From his earlier experiences as a colonial treaty negotiator
with tribes living in Pennsylvania and Ohio, Franklin knew that First
Natives were capable of all the same improvident and ill-considered
behaviors as the European colonists, but he also recognized in indigenous law ways the operation of a relatively sophisticated system of
mores and mechanisms for their maintenance that he thought the
colonists would do well to emulate.

The relationship between culture and environment also appeared
to be profoundly different from the British common law tradition,
especially in the eye of land-hungry European colonists. The concept
of individual, private, and exclusive ownership of land and its atten-
dant resources—so dear to the hearts of European immigrants intent
on establishing their own personal estates—appeared not to exist in
any of the First Native culture groups the Europeans encountered.
The focus appeared to be rather on collectively held and continually
adjusted use rights in land and resources, the maintenance of which
again occurred in tribal councils and in councils of leaders from different tribes.

But judging from the care with which they committed their observations on the subject to writing, the indigenous law ways of greatest
interest to European colonial leaders concerned intertribal relations:
norm enforcement, cultural accommodation, and (perhaps most
important) conflict resolution between the various tribes with whom
the colonists were in the most continuous contact. Interest in this
area was high because the colonies were in direct economic competition with each other, and the inability of British colonial governments
to better coordinate their efforts with each other was a source of

continuing economic and military insecurity. Their relative inability to cooperate with each other nearly caused their defeat in a war with France in 1763 and would cause equally serious problems in their conduct of the Revolutionary War against Great Britain a decade later.

The highest level of intertribal organization the colonists knew of in the eighteenth century was an alliance variously known as the Haudenosaunee (as they called themselves), or Iroquois (as they were known to the Europeans) confederacy. Originating with charismatic prophets living among the Onondaga, the "Great Law of Peace"— the confederacy's governing creed—called for the peaceable resolution of the recurring, escalating intertribal blood feuds that had all too often caused them to make war on each other. The pact also called for a commitment to mutual defense whenever a renegade tribe or faction ignored the Great Law and threatened one or more of its members.

As the alliance grew in size and strength, the benefits to neighboring tribes in joining it were as obvious as the disadvantages in opposing it. The confederacy originally consisted of five nations: the Cayuga, Mohawk, Oneida, Onondaga, and Seneca—to be later joined by the Tuscarora, a southern tribe that had moved northward to avoid enslavement in the early eighteenth century. Together, their range covered much of northern New York and southern New England.

The principles and symbolism of the Great Law flowed from a vision held and preached by its spiritual founders, Deganawidah and Hiawatha: "In his vision, Deganawidah saw a giant evergreen (white pine) reaching into the sky and gaining strength from three counterbalancing principles of life. The first principle was that a stable mind and healthy body should be in balance so that peace between individuals and groups could occur. Second, Deganawidah stated that humane conduct, thought, and speech were a requirement for equity and justice among peoples. Finally he foresaw a society in which physical strength and civil authority would reinforce the power of the clan system.... His vision was a message from the creator to bring harmony into human existence and unite all peoples into a single family guided by his three dual principles."[6]

Blood feuds between clans of neighboring tribes had been a particularly dangerous and destructive problem, for tribal custom had previously called for avenging the death of a slain relative by killing a member of the clan to which the perpetrator had belonged, if not the perpetrator himself. Feuds could (and did) escalate quickly into intertribal wars. Instead of clan revenge, the Great Law of Peace substituted a ritual called the Condolence Ceremony, in which the perpetrator's clan formally acknowledged responsibility for and apologized for the wrongdoing of their errant member and paid restitution to the aggrieved clan in the form of wampum belts. Clans and tribes were still free to resolve disputes however they saw fit within their own structures, but at the intertribal level, the Great Law of Peace and the Condolence Ceremony prevailed.

Whether resolving a blood feud or contemplating possible responses to a commonly perceived external threat, implementation protocols required consensus among the leadership of member tribes before they could take concerted action. Thus, the generally cooperative attitude and council-based decision-making model that characterized the law ways of member tribes carried over into governance of the confederacy. This arrangement served the tribes well during the volatile 1750s and 1760s, when France and England vied for commercial and military control over northeastern North America. The British colonists realized that they had no hope of prevailing over the French without the acquiescence and support of the Haudenosaunee Confederacy, whose indigenous enemies to the north had allied themselves with the French. Some historians view the confederacy's cohesiveness and well-coordinated military support for the English colonies as the deciding factor in assuring British victory in this struggle.

Well in advance of the so-called French and Indian War, Haudenosaunee leaders warned the British colonists that if they could not present a more cohesive and united front against French claims on lands and waterways of the northeast, they would fall prey to both the French and the Indian tribes allied with them. Heeding this warning, Benjamin Franklin urged other colonial leaders to create some form of intercolonial governance structure to accomplish these self-defense and commercial cooperation objectives. In an effort to use the British colonists' own sense of cultural superiority to shame them into action, as early as 1751 Franklin wrote the following: "It would be a strange thing if six Nations of ignorant savages should be capable of forming a scheme for such an union, and be able to execute it in such a manner as that it has subsisted ages and appears indissoluble; and yet that a like union should be impracticable for ten or a dozen English colonies, to whom it is more necessary and must be more advantageous, and who cannot be supposed to want an equal understanding of their interests."[7]

From a careful study of his writings, biographer Carl Van Doren concluded that Franklin's high regard for the Haudenosaunee tribes stemmed from his view that they generally conducted both themselves and their affairs of state in ways more in keeping with Western notions of justice than did the British themselves: "As between the Indians and the white settlers, he sympathized with the Indians. It was not they who broke treaties or drove greedy bargains or presumed on superior strength. He believed with William Penn that civilized justice and savage justice were much the same and could live side by side in peace. What was needed was equitable agreements between the two races, and honest trading."[8]

Van Doren also makes clear that the plan for colonial unification Franklin proposed at an intercolonial conference called in Albany in 1754 was, in fact, patterned on the Great Law of Peace: "He admired the Iroquois confederation, and plainly had it in mind in his earliest discussion of the need for union among the colonies."[9] Negotiators assembled in Albany to craft a general treaty between the British colonies and neighboring tribes; Franklin tried to use the opportunity to demonstrate to assembled colonial spokesmen both the wisdom of the Haudenosaunee governance structure and the advisability of creating a similar arrangement between the colonial governments.

Not enough colonial leaders were willing to support Franklin's Albany Plan of Union to bring it into being in advance of the French and Indian War. But the same general scheme (a voluntary confederation of independent states) did appear later, in the form of the Articles of Confederation adopted by the Continental Congress in 1781. Like the Great Law of Peace, the Articles of Confederation were more cooperative than coercive in nature, as well as more lateral than hierarchical—two features that would later render them unworkable, at least in the view of the constitutional conventioneers in Philadelphia in 1787. Unlike the Great Law of Peace, however, the Articles of Confederation were based not on an explicitly sacred vision but, rather, on a grudging, secular recognition that if the thirteen colonies did not voluntarily yield up some measure of their precious sovereignty in the service of a governing structure to represent their collective interests, they would have even greater difficulty in both paying for and winning their ongoing war of liberation against Great Britain.

In the historical record, the intertwining of indigenous and European law ways during these first two centuries of contact between them is most apparent in the language of the treaties crafted between First Natives and colonists. Frequent references to sources of spiritual authority and to the imagery of nature and human handcrafts as metaphors for the intentions of treaty makers abound in these documents. Themes of community, cooperation, lateral relationships among sovereigns in voluntary association, and, above all, connection appear again and again.

Because of its strategic importance to the British colonists, treaty making with the Haudenosaunee Confederacy receives the most frequent mention in historical documents of the time. The Iroquois constitution is metaphorically grounded in Deganawidah's vision of a Great Tree of Peace. He "explained that the tree was humanity, living within the principles governing relations among human beings.... His vision was a message from the creator to bring harmony into human existence and unite all peoples into a single *family*."[10] Leaders of the Confederacy understood Deganawidah's vision to extend to all peoples who desired to live together under the tree's branches of peace and friendship, and so they regularly alluded to this vision in treaty negotiations with European colonists, as well as with other First Native tribes.[11]

The Covenant Chain provided an even more durable and significant image and was used by both the Iroquois and the neighboring colonial governments to describe the nature of their treaty relationship during the seventeenth and eighteenth centuries. The Haudenosaunee leader Canasatego explained the imagery most fully at the convocation resulting in the Treaty of Lancaster [Pennsylvania] in 1744. He told of visitors arriving in great ships (the European colonists), whose vessels had to be made fast to the shore for them to be safe at harbor. First tied to bushes with rope, both the Europeans in their ships and the First Natives on land soon realized that the only bond durable enough to keep the ships secure in times of high wind and storm would be chains tethering them to a Big Rock, in Oneida country, ashore.[12]

Also in the Iroquois tradition, the bond would only last as long as both sides took responsibility for "keeping it free of rust"—that is, as long as they both worked collaboratively to maintain it. Based on their own oral traditions, the First Native method for doing this was a continuous retelling of the Covenant Chain story among both peoples, from generation to generation within each culture, and between cultures as well. By this means was it understood that the treaties between First Native and colonial peoples would be held as living constitutions between them. And since the Iroquois Confederacy was all that stood between the relatively uncoordinated, weakly defended British colonies and the French to the north, the colonists had every bit as much reason for keeping this chain intact as did the Haudenosaunee.[13]

Colonial Law Ways

A diversity of perspectives on social control, norm enforcement, and dispute resolution was just as true among the earliest European colonies in North America as it was among its indigenous peoples. How colonial populations accomplished these "law jobs" depended heavily on the reasons for the establishment of each colony.

Historians Henry Steele Commager and Samuel Morison make the case that the American colonies were all founded for one of three reasons: as for-profit corporate enterprises, as fiefdoms, or as theocratic religious communities.[14] In corporate colonies such as Jamestown (Virginia) and New Amsterdam (New York), the governance structure was controlled by the board of directors of the corporation underwriting the venture, and citizens of the colony were essentially employees of a company-owned town. Relationships between colonists and between colonists and colonial government were explicitly hierarchical, fairly coercive (owners initially controlled not only wages and living conditions, but access to transportation for return to Europe as well), and corporately rather than either individually or communally oriented. In terms of relations to the environment, the very purpose for these colonies' existence was extractive natural resource development.

The situation was much the same in the fiefdoms (such as Maryland), which the monarch had chartered on behalf of fellow noblemen who had supported him in political and military struggles with commoners. In these colonies, nobles sought to re-create on a smaller and geographically removed scale the same feudal conditions of wealth, privilege, and absolute oligarchic rule that the English people were then revolting against in their home country.

In neither the corporate nor the feudal colonies was a great deal of emphasis placed on religious teachings as a foundation for the moral order of the community. To the extent that corporate and oligarchic colonizers embraced any one set of beliefs to guide their enterprise, it was the ideas of John Locke, Britain's patron saint of property and secretary to the North Carolina Company (another of the early corporate colonies).

Much the reverse was true in the religious colonies, although they were a diverse lot as well. Religious dissidents immigrating to North America founded them specifically for the purpose of creating communities based entirely on spiritual rather than secular principles of governance. Thus the form of worship and the traditions of religious practice these colonists brought with them (including the relationship between clergy and congregation) carried over into structures of governance. Those of a somewhat more evangelical, coercive, and authoritarian bent (such as the Massachusetts Bay Puritans) ordered their relations accordingly, as did the more laterally organized, noncoercive groups (such as Pennsylvania's Quakers). The single greatest similarity among all the religious colonies was their belief in the importance of revealed religious teaching as the basis for creating and sustaining community, in combination with their insistence on the freedom to worship as they chose.

Moving into the eighteenth century, as more and more British subjects became American colonists, and as more and more contact began to occur between the early settlements, the colonies gradually became more alike than different in their structures of governance, their modes of commerce, and their law ways—even as their populations became more diverse. For what all the colonists also shared, regardless of religious background, wealth, or particular ethnic lineage, was the heritage of the common law. Drawn originally from the Roman concept of *jus com* (that law common to all, rather than applicable only to a single community), common law doctrines developed over a period of hundreds of years, in decisions handed down by judges appointed by the Crown to apply community-based norms and principles of justice to private disputes between citizens. These judicially crafted antecedents of the present-day Anglo-American legal doctrines of inheritance, tort, contract, and property would eventually do as much or more to define the colonists' relationships with each other, their government, and their environment as anything else in their common cultural heritage.

British inheritance doctrines at the time of American colonization do much to explain why frontier colonists were so intent on acquiring as much land as they could as quickly as they could. Land-locked Britons had long since discovered that if family estates were subdivided equally among all heirs on the death of parents, subsequent bequests of farmland over the generations would quickly become too small to support even a single family. The legal remedy was *primogeniture,* a doctrine under which the entire landed estate was willed by the sire of a family to the eldest male heir (or if there was none, to the first female to marry, at which time her estate was joined with her husband's). So for the most part it was not the landed gentry who chose to immigrate to America but, rather, those who stood no chance of ever acquiring property of their own if they stayed in England. The ownership of property became an obsession with colonists of British descent, precisely because it represented a birthright denied them in the country of their cultural origins.

According to legal historians such as Morton Horwitz, beginning in the late eighteenth century the gradual legal homogenizing of the American colonies under common law was largely responsible for heightening the status of individual rights at the expense of community wants and needs. As the colonies grew and successive waves of immigration made them more culturally and socioeconomically diverse, seeds were being planted for the growth of a "nation of strangers." When traditions, customs, and religious views were no longer shared by all or even most of the members of a given community, their legal status in relation to each other, to the government, and to the land became that much more important. As a result, the courts also assumed a newfound importance in the performance of law jobs. In culturally heterogeneous communities, religious institutions could no longer fulfill the social control, norm enforcement, and conflict resolution roles they had played in the colonies' earlier days.[15]

Nowhere was this dynamic more apparent than in changing views on the institution of private property and the consequences of those views in terms of patterns of land use. In this the colonists were mirroring changes already well under way in Great Britain. From late feudal times through the Enlightenment, an important institution of agrarian land use in England had been the Commons—originally croplands tilled collectively, but later restricted only to community pasturage for individually owned livestock. Garret Hardin's famous if ill-informed analogy in "The Tragedy of the Commons" notwithstanding, community members carefully controlled the number of animals allowed to graze at one time, to ensure sustainable use of this commonly held renewable resource over generations.[16]

The same land use patterns carried over to European colonization, especially in the religious colonies of the northeastern seaboard. In the hundreds of New England villages established in the seventeenth and eighteenth centuries, the town commons—used first as community pasturage and later as the open-space community hub around which churches, government buildings, and principal commercial enterprises were located—was the single most notable feature of their design and development. Further south, as the Quakers began to settle in the Delaware Valley, William Penn ordered that communities be similarly laid out in small townships, with "common meadows and pasturelands" at or near their center.[17] Regarding this arrangement of collective management of a commonly held resource, these early religious communities probably came as close as Anglo-American culture ever would to paralleling the land and resource management practices of the First Natives with whom they now shared the North American continent.

Around the same time the American colonies were maturing and moving toward nationhood in the late seventeen hundreds, the wealthier British landholders back in the home country were moving to "enclose" (divide up, sell, and fence off) their own commonly held pasturage. In America, communal land use patterns would also eventually give way to growing settler appetites for exclusive private ownership of the most productive farmlands. But even as the commons gradually shrank spatially to little more than landscaped open space in the middle of town, the concept of the town commons as the center of community life and hub of civic association provided the template for laying out new towns and cities throughout the young nation's nineteenth-century expansion across newly claimed territories to the west.

Revolution and Reconstitution

As important as the rising influence of the common law was during this period, the single most significant event in the evolution of the law ways of Anglo-American society in the eighteenth century was the adoption of the U.S. Constitution. The colonists fought an eight-year-long war of revolution against Great Britain in the name of liberty and to rid themselves of the hierarchical relationship with the mother country they had come to so violently resent. Having accomplished that goal, they were not about to replace monarchical rule with an equally hierarchical and coercion-based national governmental superstructure of their own making.

Therefore, the Articles of Confederation adopted in 1781 (two years before the end of the Revolutionary War) reaffirmed the existence of a one-house Congress but established neither an executive nor a judicial branch, out of fear that they would assume unwarranted powers at the expense of the states. Laws passed by the Congress were to be implemented by committees of Congress, and there was no provision for meaningful sanctions against state governments for refusing to obey congressional enactments.

States did largely ignore and refuse to enforce the unpopular tax measures Congress passed to pay off the huge and mounting war debts owed to Britain's enemies in Europe. The new United States' credit abroad collapsed. And when bankers later tried to foreclose on the farms of Revolutionary War veterans who had fallen into debt during the war, civil rebellion broke out in states like Massachusetts, where armed veterans first shut down the courts and then marched on the state capitol to shut down the legislature as well—or at least force it to pass legislation forgiving them of their debts.

This uprising—Shay's Rebellion—ultimately failed, and its leader was hanged, but it did suggest to many observers that the lateral, non-coercive government structure created under the Articles of Confederation was unequal to the task of shoring up a collapsing economy and coordinating an effective defense against both internal rebellion and external (European and occasional First Native) military threats. So, rather than simply fine-tuning the articles, as they had been instructed to do, instead the conventioneers in Philadelphia set about crafting an entirely new and different framework for national government.

The new Constitution emerged as a more hierarchical document than the old articles in several respects. First, it created a federal executive, as well as a federal Supreme Court "and such other inferior courts as Congress shall from time to time ordain and establish."[18] Second, it restricted exclusively to Congress and the presidency certain powers crucial to national economic stability and military preparedness, such as sole authority to print money, regulate interstate commerce, raise and finance a standing army and navy, and make treaties with "foreign nations and with Indian tribes."[19] At the behest of banking interests, the Constitution also specifically forbade states from passing laws forgiving indebtedness. And whenever the exercise of any of these enumerated powers was found in federal court to be in conflict with state or local law, the Constitution's supremacy clause declared with equal force and clarity that federal law would prevail.

In sum, this proposed new government could use coercive use powers when necessary against both states and citizens, acting through a considerably more hierarchical structure than had existed since before the Revolution. It would also create a higher level of national community than had theretofore existed, at the partial expense of the sovereignty of individual states.

Skeptical citizens understandably feared that, in the wrong hands, this more powerful new federal government might soon grow to oppress and exploit them in much the same way the British government had when they were colonists. So, in subsequent state conventions called for the purpose of debating its ratification, constituents demanded that the document immediately be amended to ensure that individual rights and liberties traditionally enjoyed by British subjects would also be guaranteed in writing in this new social contract. These first ten amendments, the Bill of Rights, were added in 1892, within four years of constitutional ratification. As expressed in the preamble to the original document, the Bill of Rights reflected the ratifiers' effort to ensure that their attempts to "create a more perfect union" (establishing stronger national community) would not come at the expense of simultaneously being able to "ensure the blessings of liberty to ourselves and our posterity" (concomitantly protecting individual rights).

Thus, the creators of this new form of government placed perhaps greater faith than ever before in their own law ways to make it work. John Adams asserted in its defense that they had created a "government of laws, and not of men." And in touting its ability to keep the majority from becoming tyrannical while keeping powerful individuals from becoming equally so, James Madison repeatedly emphasized in his writings advocating ratification that the distinguishing factor between majority rule and mob rule is the rule of law.

Several features of the articles and amendments to the Constitution are especially relevant to culture, spirituality, and the management of public lands and resources. First is the powers of Congress. The most important Article 1 provisions include the power of the purse (taxing and spending for the purpose of acquiring and managing the federal estate, as well as for fulfilling treaty promises made to Indian tribes), treaty and judicial appointment ratification power by the Senate, and the power to "regulate commerce with foreign nations, and among the several states, and with the Indian tribes."[20] Article 4 empowers the Congress "to dispose of and make all needful rules and regulations respecting the territory or other property belonging to the United States";[21] this is known as the "property clause."

Significant presidential powers found in Article 2 include the original responsibility to negotiate treaties and to "take care that the laws be faithfully executed"—a separation of powers principle that presidents have from time to time invoked in court in an effort to prevent what they have seen as unwarranted congressional interference with executive branch prerogatives. Also relevant to the subject of this study is the president's power to nominate federal judges (subject to Senate confirmation),[22] since different judges and Supreme Court justices over time have brought very different perspectives to bear on constitutional analysis of matters related to culture, spirituality, and public lands management.

Article 3 created the U. S. Supreme Court and authorized Congress to create a lower court system to support it. This article also empowers the federal judiciary to interpret not only federal statutes, regulations, and ratified treaties but also the language of the Constitution itself. Under the supremacy clause in Article 6, the federal courts have the power to declare local and state laws found to be in conflict with federal law to be null and void.[23]

Among the first ten amendments to the Constitution, by far the most significant one for the purposes of this book is the first sentence of the First Amendment, holding that "Congress shall make no law respecting an establishment of religion, or prohibiting the free exercise thereof."[24] Most of chapter 5 examines how, over time, the courts have applied doctrines interpreting these "religion clauses" (as they are known) to questions of public lands and resource management. Also relevant are the Fifth Amendment's guarantee that "No person shall be ... deprived of life, liberty, or property without due process of law; nor shall private property be taken for public use without just compensation,"[25] and that language in the Ninth and Tenth Amendments assuring that rights and powers not asserted by the Constitution on the federal government's behalf are retained by the people of the United States and by their respective state governments.

Thus, the Bill of Rights was fashioned as a counterbalance to the powers newly assigned to the second government of the United States, under the federal Constitution. And while the metaphorical Lady Justice might hold the scales on which this balance has historically been measured, it has been very real justices in very real cases who have determined on whose side the weight of law would come to rest.

Subduing the American Earth in the New Republic

"Exploration" and "conquest" describe dominant features of the early-nineteenth-century American experience in more ways than one. Just as government-chartered explorers such as Lewis and Clark went forth to "discover" the already thoroughly inhabited lands of the upper plains and the Pacific Northwest, so, too, were lawyers and federal judges exploring the contours and crevices of the newly created federal Constitution. And just as the explorers, surveyors, soldiers, and settlers streaming westward into the American heartland would utterly transform much of the landscape, as well as the lives of its indigenous inhabitants to meet Euro-American wants and needs, so, too, would practitioners of American law ways utterly transform the relationships between individuals and their communities, between different culture groups, and between people and their environment.

Political leaders favoring a strong central government (the Federalists) controlled Congress and the presidency until the early nineteenth century, ensuring that the justices appointed to the Supreme Court would preserve the Federalist legacy well into the future since federal judges are appointed for life. And under Chief Justice John Marshall's leadership, the Court proceeded to do just that.

One issue not completely resolved in the Constitution was whether acts of Congress, presidential proclamations, court decisions, and provisions of the Constitution itself were coequal sources of law or if, instead, they existed in a hierarchical relationship. The Marshall Court addressed this question in 1803 when in *Marbury v. Madison* it declared that the relationship was indeed hierarchical whenever these sources of law conflicted: [26] the executive was subordinate to the legislative in matters concerning the implementation of legislative intent, and acts of Congress were subordinate to the language of the Constitution, inasmuch as this social contract represented, in Lockean terms, the ultimate gesture by which the people of the United States yielded up a measure of their liberty and their property in order that the greater measure of their liberty and their property might be protected. And since Article 3 of the Constitution empowered the Supreme Court to interpret the meaning of the document, it therefore must have been the intention of its framers to grant the courts the power to declare acts of Congress unconstitutional. In 1819, in *McCullough v. Maryland*,[27] the High Court interpreted the supremacy clause as asserting the same hierarchical relationship to conflicts between federal and state law.

The transformation of relationships from cooperative to coercive and from lateral to hierarchical was nowhere more evident in Supreme Court decision making during the first third of the nineteenth century than in the legal relationship between the U.S. government and American Indian tribes. When the colonies were fighting first the French and Indian War and then the American Revolution, First Natives were a well-armed and fearsome force to be reckoned with, outnumbering the colonists by a ratio of about three to two in terms of population size. In making treaties with the Indian tribes superior sources of legal authority to state law through the supremacy clause, framers of the Constitution evidently considered the legal status of the tribes to be somewhat the same as that of European nations. However, this constitutional provision would not be tested until forty years later, by which time some western tribes resentful of settler incursions onto their lands had allied themselves with the British on the losing side of the War of 1812 against the United States. Unlike the circumstances prevailing when the Constitution was written, Euro-Americans now far outnumbered First Natives and were also a far superior military force—at least east of the Mississippi River.

In the ten years from 1823 to 1832, the Marshall Court would hand down rulings in three cases that would fundamentally transform the relationship the tribes had previously maintained with the United States. First, in *Johnson v. McIntosh,* the high court ruled that although the rights of First Natives to their lands were good against all third parties, those rights were maintained only at the behest of the federal government, which held ultimate title and "exclusive power to extinguish the Indian right"; the tribes retained only a "right of occupancy."[28]

Then in 1830 the Cherokee Nation sued in federal court in an effort to prevent Georgia law from being enforced on their lands, on the theory that they constituted a sovereign nation not subject to the laws of other governmental jurisdictions. Instead, the Supreme Court fashioned a new legal identity for the tribes, based not on their original status in the Constitution but on an analogy to the English common law of inheritance and estates held in trust.

When in England the heir to an estate was a child, either the parent's will or the court would assign a guardian to manage the estate in the best interests of the child, or ward, until such time as the heir reached adulthood and became legally competent to assume management responsibilities. So, rather than acknowledge the tribes to be sovereign nations (as they were originally alluded to in the Constitution, since that document recognized them as enjoying a treaty relationship with the United States), the Marshall Court in *Cherokee Nation v. Georgia* found them to be "domestic dependent nations" and stated that their relationship to the United States "resembles that of a ward to his guardian."[29] As discussed in chapter 5, under this common law analogy, the assertion of federal authority over the First Natives' land and resource estate brought with it a legal and morally binding responsibility to manage the estate in the Indians' best interest. The body of law interpreting this obligation—the "trust responsibility" doctrine—has played nearly as significant a role as the religion clauses of the First Amendment in adjudicating First Native claims to spiritual uses of public lands and resources.

Although substantially diminishing the legal status of the tribes, the Marshall Court was equally intent on achieving its Federalist objectives of assuring that the making of Indian policy would remain an exclusively federal prerogative. The Court made clear that, having assigned the federal government this guardianship role under law, the United States now also had moral responsibility for protecting the tribes from the economic and military predations of state governments, as well as from individual Euro-American settlers and land speculators. A year after its ruling in *Cherokee Nation,* the Court held in *Worcester v. Georgia* that the homelands occupied by the Cherokee Nation constituted a federal protectorate in which the laws of Georgia "have no force, and which citizens of Georgia have no right to enter," absent Cherokee assent or an act of Congress.[30]

In this string of decisions, the Marshall Court legally redefined the federal government's relationship with the tribes in ways that reflected a military and demographic shift that had already taken place. While its cases were in court, the Cherokees also sought relief from

Congress. In their petition to the national legislature of 1829, they described this changing dynamic: "Everything the white man asked for to satisfy his needs, the Indian hastened to grant him. Then the Indian was master, and the white man was the supplicant. Today the scene has changed: the strength of the red man has become weakness. As his neighbors grew in numbers, his power diminished more and more; and now, of so many powerful tribes which once covered the surface of what you call the United States, there barely remain a few that the universal disaster has spared.... What crime have we committed which could deprive us of our homeland?"[31] Their appeals availed them nothing. Within two years, at the urging of President (and ex-Indian fighter) Andrew Jackson, Congress instead passed legislation removing the Cherokee Nation from its Georgia homelands and relocating them in Oklahoma.

The most familiar passages from de Tocqueville's *Democracy in America* extol the virtues of America's innovative political culture, especially its unique emphasis on the value of law and legal institutions in restraining the "tyranny of the majority." But in less well-known passages in his famous treatise he took the young nation severely to task for using these same powerful ideas and institutions as instruments of oppression in its treatment of ethnic minorities—especially the Indians. The reason: "The Indians' misfortune has been to come into contact with the most civilized nation in the world, and also, I would add, the greediest, at a time when they [the Euro-Americans] are themselves half barbarians; and to find masters in their instructors, having enlightenment and oppression brought to them together."[32] Comparing the Spanish conquest of Central and South America with the Anglo-Americans' use of the law to diminish tribal status and power, he observed: "The Spaniards, by unparalleled atrocities which brand them with indelible shame, did not succeed in exterminating the Indian race and could not even prevent them from sharing their rights; the United States Americans have attained both these results with wonderful ease, quietly, legally, and philanthropically, without spilling blood and without violating a single one of the great principles of morality in the eyes of the world. It is impossible to destroy men with more respect to the laws of humanity."[33]

John Marshall and most of the Federalist Justices with whom he had served had retired from the Supreme Court by the mid-1830s, to be replaced by anti-Federalist justices much more deferential to both states' rights and private property rights. In 1857 these two trends converged in an even more egregious illustration of de Tocqueville's criticism: Chief Justice Roger Taney's majority opinion in the *Dred Scott* case, which declared that southern state laws defining slaves as property rather than people were enforceable in non-slave states.[34] To most northerners, the *Dred Scott* decision signaled that insofar as human rights were concerned, the rule of law was now divorced from the administration of justice in the nation's highest court. Questions crucial to the future identity of the American Republic—such as whether the U.S. Constitution represented a lateral, voluntary association among the states or a more hierarchical, binding, and enforceable contract—would be conclusively and definitively answered not in federal courtrooms or in the halls of Congress but, rather, on the battlefields of the Civil War.

After the Civil War, with the Union restored and postwar amendments to the Constitution striking down slavery and compelling state governments to assure all persons under their jurisdiction due process and equal protection under law, the rule of law once again assumed a dominant role in shaping the relationships between individuals, between individuals and communities, and between them and their environment. This also meant that the law would play a crucial role in determining how the economic and technological changes occasioned by the Industrial Revolution (which the Civil War had vastly accelerated) would affect these relationships.

During the first half of the nineteenth century the new American nation relentlessly acquired as much territory on the North American continent as it could, as quickly as it could, and by whatever means it could. During the second half it proceeded with equal vigor to do everything possible to transform the newly acquired landscape into economically productive, privately held real estate. This was a nation long on land and resources but short on both people and capital. The primary policy path Congress chose to follow during this period was to literally give away the federal estate to individuals and corporations willing to come west to mix their labor and capital with the land and thereby convert natural riches into private property.

First in a series of railroad acts, then in the Homestead Act, and later in various mining acts, Congress pursued a course of converting the public to the private at a rate and at a scope that had not been seen either before or since. The gilded age of eastern industrialists and the heedless, headlong privatization and exploitation of western resources represented the triumph of individualism over the wants and needs of community at every level of government. It was an age of tremendous faith in the idea that individuals and corporations freely pursuing their own private interests would collectively define what was in the public interest. Government's job was to keep the peace and facilitate economic development—nothing less and nothing more.

Seen within this context, the collectivist traditions and communal resource management practices of First Native tribes represented a serious challenge to the American nation's economic and political goals. The federal government's policy response was first to remove all Indian tribes to lands west of the Mississippi (during the early 1800s), then to confine them to reservations (during the mid-1800s), and finally to attempt their assimilation into the dominant culture by carving up the reservations into homestead-size plots and selling off the remaining lands to Euro-American settlers and land speculators.[35] For Plains tribes whose culture and subsistence depended on their relationship with wild game herds such as bison, the policy response of both the government and the railroads was to simply destroy the herds. Representatives of the Interior Department testified before Congress in 1874 that it would be impossible to "civilize" the Plains tribes as long as the buffalo remained in existence.[36]

Just as animal species such as the buffalo were sacred to these tribes, so, too, were many landscapes and landmarks in the unpartitioned public lands of the West. But as the successive federal Indian policies of removal, reservation, and allotment fully took hold, so did a severance of the tribes from contact and connection with places on which the perpetuation of their spiritual traditions depended. This understanding—that their cultural survival depended on maintaining a connection with their surroundings—caused most of the western tribes to resist by every means possible the imposition of allotment-era policies on their reservations. Nonetheless, they still lost more than half their lands during this period.[37]

Conservation and the National Commons

Even as the unrestrained, unrelenting greed that de Tocqueville had earlier decried was wreaking environmental havoc on the western lands, early conservationists such as Henry David Thoreau and (later) John Muir spoke out on the need for Americans to fundamentally redefine their relationship with the natural environment, and they did so in explicitly spiritual terms. By the end of the nineteenth century, policy makers in Washington began to take heed.

What would become the nation's first two national parks, Yosemite and Yellowstone, had already been withdrawn from resource exploitation by this time, but no one was quite sure to what uses they should be put in the future. In the 1890s Congress also began to set aside forest reserves, although it would not create the U.S. Forest Service until 1905 and the National Park Service until 1914.

An estimated sixty million bison roamed the Great Plains when Lewis and Clark set out to explore the western territories at the beginning of the nineteenth century. By the end of the century, only one thousand were known to still exist in all of North America — two hundred of them having sought refuge in the theoretically safe haven of Yellowstone National Park.[38] Poaching in the park was a problem, however. Congress passed and President Grover Cleveland signed federal legislation to protect buffalo in 1894, but the population decline continued, until by 1902 the herd size in the park was down to about twenty-five.[39]

When at the end of the nineteenth century Congress voted to save the American bison from extinction and the executive branch actually took steps to do so, it signaled a perceptible change in the heedless, headlong rush to exploit natural resources at any environmental cost that had been one of Euro-America's defining characteristics up until that time. It also signaled a shift within the dominant culture's view of itself and what it wanted to become. Along with establishment of the U.S. Forest Service and, soon thereafter, the National Park Service, this move toward the protective retention and management of resources remaining in the federal estate also marked a turning point in American macrocultural identity.

Historians still debate the significance of this national change of heart in environmental ethics, in public policy, and in law. For some, this movement from a national land use policy of privatization to one of retention and balanced management marked an unprecedented innovation in the relationship between people and environment and therefore in national identity. But for others, the rise of a conservation conscience at the end of the nineteenth century and its gradual growth in influence throughout the twentieth was simply our application at the national level of land use and resource management values dating back to our earliest historical and cultural roots. For Euro-Americans, the idea of retaining these lands in the public domain dates back to the founding of the Quaker and Puritan colonies; for First Natives, the tradition of communally held lands and use rights is from time immemorial. For both, it is the principle of the Commons: lands and resources collectively held and collectively managed by various forms established by council for that purpose.

In the case of federal lands and resources, the council has been Congress, which has delegated much of its management authority to agencies such as the National Park Service, the Forest Service, the Bureau of Land Management, and the Fish and Wildlife Service. Some of the principal federal statutes for these agencies are the organic acts creating the Park Service and Forest Service, various acts creating national parks and forests, the 1920 Mineral Leasing Act, the 1934 Taylor Grazing Act, the 1964 Wilderness Act, the 1973 Endangered Species Act, the 1976 National Forest Management Act, and the 1976 Federal Land Policy and Management Act—all of which have been amended periodically since their passage to reflect changing environmental values and interest group influences.

All of these laws grant considerable discretion to federal land managers who are trying to determine what management plan best serves the public interest for specific lands and resources at specific points in time. The political controversies and clashing interests lobbying for opposing positions in Congress have all tried to exert similar influence over day-to-day management of the public lands commons as well. Sometimes Congress has been fairly explicit in terms of what management goals it wants achieved and how (as in the Endangered Species Act); at other times and in other statutes Congress has been deliberately vague.

Political scientists traditionally offer two explanations for this vagueness. The "high road" explanation is that of deference to technical expertise: the supposedly nonpartisan, apolitical agency staff hired and promoted on the basis of technical expertise should be left alone to exercise their best professional judgment on such matters. Thus, it is a question of separation of powers. The "low road" explanation is that elected political leaders want to deflect the political heat; rather than making difficult value judgments in drafting legislation (thus appeasing some constituents while enraging others), they much prefer to delegate such unenviable decision making to unelected bureaucrats, whom they can later vilify with gusto alongside powerful constituencies whose interests may not have been satisfied in agency decision making.

This political dynamic has been especially true in the newly emerging issue area of spiritual uses of public lands and resources. There is little if any language in any of the dozens of land management statutes through which Congress governs the national commons that either explicitly or impliedly addresses the issue. Until now, federal land managers have been left very much on their own in this area, informed only by an occasional agency memo, executive order, or—increasingly—federal court decision. It is for this reason that so much attention is now being focused on how the courts are thinking about this issue, and it is why the following chapter examines these decisions in such detail.

5

Of Walls and Windows

Church–State Separation
and Religious Accommodation

Across the nation, in classrooms every school day morning and in sports arenas every weekend afternoon or evening, millions of American rise, place their right hands over their hearts, and repeat a ritual incantation that may or may not have the same meaning for all who do it. When we pledge allegiance to "one nation, indivisible," for instance, are we automatically subordinating ourselves to the edicts of that nation, even though they may occasionally conflict with those of our states, our communities, or our own conscience?

We also affirm ours to be a nation "under God." Whose God? the Christians'? the Jews'? the Muslims'? the Hindus'? the Lakota's? What about followers of the several world religions and many indigenous ones that have no one external supreme being? Are they under someone else's God anyway, whether or not they want to be? How should such questions be decided? By majority vote?

"Liberty and justice for all" gives rise to some interesting questions also. In the antebellum South, liberty for some (white Euro-American plantation owners) meant slavery for others (black African Americans). And many would argue that even though slavery no longer exists as a legal institution, the economic liberties enjoyed by some classes of persons and corporations in the present day are sustained largely at the expense of a lack of genuine opportunities for adequate education, housing, employment, and health care for others.

The preamble to the U.S. Constitution is perhaps even more stirring and more explicit in asserting the principles on which the rule of
law in America is founded. And yet it gives little guidance concerning which of its goals and objectives should take precedence over the
others. Forming a more perfect union, ensuring domestic tranquility,
providing for the common defense, and promoting the general welfare all have something of an egalitarian ring to them; that is, they
focus on doing things in common that promote the common good.
But the framers also assured us that our Constitution will "secure the
blessings of liberty to ourselves and our posterity." Justice for all
nearly always means curtailing the liberties of some—especially individual liberty to do things the majority finds dangerous or otherwise
unacceptable.

While the preamble may have been vague on the question of
which goals should supersede others (implying that they exist in a
lateral rather than a hierarchical relationship), the Constitution's
opening paragraph and several of the articles and amendments that
follow are far more explicit on the matter of *how* we should go about
determining questions of when liberty ought or ought not trump the
general welfare or domestic tranquility as policy goals. For the preamble also promises to "establish Justice," and Article 3 established
the U.S. Supreme Court and empowered Congress to develop however extensive a federal judicial branch it deemed necessary to implement federal law (including the Constitution itself) fairly.

Chapter 4 described in general terms how the Constitution created
a framework of law for resolving tensions between the individual and
community, between lateral and hierarchical power relationships,
and between cooperative and coercive means for achieving political
goals. This chapter brings those ideas more explicitly to bear on questions of diversity versus uniformity in terms of religious expression
and public lands. It begins by tracing the historical roots of contemporary constitutional law on these matters. It then moves forward to
a more detailed look at how the interplay between Congress and the
courts, between federal and state governments, and between different
ethnic groups contesting their rights in the same judicial framework
has deposited us in the uncertain and partially uncharted legal landscape we find ourselves in today.

Some of the law discussed in this chapter (especially the religion clauses of the First Amendment) applies to all persons and groups over which our national government asserts some legal jurisdiction, including American Indian tribes, while other doctrines refer more exclusively to the religious status of tribes and tribal members. This chapter begins and ends with a consideration of First Amendment jurisprudence because—as the case studies comprising part 3 of this book demonstrate—a growing number of Euro-American and First Native peoples of the United States are coming to regard our commonly held lands and resources as sacred and are seeking to use them for religious purposes. And for better or for worse, this is, indeed, the one set of legal principles that binds us all.

Law Born of Conflict: Erecting the Wall and Carving the Window

In their authoritative history of the founding of the American Republic, Samuel Morison and Henry Steele Commager identify three principal reasons why the original thirteen British colonies that later would become the United States were founded. The first was to accrue wealth through the exploitation and exportation of natural resources (as in the earliest colony, Jamestown, and in New Amsterdam, later to become New York). The second was to reward noblemen who had been loyal to the monarchy in its ongoing struggle with the Parliamentarians for control of the British government (such as Maryland). And the third was to provide a haven for religious dissidents (principally in New England and Pennsylvania).[1] Regarding the religious colonies, the monarch and the dissidents struck a rough bargain, in which the religious colonists could assume all the personal and financial risks associated with foreign colonization under the authority of the Crown and claim any lands they wished to settle on as British colonies if they would both swear allegiance to the British monarchy and forswear political and military attacks against the monarch in the home country.

Unfortunately, some of the religious colonies were as intolerant of each other as mainstream English society and the British monarch had been of them. When Quaker missionaries tried to convince New England Puritans to join their religious movement, the Puritans rewarded their efforts by tying the Quakers to the backs of wagons, stripping them to the waist (men and women alike), and dragging them from town to town while the Puritan constables beat them bloody with whips.[2]

They were also no more forgiving of doctrinal dissenters within their own ranks than they were of other religious denominations. In 1630 when the Puritan minister Roger Williams preached views at too great a variance with his Calvinist congregation and theocratic government, the community simply banished rather than beat him. In defiant response, he went on to found Rhode Island, the first British colony in the Americas established specifically for religious dissenters who by reason of their theological views were unwelcome in other American colonies. Having personally experienced government persecution because of religious difference, he was the first colonist to coin a phrase that was to become one of the hallmark principles of church–state relations in American political culture: he wrote that there should be "a wall of separation between the garden of the Church and the wilderness of the world."[3]

According to constitutional scholar Lawrence Tribe, Williams's was one of three seminal perspectives on church–state relations in American society that contributed to the drafting and subsequent interpretation of the religion clauses of the First Amendment.[4] By reason of his own experience and in light of similar oppression occurring elsewhere in the colonies, as well as in England, Roger Williams felt it essential that the "wall of separation" be erected primarily as a means of trying to protect the church congregations from assault by government leaders hostile to minority theologies. Over a century later Thomas Jefferson used the same imagery to argue against what he saw as an even greater threat: an infiltration of government by religious ideologues.[5] Both Williams and Jefferson had the same concern, which was that one or a coalition of dominant religious factions could gain control of government. The difference between their views was that Williams the religious leader wanted the wall to protect the church from the state, while Jefferson the political leader wanted it to protect the state from the church. What they agreed on was the absolute necessity of maintaining this separation, to keep American society from being further inflamed by the virus of religion-based political and military conflict that was causing such turmoil in Europe, keeping England in a state of civil war for much of the seventeenth century.

The third of these founding perspectives was that of James Madison, who wrote the first working draft of the First Amendment. As a young law student in the American colonies he had seen dissident Baptists thrown into jail for dissenting against the state (Anglican) church, which Jefferson tried to get the Virginia legislature to disestablish in 1779.[6] Madison saw first-hand the corrupting influence that state-established religion could have on the "liberty of conscience" that had been so central a founding principle of governments such as Rhode Island's and was so important to free thinkers everywhere in the colonies. In this instance, the establishment of state religion by the wealthiest and most politically powerful denomination had resulted in the loss of the free exercise of religious conscience by those who felt that it was immoral to support state religion by payment of taxes.

For this reason, Madison concluded that the intermingling of government and religion corroded not only the religious liberties of the citizenry but also these very institutions. Like Williams and Jefferson, he agreed with the importance of clear distinctions between the roles and responsibilities of church and state, but he also saw ways in which the two could mutually support the achievement of each other's mission without becoming excessively entangled in each others' affairs. It was simply a matter of recognizing what were their respective appropriate spheres of influence and activity and keeping those differences clearly in mind in conducting the affairs of both church and state.

Madison saw a role for government in keeping religious denominations from assaulting each other, holding that the "tendency to a usurpation on one side or the other, or to a corrupting coalition or alliance between them, will best be guarded against by an entire abstinance [*sic*] of the Government from interference in any way whatever, beyond the necessity of preserving the public order, and protecting each sect against trespass on its legal rights by others."[7] Madison also realized that in a religiously oriented nation such as the United States, total separation between church and state was impossible. The issue was that of the nature and extent of the contact between the two—a question of what ought to be the dimensions of the "window within the wall." Madison acknowledged that "it may not be easy in every possible case, to trace the line of separation between the rights of Religion and the Civil authority, with such distinctness, as to avoid collision and doubts on unessential points."[8] One of the central legal questions in First Amendment interpretation from the time he wrote those words to our own is what exactly are the essential versus the "unessential" points over which those "doubts and collisions" might arise?

Four of the states ratifying the U.S. Constitution agreed to do so only on the condition that Congress immediately amend it to assure citizens many of the same rights from intrusion on their civil liberties that citizens of England customarily enjoyed in relationship to their government. After he was elected from Virginia to the newly formed House of Representatives, one of James Madison's first and most important tasks was to set about adding the promised amendments to the Constitution that he had played a leading role in drafting two years earlier in Philadelphia.

The first line of the First Amendment to the Constitution largely reflects his handiwork on the matter. In seeking a balanced perspective—one in which government was not precluded from assuring the freedom to practice one's religion, while still not being unduly supportive of one denomination at the expense of another—Congress adopted and the states ratified an amendment reflecting Madison's conviction that both goals were simultaneously achievable: "Congress shall make no law respecting an establishment of religion, or prohibiting the free exercise thereof."[9]

The window in the wall of separation was (and is) a space framed by a prohibition against the establishment of state-sponsored religious behavior on one side and an equally important prohibition of denial of the freedom to adhere to one's religious beliefs on the other. All government interaction with religious institutions is not precluded, only that which would have the effect of unduly *proscribing* (prohibiting) some religious teachings and practices or *prescribing* (compelling observance of) others. How narrow or wide that window is at any given point in time is a matter very much in the eye of the beholder, of course. State action that one observer—a federal judge, for instance—may interpret as accommodating free exercise of religion (like a nativity scene in a public park) may be seen by another as state sponsorship of religious practices. Judicial views have varied widely over the nearly two centuries the federal courts have been interpreting the First Amendment's religion clauses. And judging from the diverse concurring and dissenting opinions in some recent Supreme Court decisions, that variation is no doubt likely to continue.

Contours of the Religion Clauses

Just what did the early American thinkers on the subject of church–state relations mean when they spoke in terms of "free exercise" and "establishment of religion"? More to the point, what did the framers and ratifiers of the First Amendment *think* those concepts meant when they made the religion clauses the law of the land? Legal historian John Witte offers well-documented arguments in support of the position that at least insofar as the free exercise clause is concerned, four founding principles comprise this right, each of which has found expression in some landmark decisions of the U.S. Supreme Court, particularly in the second half of the twentieth century.[10] These are as follows:

- *Liberty of conscience.* A legal and theological concept dating back to Roman times, this concept connotes the freedom to decide for oneself what moral and spiritual teachings ought to inform one's thought and behavior, at least within the limits of the maintenance of the social order.
- *Freedom of religious expression.* This concept provides the liberty to worship as one chooses, as well the freedom to choose not to worship at all.
- *Equality of religions and religious pluralism.* As the Supreme Court has expressed this principle, its essential characteristic is to create an environment in which "many types of life, character, opinion and belief can develop unmolested and unobstructed. Nowhere is this shield more necessary than in ur own country for a people composed of many races and many creeds."[11]

- *Separation of church and state.* This is the principle of governmental and ecclesiastical administration that makes possible the
  honoring of the first three ideals.

In some ways, the establishment clause mirrors the principles just
described. That is, case law interpreting this clause has over time
compelled government (1) to refrain from coercing religious expression (thereby protecting freedom of conscience), (2) to treat all religious denominations equally (thereby preserving religious pluralism),
and (3) to avoid using either the authority of government or the public wealth it controls (or both) to sponsor or actively support activities of a primarily religious nature (thereby assuring separation of
church and state).

Just how well the federal courts in general and the U.S. Supreme
Court in particular have gone about honoring these principles over
the two-centuries-old history of the religion clauses is a hotly debated
issue among constitutional scholars, lawyers, clerics, and the general
public alike. And by the end of the twentieth century there was probably as much contention and as little consensus over how the religion
clauses ought to be interpreted as there ever has been in our history.

Of the 170 religion clause cases decided by the Supreme Court
(the only federal court whose rulings are binding throughout the
United States and its territories) up through 1997, over one-half were
issued in the last three decades of the twentieth century. And with the
changing makeup of the High Court during this period has come a
discernible shift in judicial philosophy over what the religion clauses
mean and how they should be applied.

Rather than attempt to summarize those arguments, principles,
and supporting cases here, the focus of this writing is instead only
on those doctrines and cases that have a fairly direct bearing on the
management of public lands and resources for religious purposes. To
do that properly requires a review of the religion clauses not in isola-
tion but, rather, in the context of other constitutional doctrines, cases,
and congressional enactments also addressing the religious uses of
federal lands, particularly as they affect America's indigenous peoples.
To do that in historical sequence means beginning with a review of
the trust responsibility doctrine.

The Trust Relationship

As with other matters concerning religion and law in the United States, federal judicial treatment of issues regarding the spiritual practices of indigenous peoples has varied over the years, but it generally follows one of two paths of analysis. These two paths emanate from different articles and amendments to the U.S. Constitution, and more often than not they reach different destinations.

The first of these two paths is the *trust responsibility* of the United States to its indigenous "nations within," incurred by a combination of original constitutional language, early Supreme Court case law, and military subjugation of American Indian tribes by the U.S. Army. The United States had been making treaties with Indian tribes for nearly a decade by the time the Constitution was written, including within them promises that tribal lands would be acquired only through purchase or cession, and not by conquest. Thus the Article 2 powers granted to the president to make treaties (subject to Senate ratification) were assumed to extend to future land acquisition agreements with Indian tribes, as well as European nations, meaning that the supremacy clause would apply to enforcement of such treaties as against state law whenever the two were found to conflict.[12] And since Article 1 gave Congress the power to regulate commerce with "foreign nations, and among the several states, and with Indian tribes," it was a reasonable enough assumption at the time that the tribes were more like foreign nations than like states, since states are not in a treaty-making relationship with the federal government.

However, nearly four decades would pass from the time these articles were drafted until the U.S. Supreme Court first crafted a definitive declaration of the legal status of American Indian tribes within the constitutional framework. In Justice John Marshall's 1823 opinion in *Johnson v. McIntosh*, the otherwise eminent jurist came closer than perhaps anywhere else in his thirty years of administering justice to simply declaring that might makes right.[13] The court found that "discovery" of lands in North America by the U.S. government created title to all such lands in the government; that "the title by conquest is acquired and maintained by force"; that the "conqueror prescribes its limits"; and that Indian tribes hold not the rights of absolute ownership reserved to sovereign governments, but only a "right of occupancy" that the United States could extinguish at will.[14] Eight years later in *Cherokee Nation v. Georgia,* Marshall further clarified the status of the tribes by holding that they were "domestic dependent nations," with the relationship between the tribes and the federal government resembling that of a "ward to his guardian."[15]

This was a serious abrogation of the rights of self-governance over their peoples and resources that the tribes had enjoyed from time immemorial until their conquest in the field by U.S. armed forces and in court by the reasoning of John Marshall, and it was a seizure that would come at a price. Having created the analogy to the common law ward–guardian relationship, the federal government would from that time forward be bound in theory and more often than not in practice by that same jurisprudential tradition: to hold in trust for the benefit of the tribes the powers of governance and of resource management which in the *Cherokee Nation* decision it had taken away.

While it is beyond the scope of this chapter to review the trust relationship in its entirety,[16] suffice it to say that it survives as the most durable and often-referenced touchstone in federal government dealings with American Indian tribes. To be sure, the courts have recognized Congress as having broad latitude to determine through the policy process what is in the tribes' "best interest." During the nineteenth century, Congress first removed them west of the Mississippi to "Indian Country," then confined them to reservations, and ultimately tried to force their assimilation into the dominant culture by allotting reservation lands to individual tribal members and selling off the rest to non-Indian settlers and (indirectly) land developers.[17] The allotment/assimilation period also included a concerted federal effort to obliterate tribal culture altogether, by sending Indian children to English-only boarding schools many miles distant from home and family and prohibiting under penalty of criminal sanction many of the most significant tribal religious ceremonies.[18]

When policy makers finally acknowledged that these nineteenth-century efforts at forced assimilation were not succeeding, Congress had a change of heart and passed legislation in 1934 granting the tribes greater conditional powers of self-governance.[19] Except for another brief attempt by Congress in the 1950s to terminate tribal governments and sell off their natural resources, [20] the policy trend throughout most of the twentieth century was toward greater tribal self-determination and gradual restoration of sovereignty. The advent of the civil rights era in American society brought with it several federal legislative efforts on behalf of indigenous peoples' rights.[21]

More recently, in the realm of indigenous spiritual practices and related cultural properties, Congress has embarked on what might be called the "era of atonement." In frank recognition of past abuses of the trust responsibility—including actions to erase tribal culture (such as religious practices) from the national memory—Congress has enacted a series of measures designed to atone for what by today's standards appear to be nineteenth-century acts of attempted cultural extermination. This particular policy trend began with the 1978 American Indian Religious Freedom Act (AIRFA), followed by the 1990 Native American Grave Protection and Repatriation Act, the, 1992 amendments to the National Historic Preservation Act, the Religious Freedom Restoration Act of 1993, and theAIRFA Amendments of 1994.[22]

The Trust Relationship Meets the First Amendment

None of these atonement-era policies was created in a jurisprudential vacuum, however. The legislative histories of these statutes reveal a congressional awareness that while one line of federal judicial analysis has treated tribal religion-based claims primarily as a matter of intergovernmental relations (necessitating federal and state government accommodation of tribal religious interests within the ambit of the trust relationship), the second path of analysis has been to treat these disputes as predominantly susceptible to principles derived in interpretation of the religion clauses of the First Amendment. The former approach has usually—although by no means always—proved more advantageous to tribal interests than the latter, as the following discussion of relevant case law indicates.

In reviewing these cases, certain distinguishing features of fact and law are worth keeping in mind. First is the relationship between the trust responsibility and the religion clauses, in terms of which set of doctrines had the greatest effect on case outcomes. Second is the question of whether it was the free exercise clause or the establishment clause that was chiefly implicated. Third is the question of whether the religious practice in question was tied to the management of a specific sacred site or dealt instead with a ritual unattached to a land use management decision.

Preceding by four years the first of the atonement era statutes (the American Indian Religious Freedom Act of 1978) was a U.S. Supreme Court decision that encouraged the development of these laws by holding that the trust relationship provided a congressional basis for preferential treatment of tribal governments in ways not usually allowable under the equal protection clauses of the Fifth and Fourteenth Amendments. In *Morton v. Mancari*,[23] the Court upheld a tribally imposed employment preference for Indians, finding that such preferences can be viewed with less exacting scrutiny than preferences for other racial or ethnic groups because of the historical and political relationship between tribes and the federal government (i.e., the trust relationship). The court determined that "as long as special treatment can be tied rationally to the fulfillment of Congress' unique obligation toward Indians, such legislative judgments will not be disturbed."[24] The hiring preference was upheld because it was found to be rationally related to the legitimate congressional objective of fostering greater tribal self-determination; it was not racial in nature because it favored indigenous persons as members of a tribe subject to the trust relationship and not simply as individuals in a discrete ethnic group.

Thus when the 1978 act was being debated in Congress, the reasoning in *Morton* created some hope on the part of tribal advocates that the historical antipathy of federal policy makers toward tribal religion might now be truly remedied. But other legislators feared that AIFRA might create some sort of preferential "religious servitude" on public lands outside reservation boundaries, which neighboring tribes might hold sacred. Southern Arizona representative Morris Udall (the bill's sponsor) sought to allay such fears during debate on the measure by portraying it only as a "sense of Congress" to ensure that "the basic right of Indian people to exercise their traditional religious practices is not infringed without a clear decision" of the federal government to do so; that the act would "not change any existing State or Federal law"; and that, therefore, in terms of enforceability, the law "has no teeth in it."[25]

The federal courts would soon prove Congressman Udall's words to be all too true. AIRFA provided no support for the Cherokees' unsuccessful effort in 1980 to halt construction of the Tellico Dam because it would flood sacred homelands, for failed Navajo attempts that same year to prevent the filling of Lake Powell from flooding the base area of Rainbow Bridge (a sacred site) and thereby encouraging a proliferation of tourists, or for the vain efforts of the Navajo and Hopi tribes two years later to enjoin expansion of a ski resort near the San Francisco Peaks in northern Arizona's Coconino National Forest.[26]

In these cases, the tribes had sought to influence government land management decision making in recognition of their religious affinity with the site in question, based not just on the "sense of Congress" expressed in AIRFA but on arguments that their First Amendment rights to free exercise of their environmentally rooted religions were being denied as well.[27] And in each of these cases, the free exercise argument failed. In most free exercise cases not involving public lands, non-Indian plaintiffs need only show that a government action places a substantial burden on the free exercise of their religion in order for the government to then be required to demonstrate a compelling interest in limiting religious practices. But in these sacred site cases the tribes had to show more. The courts imposed the additional requirement that preservation of and access to the site in question was *central and indispensable* to the practice of tribal religion; in none of these cases could the tribes prove this to the respective courts' satisfaction. Unable to make this showing, the federal government in its defense had only to demonstrate that a legitimate (non-Indian) public interest was being served by the management decision in question to shield its actions from a tribal free exercise challenge.[28]

Perhaps the most graphic example of the relative powers of the tribes and federal government agencies in this area is the U.S. Supreme Court's 1988 decision in *Lyng v. Northwest Cemetery Protective Association*.[29] In this case, plaintiffs sought to enjoin U.S. Forest Service road construction through a traditional indigenous cemetery on Forest Service land, which was also the site of contemporary tribal

religious observances. The plaintiff tribes did establish both centrality and indispensability, resulting in a district court injunction against
logging road construction that was upheld on government appeal
before the Ninth Circuit Court of Appeals.[30] But the Supreme Court
reversed, holding that road construction did not burden Indian religion because it did not coerce individuals to "act against their faith."[31]
The court found that the Forest Service could literally destroy tribal
religion by building a road, since the construction would not coerce
Indian religious practitioners into actively violating their own beliefs.

But while the high court in *Lyng* surely did not uphold an outcome
supportive of tribal free exercise interests, it nevertheless clearly
upheld the ability of federal agencies to factor tribal religious practices into land use decision making if at their discretion they choose
to do so. While specifically disclaiming the existence of a tribal "religious servitude" on public lands by either reason of AIRFA or interpretation of the free exercise clause of the First Amendment, the court
specifically acknowledged the ability of the U.S. Forest Service to
incorporate tribal religious interests into its management practices,
in holding that the "Government's rights to the use of its own land
need not and should not discourage it from accommodating religious
practices."[32] It is thus left to the federal land management agency to
determine what constitutes a reasonable accommodation of tribal
religious needs.

In 1990, a high court majority was similarly unsympathetic to an
Indian free exercise claim outside the realm of land use. In *Employment Division, Oregon Department of Human Resources v. Smith*,[33]
the Court upheld a state statute criminalizing the use of peyote against
a free exercise challenge by two American Indians fired from their
jobs (and subsequently denied unemployment compensation) because
they had participated in sacramental use of the substance at a ritual
conducted by the Native American Church. In upholding the Oregon
statute, a five-member majority of the Court determined that the state
need only show that it had enacted a "valid and neutral law of general
applicability,"[34] the effect of which on the free exercise of religion was
"incidental."

In the majority opinion, Justice Antonin Scalia acknowledged that
"leaving [religious] accommodation to the political process will place

at a relative disadvantage those religious practices that are not widely engaged in." But he found the potential for such majoritarian discrimination greatly preferable to "courting anarchy" by more searching judicial scrutiny of religious practice restrictions, which, in his view, would result in a "system in which each conscience is a law unto itself or in which judges weigh the social importance of all laws against the centrality of all religious beliefs."[35] He therefore found the need for judicial restraint and deference to state law sufficiently strong to defeat the claim of free exercise.

Justice Sandra Day O'Connor wrote a separate concurrence, disagreeing strongly with what she saw as the majority opinion's retreat from judicial responsibility in this case. She argued that any law so completely prohibiting an important religious practice should require the state to carry the heavier burden of proof of showing a compelling interest that was being achieved by means least restrictive of religious liberty.[36] She concurred only in finding the state law constitutional because (in her view) it would survive the strict judicial scrutiny she advocated.

The dissenters in *Smith* argued that strict scrutiny should apply and that the Oregon law should not survive it, based in no small part on the judgment of Congress as expressed in the legislative history of American Indian Religious Freedom Act that "certain substances, such as peyote, 'have religious significance, because they are sacred, they have power, they heal, they are necessary to the exercise of the rites of religion, they are necessary to the cultural integrity of the tribe, and therefore, religious survival.'"[37]

Although the trust responsibility received no direct mention in this case (since it was federal judicial review of state law), the peyote use issue arose in federal appeals court again just one year later, in a case in which the trust relationship played a central role. It also implicated the establishment rather than the free exercise clause and resulted in quite a different outcome for tribal interests in the protection of spiritual practices and traditions.

In *Peyote Way Church of God v. Thornburgh*,[38] the Fifth Circuit Court of Appeals used the reasoning found in the majority opinion in *Smith* to uphold state and federal exemptions from prohibitions against the possession and use of peyote. Since membership in the

Native American Church (NAC) was predicated on enrollment in a federally recognized American Indian tribe, the court found that the federal exemption from criminal sanctions of NAC members did not represent an impermissible establishment of religion by government since the exemption arose from the intergovernmental trust relationship; the preferential classification was thus a political rather than a religious one. Exemplifying one of the judicial perspectives described in the introduction to this chapter, the court reasoned that "the federal government cannot at once fulfill its constitutional role as protector of tribal Native Americans and apply conventional separatist understandings of the Establishment Clause to that relationship" because "the unique guardian–ward relationship between the federal government and Native American tribes precludes the degree of separation ordinarily required by the First Amendment."[39]

A year later the First Circuit applied similar reasoning to a non-Indian challenge to a tribal exemption from the federal criminal prohibition against possession of eagle feathers, so the feathers could be used in Native American religious rituals.[40] Acknowledging that the exemption did represent preferential treatment of practitioners of traditional religions in federally recognized tribes, the court reasoned that such treatment was nonetheless constitutionally permissible because it "finds its source in Congress' historical obligation to respect Native American sovereignty and to protect Native American culture."[41]

In 1992 Congress amended the National Historic Preservation Act to make more explicit the need for consultation with affected tribes whenever management plans for historic sites covered by the act were being drawn up, in a way that might implicate the preservation and perpetuation of tribal culture. And in yet another congressional reaffirmation of the federal trust responsibility as instrumental in the protection of religious freedom, the 103rd Congress passed the Religious Freedom Restoration Act (RFRA). This federal legislative action was taken with the stated intent of reversing the burden of proof ruling in the majority opinion in *Oregon v. Smith*—thereby restoring the compelling interest standard to judicial review of government action burdening the free exercise of religion, as Justice O'Connor's concurrence and the dissenting opinion in *Smith* had advocated. In 1997, the Supreme Court struck down most of the

RFRA as an unconstitutional effort by Congress to override the police powers of local government, on planning and zoning matters.[42] As of this writing, the Court has not heard a case applying RFRA to Indian tribes or federal agencies.

Legal Pluralism, the Courts, and Sacred Site Management on Public Lands

In Anglo-American legal literature, "legal pluralism" has three different meanings. The first, a historic use of the term, describes the parallel existence of indigenous "law ways" in small nonindustrial cultures and the European-style colonial or national legal systems superimposed on them.[43] Much of early-twentieth-century anthropology's focus on nonliterate indigenous culture groups and their forms of social ordering relative to colonizing legalization is reflective of this original meaning of the concept.

More recently, a distinction has been made between this earlier "classic" legal pluralism and the "new" legal pluralism, which refers instead to "relations between dominant and subordinate groups, such as religious, ethnic, or cultural minorities, immigrant groups, and unofficial forms of ordering located in social networks or institutions. . . . [These] plural normative orders are found in virtually all societies."[44] This construction still includes a superordinate state-imposed legal system, within which the "plural normative orders" continue to function with varying degrees of success based in part on how well harmonized their substantive and procedural norms are with those of the state. Thus the concept is as applicable to modern industrial and postindustrial societies as the classic meaning of the term was and is to developing, postcolonial nation-states.

Yet a third use of the term makes no direct reference to culture or cultural subgroups but, rather, refers to diverse approaches to interpreting the same core texts of a given legal system. This "constitutional pluralism" may exist with or without substantial cultural diversity in the society governed by that system; the pluralist perspective arises from fundamentally different understandings and resultant interpretations of the same constitutive doctrines by scholars and jurists trained in the same legal tradition.[45]

All three meanings of the term have some applicability in the study of policies governing sacred site management on the public lands of the United States. Regarding "classic" legal pluralism, most of the roughly five hundred indigenous nations, tribes, and bands of people subject to the jurisdiction of the U.S. government (and as recognized by it) have been governing themselves as well as their subordinate and uncertain legal status would permit for at least as long as the United States has been in existence, and they continue to do so today.

The consultative process by which the National Park Service derived the Devils Tower Climbing Management Plan (described in chapter 6) exemplifies the second meaning of the term. The consultations included not only tribal representatives but also non-Indian local government officials, rural business interests, modern outdoor recreational interests, and non-Indian historic preservationists. Each group had its own value orientation and its own site management objectives based on those values. The challenge the National Park Service successfully met was to design procedures for the attainment of outcomes in which each of these subcultural groups felt that their values were sufficiently respected and their objectives sufficiently established that they could consent to the resulting plan in its final form.[46]

What do these pluralist perspectives consist of, and how might they inform judicial review of future deliberations over the derivation of management plans at such contested sites? In his survey of pluralist perspectives on constitutional interpretation, Stephen Griffin found that scholars have discerned several different frameworks the Supreme Court has applied over time in interpreting various provisions of the U.S. Constitution, from Richard Fallon's five-stage hierarchy of literal text, framers' intent, theory, precedent, and moral/policy values; to Robert Post's nonhierarchical array of the different forms of *authority* referenced by judicial interpreters (doctrinal, historical, and responsive); to Philip Bobbitt's similarly coequal modes of constitutional interpretation (historical, structural, prudential, and ethical).[47]

Within this diversity of analytic frameworks there actually lie some commonalities, including appeals to historical tradition, to logically derived structural doctrines, and to the morally compelling needs of the times and circumstances in which a constitutional dispute arises. Each of these has some applicability to the subject at hand. For instance, Post takes up modern establishment clause jurisprudence by way of demonstrating his analytic framework. He notes that the High Court did a painstakingly thorough job of articulating a clear (if controversial) doctrinal approach in its 1971 decision in *Lemon v. Kurtzman*:[48] to avoid establishment clause problems, government action must have both a secular purpose and primarily secular effect, and it must not excessively entangle government in religious practices.

Yet just over a decade later the majority of the Court would find no constitutional problem with a state legislature hiring a chaplain to open its sessions with Christian prayer.[49] In its reasoning, the majority dealt with the self-evident conflict of its decision with at least the first two elements of the *Lemon* test, essentially by ignoring this fairly well established doctrinal approach and basing its holding instead on "the fact that the 'opening of sessions of legislative and other deliberative bodies with prayer is deeply embedded in the history and tradition of this country.'"[50] A year later the Court would again abandon the *Lemon* test in favor of a history-based rationale for upholding a municipal government's practice of displaying a nativity scene on public property at Christmastime, owing to the historical origins of an event recognized as a traditional holiday.[51]

Post also demonstrates how, when extraordinary circumstances seem to require it, the Court can and does explicitly reject both "settled" doctrines and historical tradition when those past-rooted perspectives deeply offend the contemporary moral order. This enables the Constitution to function in what Oliver Wendell Holmes would term as its *organic* capacity: its ability to serve as a living, socially responsive, and contextual restatement of founding principles.[52] In Post's view, the most notable example of this moral/responsive approach is the Court's 1954 decision in *Brown v. Board of Education,* in which it rejected both the structural underpinnings of the "separate but equal" doctrine set forth in *Plessy v. Ferguson*[53] in 1896, and the half-century's worth of subsequent federal case law it had spawned.

Contemporary commentators on judicial review of government agency management decisions in sacred site controversies have mixed views on what approach should be taken. One school of thought seems to hold that the matter should begin and end with application of the trust responsibility doctrine.[54] Although this doctrine originated judicially in Justice Marshall's common law analogy in *Cherokee Nation* some 170 years ago, it enjoys renewed vitality in modern "atonement era" congressional enactments and executive orders (as well as site-based administrative actions such as the Devils Tower Climbing Management Plan) and in contemporary appellate decisions such as *Rupert* and *Peyote Way*. From this perspective, traditional religion clause doctrines are largely irrelevant and should play no controlling role in disputes implicating the federal government's trust responsibility to a tribe seeking access to a sacred site or natural resource to be used for spiritual purposes.

A more centrist position speaks instead of a range of permissible behavior between the First Amendment's twin prohibitions against government either establishing religion or prohibiting the free exercise thereof—a "window" of continuing judicial adjustment within which federal government agencies may accommodate indigenous spiritual practices for the predominantly secular purpose of aiding in tribal cultural preservation (in keeping with the trust responsibility), while still acknowledging that in extreme cases the establishment clause concerns of non-Indians might be legitimately implicated.[55]

However, an opposing perspective holds that serious dangers lie in too heavy a reliance on the trust responsibility doctrine. According to this alternative view,[56] while this approach might appear to be an appealing instrument for the assertion of tribal interests in the form of the atonement era statutes, President Bill Clinton's 1996 executive order on sacred site management, and decisions such as *Mancari*, *Rupert*, and *Peyote Way*, the doctrine can be equally as destructive of tribal interests in the hands of federal legislators, administrators, and judges who determine that legal pluralism has gone too far and more national uniformity is needed. It was only one hundred years ago, for instance, that Congress and the executive branch were forcibly removing Indian children from their homes for education at remote government boarding schools and criminalizing most tribal religious practices—all based on the rationale that it was in the best interests of the United States' indigenous peoples that their cultures be obliterated and that they be fully assimilated (by force when necessary) into mainstream American society. The courts rarely intervened during the assimilation era, on the theory that shaping the contours of the trust responsibility should be mostly a matter of political judgment and left to the political branches.

Furthermore, this argument runs, the dangers of recognizing such plenary power over the fate of American Indian tribes to reside solely in the federal government did not entirely pass away with the twentieth-century demise of the assimilation doctrine. Congress engineered a brief but radical reversal of federal Indian policy as recently as the mid-twentieth century, when states' rights–oriented conservatives controlled both houses of Congress. Some remarkably similar policy initiatives were advocated by conservative western politicians in the similarly configured 104th and 105th Congresses of the 1990s (such as Washington's Senator Slade Gorton).[57] Moreover, the recent sovereignty gains of indigenous *tribes* under the trust responsibility doctrine has sometimes been at the expense of a severe loss of legal status by indigenous *persons*. The Supreme Court has denied state court access to Native Americans for the conduct of adoption proceedings, justifying such race-based disparate treatment of individuals on the theory that it benefited the class of which they were a part.[58] The same reasoning has been applied to rationalize the denial of equal protection to Native American women in family law disputes and to bar Indian criminal defendants from access to the state judicial system, where but for their race they would have been tried under rules much less likely to result in the first-degree murder convictions they suffered in federal court.[59]

From this position, relying too heavily on the trust responsibility doctrine to shield federal agency sacred site management decision making from establishment clause attacks will work only as long as the courts are willing to rely exclusively on the "morally compelling need" category of pluralist approaches; it will work only as long as Congress perceives a need to preserve and protect tribal culture (as at present) rather than an equally compelling need to annihilate it (as it did a century ago). The exclusive emphasis on tribal sovereignty and the trust responsibility also can and occasionally does severely disadvantage the status of individual Native Americans, who would otherwise be entitled to all the rights and privileges of other American citizens.

From this view, a safer approach is to rely on equal protection arguments to safeguard the *practices* of indigenous religious observants rather than relying only on the good will of the government to accede to the wishes of the tribal government or other political entity of which the practitioners are members.[60] This grounds arguments for sacred site protection in other realms in the pluralist array, such as historical tradition (as applied in *Marsh v. Chambers* and *Lynch v. Donnelly*), and it has the added virtue of protecting the free exercise rights of individual First Natives or of assemblages of religious elders or dissidents within a tribe who hold different views from those of tribal government leaders.

Such an approach could be effective in prohibiting the physical alteration of sacred sites under the jurisdiction of agencies such as the National Park Service.[61] However, it would offer no aid in situations such as the Devils Tower climbing management controversy described in chapter 6. The trial court and even the plaintiffs readily acknowledged the National Park Service's authority to regulate tourist behavior in order to protect the physical integrity of the site (including wildlife habitat); what plaintiffs asserted the Park Service could *not* do was regulate such behavior in the interests of cultural preservation.

What all these views hold in common is the difficulty of accommodating *place*-based religious activities (a singular hallmark of nearly all indigenous worship) as distinguished from solely *practice*-based forms of worship (characteristic of nearly all Western mainstream religions) within the framework of American law. For this is a legal tradition extraordinarily sensitive to questions of the control and use of property—whether public or private. The strongest opponents to Arizona congressman Morris Udall's advocacy of the American Indian Religious Freedom Act were those convinced that to recognize at law First Natives' access rights to sacred sites on public lands would be the first step toward establishing a "religious servitude"—a prescriptive right that might eventually preclude other commercial or recreational uses. In the "either/or" world of constitutional litigation, competing rights claims (which also usually involve conflicts between competing modes of analysis) are always in a quest for hierarchical dominance rather than mutual accommodation.

But the debate (as it is currently framed in the literature discussed here) over whether the trust responsibility doctrine or religion clauses doctrines should have the stronger claim over analysis of sacred site management tends to obscure the possibility of establishing an alternative, pluralism-based framework for analysis of these issues. The concluding chapter of this book therefore contains recommendations for the design of multicultural consultation processes for sacred site management planning and for a stepwise approach to judicial review of those plans, which uses the trust doctrine as its alpha but not always its omega.

PART THREE
Management of Public Lands and Resources

6

Rising to Heaven or Risen from Hell?

Culture, Consensus, and Conflict at Devils Tower National Monument

with David Ruppert, Ph.D.

Two different creation stories for Bear's Lodge/Devils Tower began this book, because they symbolize so well how our relationship to places on the land is conditioned by the meaning our cultures have taught us to give them. To the Kiowa and many other Plains tribes, the huge monolith rising from the rolling hill country of northeastern Wyoming is Bear's Lodge, the place of refuge from which young Indian girls were saved from a giant marauding bear by being lifted into the heavens and transformed into stars. According to some tribal teachings, this is also the place where the material world first came into being and the place where, through vision quests and group rituals, First Natives renew the personal connections with each other and with the nature on which their cultural survival depends. Thus it is a place where they have come—from time immemorial—not only to reconnect with ancient teachings and the place where they were first given but also to chart their future course. It is a place of continuing cultural re-creation.

To journey across northeastern Wyoming and see this structure gradually rising above the landscape as you draw closer to it inevitably rivets the attention and energizes the imagination. But to nineteenth-century Euro-American explorers and mapmakers, this great column evidently aroused more fear than faith, and alludes more to Hell than to Heaven. Geologists have determined that its creation resulted from molten lava boiling up from Earth's inner fires to cool just as it reached the surface, and government surveyors (and eventually President Theodore Roosevelt) decided it must therefore be the figurative handiwork and aboveground abode of Satan, so they gave it a name more in keeping with their own mythic perspective on this unique natural edifice—the Devils Tower.

Names matter. Place names in particular affect our cultural construction of the world around us to a greater extent than we usually acknowledge or sometimes care to admit. Current controversies over historic place names exemplify their importance—especially the naming of places after bygone "heroes" whose exploits by today's moral standards may seem far less than heroic. For each time we repeat a place name in speech or print, we reinforce the relationship to that place of the culture group that named it. This is why members of some Plains tribes object nearly as strongly to having their most sacred site named by the dominant culture as the aboveground residence of evil incarnate as they do to the way some members of the dominant culture are allowed to treat it.

But this story is less about names than about how different culture groups regard this site and how they therefore seek to have it managed. It is a story about intercultural conflict and consensus and how two different institutions of government—the National Park Service and the federal judiciary—went about seeking to resolve the conflict before them.

There are several ways to understand the divergence between the two creation tales for Bear's Lodge/Devils Tower that appear in chapter 1. One view is of mutually incompatible accounts that cannot simultaneously be taken as true or correct. But another is of mutually accommodative perspectives that can each be deemed valid within their respective realms of meaning. As the following narrative demonstrates, the same holds true for the government institutions of the dominant culture that now have oversight authority for management of this, the United States' oldest national monument, as well as many other sites on federal public lands which indigenous peoples have identified as having particular ceremonial significance in the perpetuation of their cultural heritage. The consultative negotiation process hosted by the National Park Service sought to accommodate frankly competing perspectives and ways of understanding the conflict being experienced by all parties at the table, while the federal district court reviewing this process sought simply to determine which legal claims being made before it were superior to the others.

This tale begins with an ethnohistory of the Bear's Lodge/Devils Tower site, followed by a description of National Park Service efforts to accommodate competing interests in the derivation of its climbing management plan. Following that is an overview of the broader legal context within which these actions were taken. Thus, we contemplate two kinds of lenses through which various federal courts have viewed discretionary decision making by the government agencies responsible for factoring indigenous cultural concerns into policy implementation decisions. One is explicitly reductionist and binary; it perceives all spiritually implicated indigenous interests exclusively in First Amendment terms. Spiritual dimensions of tribal life are seen as structurally separable from other elements of indigenous culture in this mode of constitutional discourse, and deity-associated rituals are accorded roughly the same status as a Catholic Mass or a Protestant prayer meeting. Tribal spiritual life receives no greater (and sometimes far less) deference than that of the Baptists or Buddhists; agency management actions are judicially viewed solely in terms of whether they impermissibly burden the free exercise of tribal religion or defer to indigenous management preferences to the extent that they impermissibly establish tribal religion.

But the other judicial view recognizes that, as distinguished from the atomistic structuring of U.S. society into separate boxes labeled "religion," "culture," and "education," in most traditional indigenous societies in North America these are all utterly interdependent, each having little meaning without the other. To attempt such separation is like removing all the blood from a living body and then wondering why it no longer lives. The judicial approach from this other view has been to support the agencies' recognition of indigenous societies as being structurally distinct and different from the dominant culture and to accord the agencies far greater deference in their efforts to simultaneously accommodate divergent cultural perspectives in sacred site management.[1] Although there are notable exceptions in the Americas, most First Native groups in the continental United States at the time of contact were relatively small, not highly segmented or specialized, and displayed a greater degree of egalitarianism in their social structure and organization. The hierarchical nature of western immigrant societies is reflected in the highly specialized and highly structured distinctions made in what is religious and what is not; in short, the line between the sacred and the profane is sharply drawn, as are other lines drawn between the various segments of the society in general. In First Native societies, the relationship between social life and ideology can be seen to work in the same fashion. Indian religion is not usually hierarchical in character; it serves general rather than highly specialized social functions; and the line between what is sacred and what is not is often not sharply drawn, making religious functions and associated beliefs more encompassing of many aspects of social life the non-Indian would view as nonreligious. Not surprisingly, this latter view almost always takes more explicitly into account elements of the trust responsibility doctrine discussed in chapter 5.

History of the Site and of the Dispute

Ethnohistory

The Black Hills in general, and the monument itself, were the overlapping traditional territories of many Plains Indian tribes. At least six tribes share varying degrees of cultural affiliation with the monument. Archaeological evidence establishes the presence of bands of the Eastern Shoshone in the Bighorn–Powder River area (southeastern Montana) by 1500 C.E., while later sites display their presence in northern Wyoming into the eighteenth century.[2] Historic records indicate the presence of Shoshone bands living with or near the Crow at the confluence of the Bighorn and Shoshone rivers at the beginning of the nineteenth century.[3] Although originating from farther west, Shoshone use areas may have expanded and contracted, depending on the relationships with nearby tribes. Contemporary interviews with Shoshone representatives indicate a strong traditional association between the tribe and the monument. The Eastern Shoshone today are confined to the Wind River Reservation in west-central Wyoming.

Oral traditions from both tribes confirm that the Crow were once part of the Hidatsa who lived in farming villages along the Missouri River. Separation from the Hidatsa and migrations across the plains (perhaps more than one) brought the Crow to their present location on the Montana–Wyoming border location by the late prehistoric or the early historic period. Like their Shoshone neighbors and other tribes in the area, the Crow adapted to the plains as equestrian bison hunters and ranged far and wide to hunt and trade. Although the Crow area was to the west of the monument, evidence suggests that travel to and from Mandan and Hidatsa territories to the east would certainly have brought the Crow into close contact with the tower.[4]

Although the Kiowa today live in Oklahoma, their oral traditions of past migration place them in the Black Hills and nearby areas. That the Kiowa encode the tower in their oral tradition has long been known, and it is the Kiowa story mentioned previously that has long been used by the National Park Service to explain Indian affiliation with the monument.[5]

The tribes expressing the strongest affiliation with the tower and the surrounding area are the Northern Cheyenne, who today reside on the Northern Cheyenne Reservation in southeastern Montana, and the Lakota, the largest of the Sioux bands now residing on the Pine Ridge Indian Reservation in South Dakota. Numerous historic sources place both the Cheyenne and the Lakota in the general region of the Black Hills in the eighteenth and nineteenth centuries. Through oral tradition, the Lakota share with other tribes the general features of the story of the tower's origins and consider the entire Black Hills region a sacred place as the origin of their people. The Northern Cheyenne share the view of the tower as a sacred place and associate important culture heroes with both the tower and with nearby Bear Butte.

Consultation with a number of tribal groups has revealed a potential for more tribal groups to be added to the list of those having affiliation with the tower. Although research has not been conducted to document and verify these additional tribal affiliations, it is clear that the tower has played a role in the traditional belief systems of a number of American Indian tribes. The fluid nature of tribal territorial boundaries over time no doubt brought many tribes into contact with the tower itself and allowed the sharing of oral traditions between tribal groups. Continuing consultation with representatives of a number of Plains Indian tribes makes it clear that the character of the cultural landscape surrounding the tower is complex and must be viewed with an eye to the nature of Indian tribal histories, lifeways, oral traditions, and religious beliefs.

Aside from the oral traditions and variety of stories collected over the years by anthropologists, the monument staff have in recent years witnessed evidence that ritual activity by American Indians at the tower continues to the present day. Prayer offerings (e.g., tobacco or sage wrapped in brightly colored ribbon) have been found throughout the monument grounds. These ritual activities are described as very private in character and go largely unseen or unnoticed by the public or monument staff when they occur. In addition to this private activity, larger, more public ritual celebrations have been held at the monument. Segments of the contemporary Lakota have sponsored a Sun Dance at the monument each year for the past eight years. The variety of aboriginal origin stories and the continuance of both private and more public ceremonies at the monument attest to the significant role the tower has played, and continues to play, in the traditional and contemporary religious life for many Indian people.

The earliest records of Euro-Americans in the region come from trappers and government-sponsored expeditions. Many of these early visitors to the area note the Black Hills but do not specifically identify Devils Tower. The earliest mention of the hills is from the La Verendyre brothers, who traveled up the Missouri through the Black Hills as early as 1743.[6] The expedition notes of Lewis and Clark make reference to the Black Hills (Cout Noir) but do not mention the tower.[7] The earliest reference to the tower comes from a map of uncertain date and authorship. The map is thought to have been produced by a fur trapper named John Dougherty sometime between 1810 and 1814. The crudely hand drawn map indicates two concentric circles with a dot in the middle with the legend "Devils Mountain" alongside it. This feature is placed east of the headwaters of the Little Missouri River and north of the "Cheyenne River."[8]

Later references to the tower come from explorers visiting the area in the latter part of the nineteenth century. Lt. Col. R. I. Dodge, from an 1876 publication, refers to the tower as "Bad God's Tower," which may have been a faulty translation of Indian names for the place. Other visitors to the region make note of the tower but indicate names that more directly reflect Indian names. G. W. Coulton and C. B. Coulton refer to the tower as "Bear's Lodge."[9] This name is also used by G. L. Gillespie and D. N. Smith. V. L. Pirsson (1894) uses the Indian name "Mato Teepee," as do I. C. Russell and Thomas Jagger.[10] However, the name Devils Tower seems to have stuck and was used in the presidential proclamation that established the tower as a national monument in 1906.

Developments in the Bear's Lodge/Devils Tower Conflict

Over the last two decades of the twentieth century, one of the most rapidly growing recreational uses at rock formations on lands stewarded by various federal land management agencies has been recreational rock climbing. Most agencies charged with managing lands were ill prepared to deal with the increases in climbing. In 1992 the National Park Service, recognizing the growing intensity of climbing use and the potential effects this activity could have on the natural and cultural resources of protected areas, directed those parks with significant numbers of climbers to begin preparing plans that would provide a general framework for the management of climbing activities.[11] The goals of these plans would be to examine the appropriateness of climbing in specific parks areas, to provide an assessment of effects that climbing may have on natural and cultural resources, and to outline management strategies and actions that could be used to lessen these impacts. In response, most national parks applied the agency's normal public planning process and produced useful and effective plans within a short period.

Development of a climbing management plan was not to be so straightforward for Devils Tower National Monument. As reflected in its ethnohistory, Devils Tower was more than an igneous rock outcropping of interest only to western geologic science.[12] During the 1980s and early 1990s, the staff at the monument noticed an increase in the number of what were presumed to be American Indian prayer "offerings" that were left at or near the base of the tower. These offerings commonly consisted of colorful ribbon or wrapped bundles of sage (or other types of vegetation such as tobacco) and were commonly understood to be an indication of Indian religious activity at the monument. Although a general sense existed that the tower was an area of cultural significance to some Indian groups, the National Park Service needed to gain a greater understanding of this significance, and so they commissioned research on the subject.[13]

Additional factors served to make the planning process more complex than most. First, Devils Tower was the first national monument in the United States, and, as such, it is the focus of much local pride. Second, the tower is considered by most climbers to be a world-class technical climbing opportunity, and the increase over the years has come to include international and domestic rock climbers. The increase in visitors and climbing spawned tourist businesses, which had a real stake in any plan that addressed climbing activities. Third, not long before the climbing planning began at Devils Tower, regional Indian groups had been involved in a lengthy planning process over the Medicine Wheel, another site on national forest lands in northern Wyoming considered sacred by Indian tribes. Indian intertribal organizations were formed with the intent of becoming more involved in the Forest Service planning process to address the management of the Medicine Wheel.[14] After fighting to protect the Medicine Wheel and winning significant concessions for the protective care of this site,[15] these organizations turned their attention to Devils Tower and the climbing management plan.

With these factors in mind, the National Park Service understood that Devils Tower presented a rather unique case of potential conflict between climbers and American Indians. As a premier rock-climbing site, the monument was a destination point for climbers from all over the world. As a site considered sacred by American Indian groups, the monument was viewed as desecrated by climbing activities. The planning process would have to confront these starkly different cultural views in a manner that straightforwardly acknowledged the potential conflict, while at the same time trying to find solutions. To this end, the National Park Service decided on a planning process that maximized input from the various potential conflicting factions.[16]

The planning process itself was a departure from the usual procedures used by many Park Service planners. The process was designed, as all planning processes are designed in a federal agency, around the need to comply with laws and regulations related to assessments of environmental impacts and appropriate public input in an effort to reach a management decision. Normally, most planning is largely done internally within the agency and public meetings are held to gain public reaction to a range of proposed alternative actions. The Devils Tower plan followed this course, but it also added a work group to this process composed of agency and nonagency members. While the monument superintendent held authority over final decisions, this work group became a core element in the planning process.

The work group was composed of representatives of those groups that had, up to that point, expressed the greatest interest in the planning process or who were perceived by the agency to be major "stakeholders" or interested parties in the outcome of the climbing management plan. The four major stakeholders were identified as the (1) climbing community—represented by both local and national climbing organizations, (2) local and national environmental organizations, (3) local government—the county commissioners office, and (4) those American Indian communities that had been identified through recent in-house studies as having a strong affiliation with the monument.[17]

The superintendent invited two representatives from each of these interest groups to serve on the planning work group. Since at least six tribes were known at that time to have a cultural and historic affiliation with Devils Tower, the superintendent decided to invite two tribal representatives from the Medicine Wheel Coalition. The coalition's representatives were sanctioned by the tribal governments of those tribes who were *its* members. By inviting this organization to participate, the Park Service sought to preserve a government-to-government relationship with the larger group of tribes that had an interest in the climbing issues at the tower.[18]

Five meetings of the work group were held over a period of approximately one year. The first of these meetings saw the proverbial lines drawn in the sand. Representatives of the climbing group felt that there should be few or no restrictions placed on climbers on the tower and that the plan should recognize the monument as an important site for climbers from around the world. Members representing tribal interests called for an outright ban on all climbing at the tower and referred to climbing as a "desecration" of a sacred place. The Sierra Club representative focused on the effects that climbing has had on the natural resources of the tower, and the local government representative expressed concerns for the potential effects any restrictions on climbing would have on local businesses.

The distance between the work group members representing American Indian interests and those representing the climbers was the greatest at the outset of the planning meetings. Tribal representatives repeatedly referred to climbing the tower as akin to climbing St. Peter's Cathedral in Rome. Such an act, they claimed, would certainly be viewed as a desecration of a sacred place to Catholics around the world. The climbers' representatives understood that climbing may need to be managed, but they strongly resisted any suggestion that climbing be banned to accommodate any group's religious beliefs since such a ban would set, from their perspective, a dangerous precedent for the management of other climbing areas.

Path to Consensus: Education, Cultural Brokering, and Solutions Reflecting Cultural Values

Three factors dominated the evolving nature of the work group sessions and can be seen as the driving forces that brought about a compromise in what seemed to be irreconcilable differences.

First was the recognition that there was a wide and persistent cultural gap between the conflicting parties. Each group came to the table not as representatives from the same larger society, but as representatives of groups with different languages, histories, values, beliefs, and lifeways. Each member group viewed the tower in a vastly different landscape, one that was home to core values shaped by different histories and, consequently, different ways of perceiving the world and their respective places in that world.

Thus, from a practical standpoint, there was a clear need to direct the early work group sessions toward some kind of mutual cross-cultural education. The tribal elders spent many hours during the early meetings trying to explain to the non-Indian climbers how culturally important and sacred a place like Devils Tower was to Indian peoples. In an effort to impart an understanding of their cultural perspectives to the other work group members, the elders spoke of religious ceremonies and tribal origin stories related to the tower, allegorically and directly about the religious significance of the monument, and in some detail of tribal religions. Such information, it was explained, is closely guarded and often not shared with outsiders, but it was important that the climbers understood the nature and character of the monument's religious importance.

From the other side, an effort was made to explain to tribal members the importance that climbing and the climbing experience held for those who engaged in this activity. The climbers, too, it was explained, felt that for some the act of climbing was a kind of religious experience and, because of this, climbing should be afforded any accommodations provided to American Indian religious practitioners. Since the tribal elders often voiced concern over the number of bolts and pitons used in climbing Devils Tower, the climbers brought in new technical climbing equipment and explained that bolting was used only when it was considered the only safe way to climb a route.[19]

The second factor involved the emergence of a cross-cultural "broker" who helped shepherd the group through issues that both sides found difficult to address. Early in the planning process it became evident that there was a need to provide an "interpretation" or "translation" of the significance of the tower to Indian people as told by the Native American elders who were members of the work group. One individual, Elaine Quiver from Pine Ridge, was brought in; she offered explanations or interpretations of stories the elders were sharing, which helped bridge the gap of understanding; eventually, she was invited to become a member of the group. Essentially, Quiver served as an effective cultural broker between the American Indians and the climbers in the work group. Her ability to understand the at times allegorical communication methods used by tribal elders was coupled with knowledge of how to explain or retell these stories in a manner understandable to all the non-Indian members of the group.

The third factor was the character of the compromise itself. All compromise can be viewed as an assessment of mutual loss and gain. One party is often willing to alter an original position if they perceive that their adversary is also willing to adjust their original demands. Part of this process is educational—coming to at least a partial understanding by each party of what the original positions are and what they mean. These processes of education and interpretation are often hard enough within a monocultural context. However, the situation becomes more complex when the parties are separated not just by negotiating positions but by different cultural heritages. The cultural differences affect (and often hamper) the communication and learning process, and they certainly affect the process of interpretation—or understanding the meaning attached to each party's position since such meaning is normally most easily understood within the context of each group's own cultural orientation. The compromise planning solution at Devils Tower was reached by the recognition that each party was willing to change their original positions and that the new agreed-to position had important and salient cultural meanings for each group.

After it was agreed by all parties that some effort could be made to limit climbing at the tower out of respect for American Indian religious values, the discussion turned to a choice between a mandatory or voluntary closure to climbing during the month of June each year. The climbers were strongly opposed to any mandatory closure out of fear that it would set a precedent for management of other climbing areas.

Indian work group members felt that they had already compromised a great deal by limiting the closure to only one month of the summer, although it was normally the busiest climbing month of the year at the tower. At this stage in the process the American Indian representatives felt that they needed to go back home and discuss this issue with their own tribal members and seek advice on how to proceed.[20]

The mandatory versus voluntary closure debate ended when the American Indian work group members, through Elaine Quiver, announced that after consulting with other tribal members it was decided that a voluntary closure was not only an acceptable solution but also the preferred solution. She went on to explain that while many still argued for a mandatory closure to climbing, others felt that respect for Indian traditions and religions was a more important issue. A mandatory closure may keep people from climbing, but this forced restriction would not allow people to express their respect for Indian cultural values. A voluntary closure meant that climbers would have the opportunity to choose not to climb and in so doing this personal decision would express their respect for Indian people and their traditions. As it was expressed at one planning meeting by a tribal member, "if someone chooses not to climb, the respect comes from their heart."

The voluntary closure was acceptable from the climbing groups' perspective in that it would not place formidable mandatory legal controls on climbing the tower, and, as mentioned, would not set management precedent for other rock-climbing areas.[21] The climbing representatives agreed that if the plan were approved as a temporary voluntary closure, their organizations would help educate the climbing public about the closure through public announcements and articles in national climbing magazines.

The end result of this remarkable effort was the National Park Service's issuance in February 1995 of a Final Climbing Management Plan (FCMP) for Devils Tower.[22] The plan called for a prohibition on the use of climbing hardware that would damage and deface rock faces on the tower, and it implemented the voluntary June closure to climbing that had been agreed on. The latter action included a suspension by the Park Service of the issuance of commercial climbing licenses for the month of June.[23]

Three months later President Bill Clinton issued an executive order applicable to all federal land management agencies with jurisdiction over sacred sites, instructing them to assure access to and ceremonial use of such sites by indigenous peoples, as well as to ensure the physical integrity of such sites.[24] The language of the executive order closely paralleled in both intent and instruction the very actions just taken by the Park Service regarding the Devils Tower FCMP.

Recasting the Conflict as Constitutional Litigation

President Clinton's Executive Order notwithstanding, a mere two weeks after its publication Wyoming U.S. District Court judge William

Downes granted a preliminary injunction against implementation of the Final Climbing Management Plan. His order cited the likelihood that plaintiff commercial climbing guides would prevail at trial on the argument that the June moratorium on issuance of commercial climbing permits represented an impermissible establishment of Indian religion by the Park Service.[25] The monument superintendent therefore did not impose the moratorium and issued a subsequent FCMP Reconsideration clarifying the voluntary nature of the June suspension of climbing activities.[26]

As discussed earlier, the trust responsibility perspective and the first amendment free exercise approach represent two very different modes of constitutional discourse on the same subject. Choice of perspective and the precedents that inform them therefore tend to preordain outcomes in instant cases. So one might hope that any contemporary judicial pronouncements in this subject area would attempt an accounting of both perspectives, as well as at least some effort to workably articulate the two. To dwell only on one approach is to "say what the law is" after having told only half the legal story.

However, that is precisely what happened when the Devils Tower controversy was cast into constitutional terms in Wyoming's U.S. District Court. In Judge Downes's preliminary injunction against Park Service implementation of the temporary commercial climbing moratorium, he made no mention whatsoever of the federal trust responsibility to the affected tribes; it receives only oblique and implicit acknowledgment by reference to AIFRA.[27] Instead, the judge held the controlling language to be dicta in a 1980 Tenth Circuit decision regarding a free exercise claim lodged by tribes against the federal government (instead of an establishment challenge issued by non-Indians, as in the Devils Tower controversy)—the case in which the Navajos sought unsuccessfully to permanently exclude all tourist access to Rainbow Bridge National Monument.[28]

Judge Downes's hostility to and general disregard for the federal trust responsibility perspective in this case became even more apparent at trial. Plaintiff commercial climbing guides were represented by the Mountain States Legal Foundation, which asked the court to permanently enjoin implementation of the voluntary summer solstice climbing moratorium and to order the Park Service to delete references to tribal religion from the Devils Tower National Monument interpretive program as well, since in the plaintiffs' view this represented impermissible government entanglement in the teaching of religion.[29]

As plaintiffs argued the climbing moratorium issue at hearing, the judge made some remarkably candid and oddly revealing observations on the record. "As I've told you before," he said from the bench, "you're in front of the right judge on this issue, I think." He then told a poignant personal story of being humiliated as a fourth-grade student in public school when the children were called on to read the Bible in class and the teacher refused to allow him to participate because the class was using a Protestant Bible and he was a Catholic.[30]

This was very much the sort of public institutional behavior the Supreme Court would later find violative of the establishment clause in *Lee v. Weisman*,[31] and it became evident as the trial wore on that the judge's painful personal experience as a stigmatized ten-year-old member of a religious minority group—and the vindication of his feelings half a century later in *Weisman*—were providing much of the perspective through which he viewed the Devils Tower controversy. During the government's presentation, the judge encouraged the Justice Department attorney representing the Park Service to agree with his view that as a fourth grader he would have had a cause of action under *Weisman* if such a precedent had existed at that time.[32]

In their arguments, Justice Department and defendant intervenor Indian Law Resource Center attorneys both emphasized the federal government's trust responsibility to the tribes and the recent findings of two different federal appellate courts (in *Thornburgh* and *Rupert*) that the government enjoys very substantial latitude in fulfilling that responsibility in the accommodation of Native American religion. But in a one-hundred-page trial transcript, Judge Downes's only acknowledgment of the potential applicability of the trust relationship doctrine to the Devils Tower case was a two-sentence dismissal of these precedents as inapplicable because they had not been decided by the Tenth Circuit (within which Wyoming is located).[33] He had no comment on the government's observation that the Tenth Circuit had just decided a case in which it had rejected an establishment clause attack on an EPA decision to allow a tribe in New Mexico to adopt more stringent water-quality standards than the rest of the state so that the water would be suitable for ceremonial purposes.[34]

At the close of the trial the judge did make reference to government responsibility, but in quite a different context. He wondered at (what was from his perspective) the misapplication of such skilled legal talent to the defense of the government's actions to accommodate tribal cultural preservation. In his view the real threat to tribal survival was the wave of crime and alcoholism sweeping across the reservations within his jurisdiction and which Congress had not seen fit to address by the funding of programs to which he could divert the youthful Indian offenders who regularly appeared before him. He urged advocates to spend more time on these issues instead, else "we may still have preserved Native American religion into the next century, but I'm not at all certain that there'll be many Indian children left to exercise it."[35]

Finally, the attorney general for the Cheyenne River Sioux Tribe rose to make apparent the connection between the two issues. Survival is the common theme, he commented: "We appear here in federal court to protect our traditions because we believe that our traditions are in fact the root of the solution to all of our societal ills."[36]

The trial court handed down its decision on the merits in *Bear Lodge Multiple Use Ass'n v. Babbitt*[37] the first week in April 1998. As in the preliminary injunction, the decision made no reference at all to the trust responsibility doctrine; the court's findings were based entirely on a First Amendment analysis. Nevertheless, most of the holdings in this decision were in favor of the Park Service and the intercultural consultation process by which the amended climbing management plan was derived.

First, the court held moot the plaintiff's original challenge to the management plan (which had initially placed a moratorium on the issuance of commercial climbing permits in June), since the Park Service had made the commercial moratorium voluntary subsequent to the court's preliminary injunction against a mandatory one. Plaintiffs had argued that even though the ban was voluntary in print, it was not in practice, since under the amended plan the National Park Service reserves the authority to again impose a mandatory ban if the voluntary one failed to keep most climbers off the tower during the month of the summer solstice. However, the court found the possibility of a future attempted mandatory ban to be "remote and speculative," although the judge did note that were such a ban to be imposed, it might not pass constitutional muster for the same reasons given when he granted the preliminary injunction in the first place.[38]

Second, the court dismissed plaintiff complaints that the National Park Service's interpretive program was indoctrinating children into the religious beliefs of Native Americans and the signs asking visitors to voluntarily stay on trails (referencing its sacred status) represented a coerced observance of indigenous religions. However, these dismissals were made for lack of plaintiff standing to sustain their complaints and without comment on the substance of the issues. (For the interpretive program, this probably would have involved a painstakingly detailed and inevitably subjective parsing of interpretive program materials and public address transcripts to determine whether the program is merely educational or had impermissibly crossed the line into indoctrination and compelled observance of indigenous religious tenets.)

As discussed earlier, one of the more noteworthy features of the trial court ruling was that it substantially upheld the tribal and Park Service positions without any acknowledgment of the federal trust doctrine per se. Instead, the court cast the Park Service's actions as a permissible accommodation of religious worship (alleviating a burden on the indigenous freedom to practice) in much the same way that the Supreme Court had shielded the Mormon Church from an establishment clause attack on its religion-based hiring practices a decade earlier.[39] After the *Amos* decision, Judge Downes ruled that "the purposes underlying the [voluntary June climbing] ban are really to remove barriers to religious worship occasioned by public ownership of the Tower. This is the nature of accommodation, not promotion, and consequently is a legitimate secular purpose."[40] In other words, the degree of accommodation is no more or less than for any other religious denomination—the only difference being that the tribes' place of worship happens to be on public lands.

Ironically, this accommodation is precisely the policy objective Representative Morris Udall was trying to achieve twenty years earlier in his drafting and advocating passage of the American Indian Religious Freedom Act (AIRFA) at the outset of the atonement era. But AIRFA's constitutional basis lies in both the trust responsibility doctrine *and* the First Amendment, and Judge Downes seemed determined to make his findings without any reference to the former. The significance of this choice is that applying an exclusively establishment clause frame of reference operates by trying to demonstrate similarities in law between tribal spiritualism and Anglo-American religious denominations; while the trust responsibility approach instead emphasizes the uniqueness of the federal government relationship to the tribes as semi-sovereign peoples rather than religious practitioners. As applied in the Devils Tower trial court decision, pure establishment clause analysis seeks to accommodate pluralism by focusing on perceived sameness, while trust responsibility doctrine seeks the same objective by focusing on difference.

The distinction between the two is more than strictly academic. Confining the analysis solely to establishment clause discourse denies both the Park Service and the affected tribes the moral authority to seek any accommodation beyond that allowed by the decision (such as the temporary mandatory commercial climbing ban the superintendent first tried to impose at the tower). Following this approach, the superintendent may have potent discretionary authority to prohibit all commercial and recreational activity in order to protect the physical integrity of the monument or the well-being of its wildlife, but not to assure the unimpeded replication of spiritual aspects of tribal culture.

First Amendment analysis provides a more crisply defined, familiar, and fairly predictable unifying framework within which to debate and make decisions on these matters, but it does so by ignoring the fact that the spiritual dimensions of tribal societies are inextricably woven into the fabric of daily life in specific (publicly held) landscapes. It also ignores the nineteenth-century history of forcible removal of indigenous peoples from these sacred landscapes and of recent congressional efforts (starting with AIRFA) to foster some degree of reconnection between indigenous peoples and the sites they hold sacred.

In contrast, the trust responsibility doctrine takes full account of these realities. But in so doing, it requires the continuing education of the dominant culture (both nonindigenous public land users and the federal judiciary) as to why particular deference must be accorded peoples whose cultural survival depends on periodic unimpeded access to sacred places.

Epilogue

The place is the white marble plaza before the main entrance to the Byron White Federal Courthouse, on a cool, crisp, brilliantly sunny Denver morning in March 1999. The Tenth Circuit Court of Appeals was preparing to hear oral arguments on an appeal of the trial court's decision in the Devils Tower case brought by the same commercial climbing guides who had been the unsuccessful plaintiffs at trial.

I am standing in a ceremonial circle in the plaza with several Lakota tribal members, the attorneys defending the Park Service and several Indian tribes in the appeal, and the superintendent of Devils Tower National Monument. Steve Emory, the Cheyenne River Sioux Reservation attorney general who had attested at trial to the linkage between the place-based spiritual renewal of his culture and the resolution of the social ills afflicting his tribe, offers burning sage to the six directions (north, south, east, west, the sky, and the Earth) while performing a chant that had woven into it the names of the attorneys standing in the circle. He later told me this had been a warriors' blessing ceremony, traditionally performed for combatants setting forth to do battle in defense of their tribe.

A few moments later in an elegant, wood-paneled courtroom, the battle was joined. The director of the Mountain States Legal Foundation (one of whose former directors, James Watt, had briefly served as President Reagan's Interior secretary) argued on behalf of the guides that even though the commercial climbing ban is voluntary, it still has a "chilling effect" on business and on the guides' decision as to whether to take clients up the tower, since too high a rate of noncompliance with the voluntary ban might result in stricter controls on climbing activity.

A month later the appellate court issued its unanimous ruling, upholding the Park Service and tribal position in the dispute.[41] While the holding itself simply dismissed the case for want of the appellants' ability to demonstrate that they had actually suffered harm by reason of Park Service actions in implementing the management planning and otherwise administering the monument, the court made a point of reiterating some of its views on issues of law raised in the case that apply to similar conflicts over sacred sites on public lands generally.

First, the appellate judges described at some length the religious significance of the monument to its neighboring tribes, as protected by the several acts of Congress explicitly upholding federal agency authority to accommodate First Native religious beliefs and practices in the management of sacred sites on federal lands. They also made note of congressional enactments authorizing the temporary closure to all but Indian worshipers of sites such as El Pais National Monument and Cibola Historical Park[42]—actions much more restrictive of general public access to these sites than the voluntary June climbing moratorium requested by the National Park Service at Bear's Lodge/Devils Tower.

Although the court could have disposed of the appeal with a one-sentence denial of standing to the commercial climbers for failure to show injury, the judges were evidently trying to signal future would-be litigants initiating similar disputes elsewhere in its jurisdiction (the Rocky Mountain region and western Great Plains) what would likely be the eventual fate of such lawsuits. For even as the Mountain States Legal Foundation was arguing the Devils Tower case on appeal, it had just finished filing suit against the U.S. Forest Service on behalf of a lumber mill in Wyoming, challenging the consensus-based forest management plan protecting the viewshed around the sacred Medicine Wheel in the Bighorn National Forest. In its Medicine Wheel complaint, Mountain States made arguments analogous to those in the Devils Tower litigation: that in protecting the viewshed, the Forest Service was impermissibly establishing Indian religion rather than accommodating its free exercise.

Undaunted by its defeat at the Tenth Circuit, Mountain States appealed that decision to the U.S. Supreme Court. However, in April 2000 the High Court declined, without comment, to hear the case—thus letting stand the Tenth Circuit ruling. It remains to be seen whether future presidential appointments to the federal bench might result in rulings on such matters more favorable to cause advocacy litigation groups such as Mountain States than the ones handed down so far by federal courts in the western states.

Finally, in this saga it was not the courts alone that were seeking to educate. Some of the First Native representatives participating in the Devils Tower management plan negotiations in the early 1990s wanted the superintendent to order a mandatory closure of the tower to all climbing activities—recreational and commercial alike—for the month of June. But after conferring with tribal elders, they changed their negotiating position. As they explained this shift to the Park Service anthropologist facilitating the intercultural consultation process, the elders wanted climbers not to climb not because they were forbidden from doing so but because they chose not to.

For a rock climber skilled enough to ascend any of the tower's routes to voluntarily forego such an opportunity during a prime climbing month necessarily involves some serious soul-searching and moral deliberation. For more than 80 percent of the recreational climbers who would otherwise have climbed the tower to agree not to do so, as they have annually since 1995, is a major testament to the effectiveness of the intercultural education process that took place in the Devils Tower consultations leading up to adoption of the climbing management plan. It also means that most climbers respect the cultural history and spiritual meaning of the sites they climb to the same extent that they respect the rock itself.

But on the summer solstice afternoon in June 1998, I watched as several defiant local climbers ascended the west face of the tower, at a location where they knew they would be in full view of the large Sun Dance ceremony Charlotte Black Elk was hosting behind a ridge a quarter-mile to the west. As one of the climbers told me later, "It's my rock, too; and no one can tell me to stay off it as long as I'm not hurting it." So from the First Natives' perspective, is the glass 15 percent empty or 85 percent full? In a country as ethnically and politically diverse as the United States, 100 percent compliance with a voluntary climbing ban at sites as tantalizing as Devils Tower may be difficult if not impossible to achieve, especially considering the intensity of anti-Indian sentiments among some local Euro-American climbers in northeastern Wyoming.

To acquire the strength, skill, and stamina necessary to safely climb some of the routes at a site like Bear's Lodge/Devils Tower is to meet a great challenge. But as the importance of the issues raised by cases such as this one comes more clearly into focus, perhaps just as significant a challenge and just as great an accomplishment is developing the discipline and the insight to—under some circumstances—train oneself not to climb as well.

7

Other Spaces, Other Cases

Worship and Multiple-Use Management of Public Lands

Time and Purpose in Federal Lands Policy

Historians face the considerable challenge of trying to find order in the chaos of our past—to find patterns of meaning in the record of events that help us better understand not only *what* happened in bygone days but also how and why. As they go about determining the meaning of our past, they also play a major role in shaping our contemporary cultural identity—our current understanding of *who* we are and why.

Environmental historians tell us that the public's relationship to public lands—and thus the national identity to the extent that it is defined by that relationship—has changed quite a lot over the two centuries the United States has been a nation. Historians generally divide this history into four distinct if partially overlapping periods—the following eras:

1. *Acquisition* (colonial times to the late nineteenth century)—acquiring as much North American real estate as possible from whomever controlled it by whatever means were necessary to that end, through actions such as the Louisiana Purchase, the Mexican-American War and its resulting Treaty of Guadalupe Hidalgo, and the Gadsden Purchase
2. *Disposition* (throughout the nineteenth century)—selling off or

giving away the national estate as quickly as it was being acquired, through legislation such as the various railroad acts, the Homestead Act, and the General Mining Law

3. *Retention* (late nineteenth through early twentieth century)— ceasing to sell public lands, and reserving or protecting certain public lands from resource exploitation, through executive and congressional actions such as the founding of Yosemite and Yellowstone National Parks and the establishment of some national forests

4. *Management* (twentieth century)—active stewarding of the public estate by various public land and resource management agencies on the public's behalf, as directed by Congress in laws such as the organic acts creating the U.S. Forest Service and the National Park Service, the acts providing for pasturage and minerals leasing on the federal estate, along with the Wilderness Act, National Forest Management Act, Federal Lands Policy and Management Act, and the Endangered Species Act.[1]

In moving through each of these eras, Congress created new bureaucracies with new policy mandates, some of which directly conflict with earlier mandates and older bureaucracies that still exist. Federal land managers in the present day face the considerable challenge of stewarding the federal estate in ways that try to simultaneously accommodate sometimes diametrically opposing mandates from Congress, the degree of opposition depending on when these various laws were passed and what powerful political constituencies are advocating their enforcement.

Just as federal lands management policy has changed over time, so has federal policy with regard to American Indian tribes. As described in chapter 4, federal Indian policy has likewise moved through four distinct phases:

1. *Removal*—strongly encouraging and eventually forcing all Indians to move west of the Mississippi in the early nineteenth century

2. *Reservation*—confining tribes to reservations within the federal estate in remote areas of newly formed western territories and states in the late nineteenth century

3. *Assimilation and allotment*—carving reservation lands up into private homestead plots and selling off or giving away all lands not allotted to Indians to Euro-American settlers and land developers, while also forcibly educating Indian children in government boarding schools and forbidding tribal religious worship in the late nineteenth century
4. *Self-determination*—a gradual policy change during the twentieth century toward greater powers of self-governance and control over the reservation resource base, as well as facilitating cultural preservation.

Not surprisingly, these two courses of policy evolution have followed similar paths through the course of American environmental history, as federal lands policy and federal Indian policy conveniently found ways to meet each other's needs. While Congress was expanding its control over the North American continent during the nineteenth-century acquisition era of federal lands policy and just as quickly selling or giving it away to homesteaders, miners, ranchers, and the railroads, it was also driving the Indian tribes west of the Mississippi and onto reservations, then allotting reservation lands to non-Indians.

Federal government and missionary efforts at the forced assimilation of American Indian peoples into mainstream American society did not officially end until 1934, although many First Natives would argue that the process continues still, if not so explicitly. Not until the modern environmental era of the late twentieth century (when Congress instructed the federal bureaucracy to begin managing the federal estate for purposes additional to simply maximizing financial gain) did the religious relationship between First Natives and public lands begin to figure at all in government land use decision making.

While it may be a stretch to contend that federal land use policy and federal Indian policy coevolved, it is apparent that they have paralleled each other in some interesting respects. Therefore, in considering the case studies described in this chapter, the three most important factors to keep in mind are the time period during which key events unfolded, the law(s) being interpreted and enforced, and the federal agency responsible for making management decisions. For example, in the Devils Tower case study featured in chapter 6, the federal agency in question was the National Park Service, which generally has the most preservation- and conservation-oriented statutory mandate of any of the federal land management agencies, and it was seeking to comply with the most recent congressional enactments, executive orders, and court orders relative to sacred site management. These factors are significant, for they do much to explain why earlier sacred site case law involving multiple-use agencies such as the Forest Service and the Interior Department as a whole (not just the Park Service) have been so universally dismissive of Indian efforts to protect their sacred sites on First Amendment grounds.

Rangers in the National Park Service face a management dilemma somewhat like that of librarians: the congressional enactment creating the NPS instructs it to provide for public use and enjoyment of our national parks and monuments on the one hand, but to preserve and protect them for the educational and recreational benefit of current and future generations of visitors on the other. Finding the correct balance between public use and protection is the continuing management challenge of nearly everyone working in that organization.

Would that the balancing act were as simple for either the U.S. Forest Service (in the Department of Agriculture) or the Bureau of Land Management (BLM; which, like the Park Service, is organizationally situated within the Department of the Interior). Both the Forest Service and BLM are *multiple-use* management agencies; that is, Congress has charged them with responsibility for balancing not just recreation against preservation but with coordinating mining, oil and gas drilling, logging, and grazing against each other, as well as against recreation and preservation. And while each of these separate activities has its own well-organized and politically powerful advocates, there are no champions for multiple use as a concept outside the halls of Congress itself and perhaps upper management in the Forest Service and BLM bureaucracy. To work in a multiple-use land management agency is to live in a world of perpetual conflict.

The modern statutes governing the activities of federal land management agencies tend to go into considerable detail in terms of *how* the Forest Service and BLM should go about their work, but they are remarkably brief on the topic of *what* these lands should be managed for. For example, the Forest Service's primary multiple-use statutory mandate is the Multiple Use and Sustained Yield Act of 1960, which simply declares that "the national forests are established and shall be administered for outdoor recreation, range, timber, watershed, and wildlife and fish purposes."[2] The Bureau of Land Management's substantive instructions from Congress are no less cryptic: the Federal Lands Policy and Management Act directs BLM to manage the lands under its jurisdiction "in a manner that will protect the quality of scientific, scenic, historical, ecological, environmental, air and atmospheric, water resource, and archeological values; that, where appropriate, will preserve and protect certain public lands in their natural condition; that will provide food and habitat for fish and wildlife and domestic animals; and that will provide for outdoor recreation and human occupancy and use;... [but also] in a manner which recognizes the Nation's need for domestic sources of minerals, food, timber, and fiber from the public lands including implementation of the Mining and Minerals Policy Act.[3]

While these laws are the Forest Service and BLM's respective multiple-use mandates, from time to time Congress has overlaid them with a variety of single-purpose statutes, such as the 1964 Wilderness Act (providing for the creation of protected wilderness areas within lands managed by the Park Service, Forest Service, and BLM), the 1973 Endangered Species Act, the 1978 American Indian Religious Freedom Act, and the 1992 amendments to the National Historic Preservation Act. Additionally, citizen rights and liberties arise directly out of the federal Constitution that federal land managers must also take into account in regulating behavior on public lands. These include the free exercise of religion, free speech and assembly, and due process. Citizens do not lose access to the Bill of Rights when they enter onto federal lands, and federal land managers need to ensure that public land laws are not implemented in a way that more than incidentally impinges on one or more of these rights.

Whether arising directly out of the First Amendment free exercise clause, the trust relationship, or a congressional enactment, religious worship as a multiple use of the federal estate is a late-coming concept to these agencies; they are just now beginning to recognize it as an inevitable if not altogether welcome aspect of their management mandates. As the following discussion points out, the courts have generally found agencies such as the Forest Service to have very broad discretion in deciding to what degree they choose to regard religious worship—whether by American Indians or Euro-Americans—as a recognized use of the public lands within their jurisdiction. But atonement-era congressional enactments (including the Religious Freedom Restoration Act and the National Historic Preservation Act, as they apply to First Native interests), along with executive orders regarding religious access, are encouraging the Forest Service and Bureau of Land Management to take religious claims on the uses of these lands more seriously than they ever have before.

Religious Accommodation and the Multiple-Use Dilemma

In the Bear's Lodge/Devils Tower case, the climbers and the tribes may have been at odds over limitations on both access to the site and how visitors behaved once they were there, but neither party wanted to use the site in ways that would be visibly and grossly physically destructive of it. However, the same is not true of land use conflicts that come before National Forest and BLM managers. In some of the most notable legal conflicts on record, logging companies, ski resort operators, and university astronomers all succeeded in persuading U.S. Forest Service officials that their preferred uses of national forest lands should take precedence over First Native requests that the sites be kept physically intact and preserved for the exercise of their religious freedoms. Especially in those disputes where the profits of resource-extractive industries have been at stake, both the Forest Service and the federal courts reviewing agency decision making have easily concluded that when the contest was between religious values and market values, in reality there was no contest.

This is why the Bighorn Medicine Wheel case that ends this chapter is so noteworthy. It demonstrates the growing realization within the multiple-use agencies that sacred sites are indeed national treasures and are worth preserving for the benefit of the cultural heritage not only of First Natives but for all the peoples of the United States on whose behalf these lands and resources are being managed.

And the multiple-use dilemma is not the federal government's alone. Many state and local government lands, whether being managed as parks and open space, for resource extraction, for scientific research, or for other public uses such as transportation (e.g., highways and airports) share the same pre-Columbian archeological history as the rest of the American landscape. Both indigenous peoples and other religious minority groups are moving to draw attention to the religious dimensions of multiple-use management on these non-federal lands as well.

As of this writing, the highest-profile dispute in this category—literally—is the University of Hawaii's construction of multiple observatories on the radically rearranged summit of the fourteen-thousand-foot Mauna Kea volcano at the center of the Big Island. This site is one of the most revered sites in all of Polynesia, and the university's management of it (much of the observatory equipment was purchased with federal funds and is operated by federally funded employees), as well as the plans of a consortium of its scientific tenants to significantly expand the number of structures and the visual effect on the landscape, has stimulated a growing chorus of opposition from both Native Hawaiians and conservationists. State government treatment of the Mauna Kea summit stands in stark contrast to the preservation and conservation emphasis at nearby Hawaii Volcanoes National Park, which has its own unique set of intercultural management issues to deal with. Like the U.S. Forest Service, the Hawaii state government has only recently begun to take into serious consideration the religious interests of native Hawaiians in managing this site. Whether that consideration will actually translate into site planning that actually accommodates Hawaiian elder efforts to treat the mountain and its summit in a more culturally respectful way remains to be seen.

The balance of this chapter presents a series of case studies that, over time, indicate a trend toward multiple-use management agencies at least taking more fully into account the religious uses of lands they control than they have historically. It must be left to future historians to determine whether this trend bespeaks a temporary deviation from the familiar dialectic over traditional multiple uses, or if, instead, we are in the early stages of a major shift toward the recognition of cultural and spiritual values as legitimate—if infrequently predominant—factors to consider in multiple-use planning and management.

Looking unto the Hills

Traveling anywhere in the Mountain West is to move through landscapes where the dominant features are usually distant snow-capped peaks, which grow larger and more imposing as one draws closer. For many First Native cultures—especially in the Southwest—these places are either the abode of spirit beings or are literally the bodies of deities themselves; respecting the tenets of their faith and traditions includes respecting the physical integrity of these sites. But if First Natives, like the Old Testament psalmists, look on these places to be reminded of their spiritual connection with all creation, others have seen these sites with very different eyes and have treated them in very different ways.

During the nineteenth-century acquisition and disposition eras, Anglo-American trappers, miners, loggers, ranchers, and railroad construction workers intruded into these high country places at will, taking whatever they wanted with relative impunity—except in areas where renegade bands of Apaches or other warlike tribes still commanded the landscape. The connection this new wave of immigrants had with the lands around them—like that of the conquistadors before them—was explicitly and exclusively material in nature. When they looked to the high country, they saw not deities but dollars waiting to be made—from the wildlife, timber, minerals, and pasturage that might be found there.

By the time the last of the renegade bands had been killed, captured, jailed, or confined to reservations at the end of that century, and the National Park Service and U.S. Forest Service came into being, continuously arriving settlers, as well as the federal government itself, all assumed that the First Native cultures of the West were doomed. Disposition-era federal Indian policy had decreed that indigenous peoples were to be "assimilated" into Euro-American society. Enrollment in either government or missionary-sponsored boarding schools hundreds of miles from family and sacred sites was the fate of Indian children, and the practice of indigenous religion was declared a federal crime. The sixty million buffalo on which tribes throughout the Great Plains had subsisted had been reduced to a herd size of fewer than a thousand animals, and it appeared that they, like the First Native cultures who revered the buffalo as spiritual intermediaries, were headed for extinction.

During this period, when the federal government first began to actively manage the federal estate for either recreational or resource-extractive purposes, it also began to eject from some public lands all who did not have a right under federal law to be there. While this did cut down on the poaching of increasingly endangered wildlife (such as the bison), it also began to bring to an end the unfettered access to sacred sites that Indian tribes had previously enjoyed. Until 1934, these tribes had no legal standing to challenge anything the Forest Service chose to do with these sites, which had formerly been their places of worship. In summary, from the time of their founding until passage of the "atonement era" statutes of the 1970s and 1980s, both the Park Service and the Forest Service managed the lands entrusted to them without particular regard for the spiritual affinity First Natives held for sacred sites on the federal estate. Both agencies are historically rooted in institutional traditions in which the religious uses of public lands and resources—whether by First Natives or Euro-Americans seeking divinity in nature—played no meaningful role.

When the Forest Service first undertook its mission to manage the national forests for a wide variety of uses in the early twentieth century, Indian tribes had no independent legal authority to challenge anything the agency chose to do in these newly created national forests. And it was not until 1978 that Congress recognized a First Native religious interest in the management of the national forests— especially the treatment of sacred sites. When Congress in that year passed the American Indian Religious Freedom Act (AIRFA), opponents of the measure contended that it would create some form of preferential use right on the part of Indian religious observants, a *use* right that might eventually come dangerously close to ripening into a prescriptive *ownership* right. To obtain passage of the measure, its author—Arizona representative and House Interior Committee Chair Morris Udall—had to assure fellow legislators that the act did no more than recognize that the tribes did indeed have a spiritually based First Amendment interest in management of the federal estate and that this interest should at least be considered in public lands management. This was not a matter of creating new rights, he insisted, but only recognizing those access and worship rights that had inhered in the First Amendment all along.[4]

Therefore, when the tribes first tried to use AIRFA in conjunction with the religion clauses of the First Amendment to protect sacred sites against destructive federal land management decisions, the courts took this legislative history seriously. The first tests of the law came two years after its passage, in the form of court challenges to federal dam building and management: the Cherokees' opposition to the flooding of sacred homelands by the Tennessee Valley Authority's Tellico Dam, and the Navajos' resistance to the raising of Lake Powell, thereby permitting waterborne tourist access to Rainbow Bridge.[5] The tribes prevailed in neither of these cases, for they failed to convince the court that the sites in question were both *central* and *indispensable* to their religious practices—a burden of proof not levied on plaintiffs who are not making place-based claims to the free exercise of religion. And in neither of these cases could the tribes meet this court-set standard.

The next major court test of AIRFA involved the San Francisco Peaks, in northern Arizona. Rising majestically above the Colorado Plateau and visible on a clear day for nearly a hundred miles, this site is sacred to both the Hopi and Navajo tribes, among others:

> The dominant geological formation visible from the Hopi villages and much of the western Navajo reservation is the San Francisco Peaks, which ... have for centuries played a central role in the religions of the two tribes. The Navajos believe that the Peaks are one of the four sacred mountains which mark the boundaries of their homeland. They believe the Peaks to be the home of specific deities and consider the Peaks to be the body of a spiritual being or god, with various peaks forming the head, shoulders, and knees of a body reclining and facing to the east, while the trees, plants, rocks, and earth form the skin. The Navajos pray directly to the Peaks and regard them as a living deity. The Peaks are invoked in religious ceremonies to heal the Navajo people. The Navajos

collect herbs from the Peaks for use in religious ceremonies, and perform ceremonies upon the Peaks. They believe that artificial development of the Peaks would impair the Peaks' healing power. The Hopis believe that the Creator uses emissaries to assist in communicating with mankind. The emissaries are spiritual beings and are generally referred to by the Hopis as "Kachinas." The Hopis believe that for about six months each year, commencing in late July or early August and extending through mid-winter, the Kachinas reside at the Peaks. During the remaining six months of the year the Kachinas travel to the Hopi villages and participate in various religious ceremonies and practices. The Hopis believe that the Kachinas' activities on the Peaks create the rain and snow storms that sustain the villages. The Hopis have many shrines on the Peaks and collect herbs, plants and animals from the Peaks for use in religious ceremonies. The Hopis believe that use of the Peaks for commercial purposes would constitute a direct affront to the Kachinas and to the Creator.[6]

At about the same time that Congress was debating AIRFA, the concessionaire at the San Francisco Peaks sought permission from the supervisor of the Coconino National Forest to expand a downhill ski facility and tourist lodge. When the Forest Service eventually granted permission for a modified expansion plan to go forward, Hopi and Navajo elders argued that this development would seriously impair their ability to sustain their religious beliefs and practices in relationship to these sites. However, first the trial court and later the D.C. Circuit Court of Appeals agreed with the Forest Service that as long as there was space remaining on the mountain for the tribes to use as they traditionally had, there was no free exercise burden.[7]

This analysis was essentially a spatial one that assigned different uses to different quadrants of the mountaintop: as long as there was still space for the Navajos and Hopis to undertake religious observances, it did not matter that other sectors of the same general site were being permanently modified and used in ways radically at odds with the tribes' religious ones. The idea of incompatible character of use did not receive much judicial notice or attention; it was enough that the Forest Service simply left enough room on the mountaintop for worship, as well as tourism and mechanical recreation.

At about the same time, a similar controversy was brewing in the coastal ranges, in the Six Rivers National Forest in northern California. The Forest Service proposed to build a backcountry road and permit logging in an area where members of nearby tribes regularly performed a variety of religious rites where their ancestors were buried. In response to a suit filed by tribal representatives and environmental groups, a federal district court enjoined the Forest Service from undertaking these activities, citing probable violations of both the Clean Water Act and the American Indian Religious Freedom Act; the Ninth Circuit Court of Appeals, sitting in San Francisco, upheld the trial court ruling. While the litigation was pending, Congress passed the California Wilderness Act of 1984,[8] which declared the area around the proposed road to be wilderness (thereby precluding logging), but also set aside a narrow strip of land within the newly created wilderness to allow the road to be built. Having obtained their objective, the environmental groups withdrew from the litigation, leaving the Indians alone to argue their AIRFA claims on appeal to the U.S. Supreme Court.

In 1988, the High Court reversed the lower courts on the First Amendment and AIRFA questions. The five-member majority in this decision held that all the Forest Service needed to do was take notice of the Indians' religious interests in the site in question, but that it had no duty to give greater weight to the Indians' claims than any others. In fact, the court said, the Forest Service could completely destroy the Indians' place of worship if it found it necessary to do so in pursuit of its multiple-use mandate: "Even if we assume that we should accept the Ninth Circuit's prediction, according to which the G-O road will 'virtually destroy the Indians' ability to practice their religion,' . . . the Constitution simply does not provide a principle that could justify upholding respondents' legal claims. However much we might wish that it were otherwise, government simply could not operate if it were required to satisfy every citizen's religious needs and desires."[9]

The High Court thus granted enormous discretion to the Forest Service in taking (or not taking) tribal religious interests into account in drawing up and implementing forest management plans—an outcome it could achieve only by completely ignoring the federal government's trust responsibility to Indian tribes. But the same majority opinion also expressed this view:

> The Constitution does not permit government to discriminate against religions that treat particular physical sites as sacred, and a law forbidding the Indian respondents from visiting the Chimney Rock area would raise a different set of constitutional questions. Whatever rights the Indians may have to the use of the area, however, those rights do not divest the Government of its right to use what is, after all, its land....
>
> Nothing in our opinion should be read to encourage governmental insensitivity to the religious needs of any citizen. The Government's rights to the use its own land, for example, need not and should not discourage it from accommodating religious practices like those engaged in by the Indian respondents.[10]

So the Supreme Court basically handed the Forest Service a very heavy, very sharp, double-edged sword for managing forest lands for spiritual purposes. If it chose to do so, the agency could obliterate a sacred site if in its judgment the implementation of some federal statute called for this to be done. Alternatively, the *Lyng* decision clearly signaled to the Forest Service (as well as other federal land management agencies) that accommodating place-based religious practices on public lands was a legitimate secular purpose of government and one that it should not be discouraged from fulfilling.

In the wake of *Lyng* and the generally higher profile that Indian religious claims on public lands management were receiving in the media, the Forest Service did, in fact, begin to pay closer attention to these First Amendment issues. While ski resort operators were laying claim to the slopes of the San Francisco Peaks and loggers and road builders to indigenous burial grounds in the Sierras, astronomers were training yet another multiple-use vision on yet another high country site in the Southwest. The place was Mount Graham, in the Pinaleño Mountains of the Coronado National Forest in southeastern Arizona. The intended use was construction of the world's largest array of telescopes, to be built by a consortium of research observatories led by the University of Arizona.

When the Forest Service undertook its environmental assessment on this project in 1985, the news was not good for proponents. It revealed this site to be the home of an endangered animal, the Mt. Graham red squirrel, which relies on the pinecones from the large old-growth conifers growing on this high country "biological island" for its existence. After consultation, the U.S. Fish and Wildlife Service ruled that to undertake site development as proponents originally intended would threaten the squirrel's habitat. One measure of the political power marshaled in support of this project is what happened next: instead of abandoning the project, Arizona Senators John McCain and Dennis De Concini steered a measure through Congress that legislatively exempted the Mt. Graham project from the normal review processes of the Endangered Species Act.[11]

Nor was this site exactly devoid of previous human disruption. Some areas around the Pinaleño peaks had already been logged, and Mt. Graham itself (one proposed site for the telescope complex) played host to several summer homes and a Bible camp—a summer retreat built by one of the many religious denominations that had been establishing religious facilities on leased land in or near national forests in the American West since the early days of the twentieth century.

As an element of the environmental review process, in the late 1980s the Forest Service also initiated consultation with several neighboring Indian reservations—among them the Hopi, the Zuni, and the San Carlos Apache. Receiving no formal objections from any of them, the university and the Forest Service concluded that sacred site complications were not an issue here. However, in 1990 and again in 1991, the San Carlos Apache tribal chairman communicated to the Forest Service that Mt. Graham was a sacred site—the home of the Gaans, deities who had given original medicine to the Apache.[12] The tribe's lateness in responding to the Forest Service consultation notice had evidently been occasioned by dissension within the tribe (actually a confederation of disparate tribes confined on the same reservation by the U.S. Army in the late nineteenth century) as to whether the Mt. Graham site was sacred and what activities should and should not be permissible thereon.[13]

Like the Fish and Wildlife Service's efforts to preserve red squirrel habitat, the Apache Survival Coalition's efforts were too little, too late, and against insurmountable political odds. What this case also points up is a phenomenon familiar to any government official involved in consultations with tribes over sacred sites on public lands, which is "Who speaks for the tribe?" Not unlike American society as a whole, religious leaders and spiritual elders within a given tribe or band often do not necessarily see eye to eye with elected tribal officials as to how reservation lands ought to be managed or how tribal spiritual interests in sacred sites on public lands ought to be represented to other governmental entities. By the time the Apaches had sorted out their internal differences on this matter, it was too late for them to have any meaningful effect on Forest Service decision making.

One of two problems here is that of institutional design. In the words of Lumbee tribal member Rob Williams, a law professor and director of the University of Arizona's Office of Indian Programs during this controversy:

> There are no alternatives by which the great diversity within Indian communities and across Indian country can be recognized and reflected in our environmental law. Thus, our environmental law tells Indians that they must run their governments the same way that the dominant society runs its governments. This means that when the tribal government in a factionalized Indian community fails to respond to a request from the Forest Service about the tribal community's religious interests in a mountain, our environmental law can treat the tribe as having no religious interests in that mountain at all. Indians can only engage in the federal land use and environmental regulatory process through cultural and political institutions determined by the dominant society.[14]

And the other problem is one of how diverse cultures know the environment:

> For Indians, stories and narratives like the Gaan creation myth invoke the imaginative capacity to visualize the connections between the physical

environment, the social welfare of the community, and the spiritual values that create the consensus in Indian communities as to whether a particular use of the environment is beneficial or harmful to the human community. For non-Indians, there are no stories and myths which can help us imagine why preserving biodiversity is something deeply connected to who and what we are in the world—only science, economic analysis, vaguely stated appeals to aesthetic sensibility, and symbols generated by the Endangered Species Act such as the red squirrel. None of these has proven capable of generating consensus in our society about the importance of environmental values such as biodiversity to the human community.[15]

Professor Williams's statement is only partially correct. Clearly, there is no consensus within American society as to whether "a particular use of the environment is beneficial or harmful to the human community," just as there was no consensus among the San Carlos Apache when it most mattered. But as to the "stories and myths which can help us imagine why preserving biodiversity is something deeply connected to who and what we are in the world," this continues to be very much a work in progress. In fact, one of the principal theses of this book is that the renewed appreciation for the divine in nature among the major religious traditions of the West—along with rediscovery of pre-Christian European Earthen spiritual traditions and growing respect for diverse indigenous traditions embodying these teachings—represents yet another historic shift in Americans' relationship to their natural environment. It reflects an almost instinctive, survival-oriented movement toward developing a more complete, extrarational understanding of "why preserving biodiversity is something deeply connected to who and what we are in the world." And this goes not just for the preservation of biodiversity itself, but for the preservation of both the teachings on these matters and the places where they were rendered. Wilderness and worship have always gone hand in hand in indigenous American culture groups, and they are doing so in other spiritual and religious institutions in mainstream American society to a greater extent than any previous time in our history.

Similar management issues are arising elsewhere in the western

United States, anywhere the mountains are high enough and the view is good enough either for telescopes to be aimed heavenward or for telecommunications towers' transmission signals to be aimed earthward. And elsewhere, as at Mount Graham, so far it has always been technology that has prevailed, whether it be the microwave transmission towers near War God Springs on Navajo Mountain or the observatories on Hawaii's fourteen-thousand-foot Mauna Kea.

In some of these cases, environmental groups acted in alliance with Indian tribes to focus attention on the moral aspects of public lands management. But this relationship is a tenuous one: in the dispute giving rise to the *Lyng* decision, environmentalists abandoned the cause once Congress had voted the contested area off-limits to logging, even though the compromise road route still disturbed Indian burial grounds. The relationship between religious leaders (within Indian tribes and in the dominant culture), political leaders (within Indian tribes and in the dominant culture), and conservationists (within Indian tribes and in the dominant culture) is a complex, dynamic, and continuously evolving one, as cases throughout the rest of this book illustrate. Suffice it to say that the dynamic among these is very much worth watching, for it points the way to the future of how disputes over the spiritual uses of public lands and resources will be managed.

Single Use, Multiple Use, and the Turning of the Wheel

The classic resource management dilemma faced by federal agencies such as the Forest Service and the Bureau of Land Management is that while both are governed by general-purpose statutes calling for multiple-use management of the lands and resources entrusted to them, they must also adhere to the requirements of several other single-purpose statutes, such as the Wilderness Act, the General Mining Law, the Endangered Species Act, and the National Historic Preservation Act. Deciding which of these statutes should take precedence under which circumstances with regard to what specific areas, sites, and resources on the public lands is a decision-making exercise requiring the wisdom of Solomon, the patience of Job, and—now— the intercultural insight of Sacagawea. And in these opening years of the twenty-first century, there is probably no better example of the multiple-use agencies' newfound focus on sacred site management dilemmas than the Bighorn Medicine Wheel.

The site is located in what is now the Bighorn National Forest in Wyoming along the northern tier of some of the state's most remarkable landscapes, roughly midway between Bear's Lodge/Devils Tower to the east and Yellowstone National Park to the west. It consists of a circle of stones approximately ninety feet in diameter, with twenty-eight spokes radiating out from a central cairn (a Celtic term for stones stacked into a pyramid as an altar, place marker, or reference point). Other cairns arise along spokes of the wheel to the west and southwest of the center, at a distance of twelve to twenty feet from the center.

Archeological research and stories shared from the contemporary oral traditions of the Arapaho, Cheyenne, Crow, and Shoshone suggest that this particular wheel (there are over two dozen such structures of various sizes scattered along the eastern slopes of the Rocky Mountains from Wyoming on up into Canada) was constructed well before the coming of the first Euro-Americans.[16] Although now perhaps most closely associated with the cultural traditions of the four culture groups named above, Forest Service records indicate that in 1999 alone, representatives from sixty-six different Indian tribes conducted a total of 241 different ceremonies at the site.[17]

Interviews with cultural consultants from several of these tribes indicate that different culture groups may use the site for similar but also slightly different purposes. Common practice themes include vision quests, Sun Dances, fasting, chanting, invocations, other spoken prayers, and silent meditation. Until the 1970s the possible ancient uses—and therefore, reasons for the original layout—of the site were sources of speculation but little firm knowledge. It was then that astronomer John Eddy of the High Altitude Observatory at Boulder's National Center for Atmospheric Research undertook precise measurements of rock cairn placements at the wheel in relation to certain celestial events.[18] What he found is that, using the wheel somewhat like a true-north compass, moving to a location just outside the wheel where one of the peripheral cairns lines up with the center cairn does indeed position the observer's line of sight precisely to the point on the eastern horizon where the Sun rises at the summer solstice (sunsight cairn) and where various other celestial events predictably materialize (such as the brief dawn appearance of various Magnitude I stars off the starsight cairns).

This research revealed that the original designers and creators of the wheel quite probably constructed it for somewhat the same reasons as the Celts who built Stonehenge, as a site on Earth from which it was possible to realize an intelligible relationship with the cosmos—to orient oneself in space as well as in time. In sum, it may have been and may well continue to be (depending on one's spiritual orientation and understanding) a place where one comes *to be reminded of* one's place in all creation—neither less than nor more than all else around us, but simply a part of it.

Whatever spiritual meaning different First Native culture groups and other visitors might attribute to the site, its historical significance as an ancient human construction earned it National Historic Landmark status in 1970, at which time then–Interior Secretary Walter Hickel described it as "the largest and most elaborate Indian structure of its type."[19] From that time forward, public interest in the site and public visitation to it grew steadily. From 1990 to 1993, the annual visitor count (visitations can only occur in the summer when the snow melts and the wheel becomes visible) rose from twelve thousand to seventy thousand persons.[20]

Trying to find the balance point between use and preservation, the Forest Service initially proposed to pave the road up to the site and to construct a visitor's center and rest rooms. However, tribal representatives argued that to do this would encourage even more extensive and continuous visitation, making the site even less suitable for ritual observances. Since it had already been designated a National Historic Landmark (which encourages public attention but does not in and of itself assure greater protection), the Wyoming State Historic Preservation Office also expressed concern that the site be preserved, but not in a way that would fundamentally change its character by altering its surroundings.

During this period of both growing visitation and growing concern, in 1992 Congress amended the National Historic Preservation Act to require, among other things, that any federal agency contemplating action on federal properties that would affect the character of a national historic landmark which an Indian tribe considered to be of significant cultural value had to consult with such tribe or tribes before undertaking the proposed action, thus including tribes within the ambit of consultations already required under section 106 of the Historic Preservation Act.[21]

The Forest Service then undertook an extended consultation as called for under the act, which in 1994 resulted in the supervisor of the Bighorn National Forest entering into a programmatic agreement with the act's Advisory Council on Historic Preservation, the Wyoming State Historic Preservation Officer, the Bighorn County Commissioners, and the Federal Aviation Administration (to keep the air space clear over the site), and two different groups representing American Indian tribes that have a direct cultural affiliation with the site (the Medicine Wheel Coalition and the Medicine Wheel Alliance). As called for in the agreement, two years later and in consultation with the same parties, the Bighorn National Forest supervisor adopted a Historic Preservation Plan (HPP) that provided "a process for integrating the preservation and traditional uses of historic properties with the multiple use mission of the Forest Service."[22] In other words, as called for under the NHPA, in this Historic Preservation Plan the forest supervisor was formally taking on the responsibility of integrating the single-use purposes of the National Historic Preservation Act (insofar as the Medicine Wheel was concerned) with the multiple-use provisions of the 1960 Multiple Use and Sustained Yield Act and the 1978 National Forest Management Act (which calls on the Forest Service to adopt and maintain a detailed resource management plan for every national forest in its system).

To achieve this integration, the decision notice for establishment of the HPP for the Medicine Wheel area included an amendment to the Forest Plan already established for the area in compliance with the National Forest Management Act. This took place in 1996, shortly after President Clinton had also weighed in on such matters, by directing that "each executive branch agency with statutory or administrative responsibility for the management of Federal lands shall to the extent practicable, ... accommodate access to and ceremonial use of Indian sacred sites by Indian religious practitioners and avoid adversely affecting the physical integrity of such sacred sites."[23]

What the HPP and Forest Plan Amendment 12 did was to establish an eighteen-thousand acre "area of consultation" around the two-hundred acre National Historic Landmark site, with the understanding that the character of the site itself could not be maintained unless there were also some controls on other resource uses in the immediate vicinity (and within immediate view) of the wheel itself. In the consultation process leading up to drafting the HPP, several tribal ritual observants had testified that the continuous use of unpaved, unimproved Forest Service roads (one of which came within fifty feet of the site) by logging trucks and other increased traffic was severely degrading their ability to use the site for any form of spiritual practice at all. Uncontrolled tourist access also appeared to be taking a physical toll on the site, including the impact of numerous footpaths and the removal of some stones from the structure.[24]

Implementation of the HPP involved closure to commercial traffic of the road passing closest to the Medicine Wheel, and it also prompted reconsideration of a timber sale proposed earlier in the vicinity of the wheel because of the degrading effect it would have had on the character of the site within the expanded area of consultation. In response, a local sawmill that relied on commercial logging in that vicinity of the Bighorn National Forest appealed the supervisor's decision not to let the timber sale proceed, pending further consultation. Represented by the same conservative legal foundation that was already litigating the Devils Tower case on behalf of the plaintiff commercial climbing guides, Wyoming Sawmills filed a similar action in the U.S. District Court for the District of Wyoming in February 1999.

In its brief on behalf of the sawmill, attorneys for the Mountain States Legal Foundation charged that in adopting and implementing the Historic Preservation Plan, the Forest Service was doing the following:

1. Violating the First Amendment and impermissibly engaging in the establishment of Indian religion, by curtailing logging activities in order to accommodate spiritual uses of the site
2. Violating the Federal Advisory Committee Act, by allowing the Medicine Wheel Coalition and Medicine Wheel Alliance to have too much influence in the HPP implementation consultation process

3. Violating the National Environmental Policy Act, by not taking a close enough look at the socioeconomic effects of the decision to curtail logging activities in the vicinity of the wheel
4. Violating the National Forest Management Act (NFMA), by following National Historic Preservation Act (NHPA) procedures for consultation and public participation instead of NFMA procedures, when it amended the Forest Plan to mitigate the effects of logging within the expanded consultation area.[25]

In sum, the plaintiff's suit embodied the classic single-use/multiple-use dilemma faced by all federal land managers to one degree or another: by adhering too closely to the consultation requirements of a single-use congressional mandate (the National Historic Preservation Act), in the view of the plaintiff sawmill, the Forest Service was violating the requirements of a multiple-use congressional mandate (the National Forest Management Act).

In defense of the Forest Service, the U.S. attorney argued that the agency was simply accommodating the free exercise of Indian religion rather than establishing it, that it was simply taking First Native views into account (just like those of local government officials) in NHPA consultations rather than delegating Forest Service decision making to them, that it had indeed adequately considered the effects of its actions, and that its public participation and consultation activities had been consistent with the requirements of both the NHPA and NFMA.[26]

Of all these various causes of action, the one garnering the greatest attention is the first one: that in creating the buffer zone "area of consultation" around the wheel and not permitting traditional resource extractive activities in the zone in the absence of consultation with all the parties to the programmatic agreement and HPP, the Forest Service was impermissibly engaging in the establishment of Indian religion. This is basically the same charge the Mountain States Legal Foundation leveled against the voluntary June climbing moratorium in the National Park Service's Final Climbing Management Plan for Devils Tower, when it filed suit in that case in 1997. When Mountain States lost at trial in that case, it appealed to the Tenth Circuit Court of Appeals (based in Denver), which hears appeals from federal trial courts in states throughout the western Great Plains; and in April of 1999—just two months after Mountain States filed the Medicine Wheel case—the Tenth Circuit handed down its decision on the appeal of the Devils Tower decision.

The appellate court dismissed the Devils Tower appeal for lack of standing; that is, the commercial climbers had failed to demonstrate that they had been harmed by the voluntary moratorium in a way that would give rise to a legitimate legal claim against the Park Service. Thus it also let stand the trial court's ruling that the Park Service was reasonably accommodating tribal spiritual practices at Bear's Lodge/ Devils Tower in compliance with the free exercise clause of the First Amendment rather than impermissibly embracing Indian religion in contravention of the First Amendment's establishment clause.

In some respects, the suits filed by the Mountain States Legal Foundation represent efforts to defend the past (a time when federal land managers completely disregarded Indian and other spiritual concerns in resource planning) against the present—a new policy era in which the spiritual uses of public lands and resources represent yet another management consideration to take into account. The problem for the organization is that in filing these actions, it is beginning to appear more and more antireligious as well as anti-Indian in nature, which is an uncomfortable position for this otherwise highly conservative public interest law firm to be in. Sensitive to this point, on its filing of the Medicine Wheel case, one of its attorneys commented that "the Mountain States Legal Foundation is not an anti-religious organization in any way. . . . We just don't think religion is a good tool for forest management."[27]

At federal shrines such as the Arlington National Cemetery, at old Catholic missions throughout the southwest that are also national monuments, and at Sunday morning church services in national parks throughout the United States, National Park Service regulations forbid behaviors that would be antithetical to religious worship or spiritual reflection, which is also one of the purposes of the Medicine Wheel Historic Preservation Plan. Euro-American society as a whole is quite accustomed to treating missions and cemeteries—and the worshipers and mourners who congregate there—with the respect they deserve. Now this society is being called on to extend that same respect to sites held just as sacred by other culture groups, and some elements of that society are clearly finding it harder than others to do so.

As the Medicine Wheel case works its way through the federal court system, it may also come before the judges of the Tenth Circuit and then possibly before the U.S. Supreme Court, as the Devils Tower case eventually did.[28] Whether or not they are resolved in the same way, both the Medicine Wheel and the Devils Tower disputes illustrate that we are indeed living in changing times. Congress initiated the process with atonement-era statutes such as the American Indian Religious Freedom Act, the Native American Graves Repatriation Act, and the 1992 amendments to the National Historic Preservation Act. The executive branch followed up with regulations implementing these statutes, as well as President Clinton's executive order clarifying federal agency responsibilities under some of these laws and the First Amendment itself. And over the last two decades of the twentieth century the federal courts have been called on to adjudicate the pace and direction that these changes should take.

This movement from the legislative (policy making) to the executive (policy implementation) to the judicial (policy adjudication) and back to the legislative (policy amendment, in light of implementation and adjudication outcomes) can in itself be understood as a great cycle, or wheel, of sorts. Students of Western environmental history, as well as participants in this policy process, also understand it to be a wheel that is constantly turning. Tom Graff, regional counsel for the Environmental Defense Fund and a very successful legal advocate, once remarked, "There's no such thing as a final decision in environmental law,"[29] and this is what he meant.

Now set in motion, this wheel will no doubt continue to turn. Despite personnel and policy changes in Congress, in the executive branch, and in the federal judiciary, once brought into the policy process, the theme of spirituality in the uses of public lands and resources can be seen as either a recent innovation in public lands policy or a return to its most ancient roots. And for anyone who doubts that it is the latter, try standing just southwest of the Bighorn Medicine Wheel at the spot where the sunsight cairn lines up with the center cairn on a summer solstice dawn.

To be in that place at that time, just as to stand in alignment with the sunsight notches in the kivas at a site like Chaco Canyon, is not only to be reminded that you are there on the solstice. It is also to remember that other humans—including the ancient ones who built these structures—have been standing at just the same spot and seeing just the same relationship between themselves, the sky above, and the Earth below come into being for many hundreds of years gone by. It is to be connected in both place and time to those who have gone before, just as—depending on how the policies discussed in this book are carried out—for both First Natives and members of American society as a whole, these places may also serve as a connection point between us and those who are yet to come.

8

Birthing the Woolly Cow

The Contested Legal Reconstruction
of the American Bison

So far the focus of this book has been on the combined influences of culture, religion, and constitutional law on the management of places—sacred sites and the public lands around them. By contrast, chapters 8 and 9 feature the treatment of the entities that move about on, fly over, grow on, or flow through the public lands—that is, wildlife, plant life, and water.

Like sacred sites, different cultures see these things in different ways and call them by different names. In traditional multiple-use public land law, these are *natural resources*, a term reflecting perceptual construction of the natural environment as a vast supermarket, where resource-extractive industries go shopping for the food, fiber, minerals, and water needed to sustain human life and society. In other federal statutes (such as the Wilderness Act, Endangered Species Act, and Marine Mammal Protection Act), plants and animals are simply other life forms we humans have responsibility for taking care of because we hold the power of life and death over them. In the teachings of various First Native culture groups, however, plants and animals are relatives, deities, sacred intermediaries between humans and the spirit world, or some combination of all the above.

How we see these entities and what we call them certainly influences how we treat them. This chapter is about a serious and contentious conflict being waged in the American West over the treatment of one such being: the American bison. The saga begins at the end of the last Ice Age in Europe and in North America, with the histories of two great horned ungulates—the bison in North America and the aurochs in Europe—both of which were once revered by the human cultures that relied on them for their survival.

Context for the Conflict

Poachers killed the last surviving aurochs in northern Europe about four hundred years ago. But by then the animal was no longer of much use to humans anyway. Through selective breeding, for the previous six millennia humans had been gradually transforming captive herds of this huge, once-revered wild animal into the smaller, fatter, slower, dumber domestic cow. Today, cattle ranchers in the United States are beginning to do the same thing to the bison, also commonly known as the buffalo. It is happening biologically, and it is happening legally. In recent years, some western state legislatures have begun to transfer regulatory jurisdiction over bison from their wildlife management agencies to their departments of agriculture, thus transforming them in the eyes of state law from wild animals into livestock.

The distinction is more than academic and legalistic. In the unusually severe winter of 1996–1997, agents of the Montana Department of Livestock and private ranchers stood with hunting rifles just outside the north entrance to Yellowstone National Park, killing over a thousand buffalo (a third of the herd) as they migrated down out of the deep snows in the high country in search of forage.[1] The state government rationale for this action was that the bison might infect cattle herds with brucellosis, a disease known to cause miscarriages in the latter species. However, bison-to-cattle transmission of this infection has never been demonstrated to have actually occurred in the field, and cattle are susceptible to the disease only during the late spring calving season, by which time the Yellowstone herd migrates back up into the park's protected pastureland.[2] These same state officials captured and slaughtered Yellowstone bison just outside the park in the winters that followed.

These actions did not go uncontested. A coalition of American Indian tribes and environmental conservation groups soon organized to oppose state efforts to legally transform bison into woolly cows. The tribes see the future biological and legal status of the bison as inextricably linked to their own cultural survival, while for environmental groups the legal redefinition of wildlife as livestock for state management purposes represents extreme commercial intrusion into the manipulation of the very life forms that comprise American wilderness.

This chapter begins with consideration of the aurochs' and bison's ancestral relationship to their neighboring human populations in Europe and North America, then moves to an analysis of human cultural and legal conflict over the bison–human relationship in the present-day United States. In so doing, this narrative demonstrates how state legislative efforts in some areas of the American West to legally reconstruct the bison from wildlife to livestock bespeak a much more fundamental conflict. It goes to the far deeper question (explicitly cultural in nature) of how different groups perceptually construct their environment and ascribe significance to it.

To legislatively reconstruct the bison in this way is also to desacralize it. And this political effort is also deeply dividing mainstream society in the American West as well. As they work in consort with various Plains tribes to stop the destruction of the Yellowstone bison herd when it migrates out of the park during the winter months, the actions of some environmental groups are based on a worldview that is much more closely aligned with their indigenous partners in this endeavor than with the Euro-American state legislators and bureaucrats who are doing the legal reconstructing. Thus the struggle to preserve the bison reflects an effort at cultural survival on the part of the Plains tribes; it also exemplifies a powerful conflict over the ascriptions of significance to nature within American society as a whole. In seeking to chart a course through this essentially intracultural conflict, this chapter ends with the suggestion of policy alternatives that will avoid the default policy option of, as one tribal herd manager warns, killing the buffalo while keeping the meat machine alive.

From Sacred to Satanic: Horned Beasts in European Religious History

In the European imagination, wild horned animals have undergone quite a metamorphosis since the Ice Age. Among the oldest known works of art in all of human history is the depiction of the aurochs and other horned game species (archeological evidence reveals that these Stone Age artists ate as well as admired them) on the walls of the caves of Lascaux, France. Horns of the aurochs and their domestic progeny surrounded the altars to the goddesses of the Neolithic civilizations of the Near East, and the animal figured prominently as the male half of the fertility equation in many of the pre-Christian nature-based spiritual traditions of early Western civilizations.[3]

But at about the same time that their domestication firmly took hold, so did their desacralization by the Judeo-Christian monotheistic traditions. Celtic deities like the horned god Cernunos were later to be imbued with a very different persona. The Christians' icon for evil incarnate was soon to become a half-man, half-beast who sported cloven hooves, a tail, and horns. The sacred no longer existed in nature itself—not in flowing water, not in groves of trees, and certainly not in animals, either domestic or wild. Instead, there was a vertical Great Chain of Being (a Christian appropriation of a neo-Platonist formulation), with God in the heavens above, struggling humanity suspended on Earth below (afflicted, according to Genesis, both by self-knowledge that set them apart from the animals and animal instincts that set them apart from God), animals below them, plants below the animals, and vile demonic human/beasts inhabiting the dark nether regions of the Earth. Salvation and spiritual purity resulted from rising above our "animal nature" rather than reveling in it.[4]

The Bison's Path, Part 1: Out of the Past

Early European immigrants to North America's Atlantic shores brought along both a burgeoning enthusiasm for the manipulation of nature and a deeply ingrained religious antipathy to all things wild. They encountered here a physical environment and a diversity of indigenous cultures unlike anything they had ever known. When they crossed over the eastern mountains into the Great Plains, the immigrants beheld another sight unprecedented in their experience: sixty million buffalo.[5] They also discovered indigenous peoples who had been living with and off of these vast herds for at least ten thousand years.

Among First Natives, bison did not suffer the same fall from grace in North America as had the aurochs and its domestic progeny in Europe. Tribes from Canada to Mexico depended on the animal to varying degrees for sustenance and revered it in their religious practices. It was perhaps most central to the lifeways of the tribes of the western Great Plains.[6] In addition to being almost the entire basis for their subsistence, bison were (and are) also crucial to indigenous religious beliefs. They are understood to be important intermediaries between humans and the spirit world. The gift of the Sacred Pipe to the Sioux from White Buffalo Calf Woman, who appeared to hunters first as a woman but reverted to the form of a white buffalo on completion of her mission, remains as one of the most enduring teachings in Sioux spiritual traditions.[7]

The Plains Indians' reliance on the buffalo for every aspect of their physical and cultural survival was a lesson not lost on the Euro-American immigrants who would eventually fight them in the latter half of the nineteenth century. Fierce and feared combatants, the most effective (and safest) long-term strategy for making war on the Plains tribes turned out to be making war on the buffalo. Representatives of the Interior Department testified before Congress in 1874 that it would be impossible to "civilize" the Plains tribes as long as the buffalo still existed.[8]

The enormous migrating herds of bison also made impossible the "civilizing" of the soil by newly arrived settlers and played havoc with railroad operations along the just-completed transcontinental rail lines. Railroads hired hunters like Buffalo Bill Cody to start decimating the herds; he claimed to have killed over four thousand alone in his year as a Union Pacific employee. Passengers also were encouraged to shoot them from moving trains as a form of entertainment. Bison were being killed at the rate of about five million per year by the early 1870s. Congress actually managed to pass a Buffalo Protection Act in 1874, but President Ulysses Grant blocked its enactment by allowing it to succumb to a pocket veto.[9]

By 1899, only a thousand buffalo were known to still exist in all of North America—two hundred of them having sought refuge in the theoretically safe haven of Yellowstone National Park. Poaching in the park was a problem, however. Despite legislation passed to protect buffalo in 1894, the population decline continued so that by 1902 the herd size in the park was down to about twenty-five. Once the poaching law started to be enforced, the herd made a gradual comeback. By 1995, the Yellowstone herd was estimated to number about 3,900 animals.[10]

Federalism, Cultural Conflict, and American Wildlife Law

The near-extinction and subsequent recovery of bison herds in Yellowstone and elsewhere in the American West occurred against the background of a gradual but steadily shifting relationship between federal and state governments concerning control over wildlife management. The relationship began with the end of the American Revolution, when state governments formally "received" the essential doctrines of English common law as the basis for their own legal systems.[11]

One of these principles was that all wildlife was the property of the sovereign. In state constitutions and statutes, this was generally translated into the concept of collective ownership in the citizens of the state, with authority to manage wildlife vested in state agencies empowered to act on their behalf.[12]

This principle held true even as new states were created in the course of westward expansion—states in which some or even most of the land stayed in federal ownership. State authority to manage wildlife populations was assumed to be complete, regardless of whose land they were on, until early in the twentieth century. It was then that the U.S. Supreme Court began to find residual federal authority to exist in the form of international wildlife preservation treaties. In *Missouri v. Holland*,[13] the Court ruled that when the federal government entered into a treaty with Canada for the international protection of waterfowl in transboundary north–south migration, that action superseded the authority of state governments to manage those species in ways that violated treaty provisions.

Congress further trimmed state wildlife management authority in the Bald Eagle Protection Act of 1940.[14] But for sheer federal effrontery in terms of both diminishing state agency authority and raising western cattle rancher ire, the prize goes to two statutes enacted by Congress at the outset of the modern environmental era: the 1971

Wild Free-Roaming Horses and Burros Act (WF-RHBA) and the 1973 Endangered Species Act (ESA).[15]

The horses and burros law was a product of public outrage at western ranchers' mass killings of mustangs and burros (wild herds who escaped from the Spanish conquistadors of the 1500s and from gold prospectors in the 1800s), who were eating the forage and drinking the water on federal lands for which the ranchers had purchased permits to graze their livestock. Under state estray law, livestock regulation agencies also have the authority to round up, remove, and destroy unclaimed, unbranded livestock. Shortly after Congress enacted the WF-RHBA to forbid both private ranchers and state agencies from destroying these animals on or removing them from federal land, New Mexico declared its intention to ignore the statute, and its livestock board removed the mustangs and burros per their previous authority and customary practice. The state also sued the Interior secretary to enjoin enforcement of the law, and in 1975 a three-judge panel in New Mexico's U.S. District Court struck it down as violating states' rights and in excess of Congress' authority to manage the federal estate as granted by the property clause of the U.S. Constitution.

But a year later, in *Kleppe v. New Mexico*,[16] the U.S. Supreme Court unanimously ruled that whenever Congress is acting under its property clause powers to manage federally owned lands and resources on behalf of the people of the United States, its power to do so is "without limitations." The Court also found that it was within that authority to declare mustangs and burros to be wholly under federal protection as long as they stayed on federal land, and thus to forbid the state and private parties from harming them. In the statute, Congress did not go quite so far as to legislatively redefine this feral livestock as wildlife (the reverse of what state legislatures have been doing to the buffalo lately), but federal legislators did characterize them as "an integral part of the natural system of the public lands"[17] and therefore immune from traditional state removal and destruction practices.

Later developments suggested that the act might have worked too well. Since ranchers in the western states, with the full support and cooperation of both state and federal governments, had long since succeeded in eradicating large predators (like wolves, grizzly bears, and mountain lions) from the western range, there were no meaningful controls on the population size of any wild, hoofed animals, except for hunting. Once the mustangs and burros received federal statutory protection, these liberated livestock used it to full advantage.

By 1978 the numbers of mustangs and burros had increased so greatly that, in combination with the level of cattle grazing on public lands (which had not been diminished subsequent to passage of the wild horse bill), some form of wild horse and burro population control seemed necessary. Therefore, Congress amended the law at that time to grant federal land management agencies authority to "expeditiously" remove excess populations of horses and burros whenever they are determined to be causing clear degradation of federal rangeland quality (leaving unanswered the question of whether it was population growth among horses and burros or undiminished levels of commercial cattle grazing that was chiefly responsible for rangeland damage). Federal courts have since upheld federal agency authority to remove excess protected animals from the range.[18]

Less idiosyncratic and far more pervasive in its effects on federal lands and resource management was the Endangered Species Act of 1973. Judging from the legislative histories of the two statutes, it seemed to have a somewhat more thoughtful philosophical basis than the WF-RHBA and has stood the test of time a little better. The ESA frankly acknowledged the awesome power humans now wield over the natural environment—and likewise acknowledged that with that power comes more responsibility for the well-being of plant and animal species on the verge of extinction than American society had theretofore been willing to accept.

Of the many actions taken in pursuit of the ESA's objectives, the one most irritating to western livestock operation interests has probably been the reintroduction of endangered predator species such as the wolf, which ranchers had been working hard to rid the rangeland of throughout the latter nineteenth and early twentieth centuries—some wolves, of course, having long since discovered that they could make an easier, safer living by dining on domesticated calves and lambs instead of having to run to ground deer, elk, and moose fawns or buffalo calves. And just as with the bison, the epicenter of this particular cultural and legal conflict has been Yellowstone National Park. Livestock operators in Montana and Wyoming have opposed by every means possible the reintroduction of wolves to Yellowstone, for reasons that ultimately are probably as much symbolic as economic. It is a question of who actually controls the range: the federal governments or the states, the ranchers or the wildlife?

Contested Legal Reconstruction

Once the Yellowstone buffalo herd had survived its extinction crisis and grown to the status of a viable, self-sustaining population, the herd also reestablished its seasonal migration patterns down out of the park when winters were especially harsh and forage scarce, then back up into the high country in the spring. Although much of the rangeland to the north and west of the park is federal land managed by the U.S. Forest Service, most of that pasturage is leased to private cattle ranchers. Thus, ranching interests doubly resented the migrating bison: first because of an as-yet unsubstantiated risk of brucellosis transmission and, second, because of competition with their cattle for water and forage on the public range.

The Yellowstone bison represent the largest free-ranging noncommercial wild buffalo herd in the United States. Collectively, the greatest number of buffalo in the country now reside on commercial ranches. The ranchers in southern Montana and elsewhere in the West are not trying to eradicate buffalo altogether. Far from it: as both demand for beef products and their prices continue to fall, commercial bison ranching may well provide a crucially important economic boost to this sagging industry. The concern of some (but by no means all) ranchers is with *wild* buffalo—that is, bison populations which left to their own devices would happily reinhabit much of the federal rangeland that is now being leased to private ranchers.

Different states have taken different approaches to regulating bison populations within their borders. The citations in table 1 show that some simply define them as wildlife and others solely as livestock, while still others define them to achieve different policy objectives: as wildlife for the purpose of regulating hunting and prosecuting poaching, and as livestock for the purpose of food regulation and animal disease control. Among these "dual-designation" states, Montana calls for coordination between the department of livestock and the fish and game commission regarding the status of wild buffalo but gives preemptive authority to the livestock department whenever disease control or estray control is implicated. Montana law also indemnifies any rancher who kills a wild buffalo on the rancher's private land from prosecution under the state's poaching statute.

Table 1 Constructing the Bison

State	Statutory Citation(s)
As Wildlife Only	
Arizona	A.R.S. § 17-101.B.2, 3. (1998)
California	Cal. Fish & G. Code § 2118(b) (1999)
New Mexico	N.M. Stat. Ann. § 17-2-3(2)(a)
As Livestock Only	
Colorado	C.R.S. 35-50-136(4) (1998)
Nebraska	R.R.S. Neb. § 54-1368(3)(b)
Oklahoma	2 Ok. Stat. 6-121(2) (1998)
North Dakota	N.D. Cent. Code § 36-01-00.1.3 (1999)
South Dakota	S.D. Codified Laws § 40-7-1.1 (1999)
Dual Designation	
(upper cite is to wildlife designation; lower is to livestock)	
Idaho	Idaho Code § 36-1120 (1998)
	Idaho Code § 25-3301(3) (1998)
Kansas	K.S.A. § 32-1005(b)(3)
	K.S.A. § 65-6a118(z)(aa) (1997)
Montana	Mont. Code Ann. § 87-2-101 (1998)
	Mont. Code Ann. § 87-2-120(i) (1998)
Utah	Utah Code Ann. § 23-13-2(46)(g) (1998)
	Utah Code Ann. § 4-7-73(5) (1998)
Wyoming	Wyo. Stat. 23-1-101 (xiii) (1999)
	Wyo. Stat. § 11-20-124 (1999)

Wildlife are notoriously disrespectful of political borders and property boundaries. But when bison set foot outside the border separating the sanctuary of Yellowstone National Park from other federal lands in Montana, or the sanctuary of Grand Teton National Park from other federal lands in Wyoming, they unknowingly cross into a different and far more dangerous, uncertain situation than just the climatic extremes of these high country parks. At least through the end of the twentieth century, whether they survived depended less on the suitability of the winter habitat than it did on which federal judge was chosen to decide their fate. As the following comparison of two recent district court decisions demonstrates, some judges find it far easier than others to see bison as woolly cows rather than as wild sacred icons and to allow state wildlife officials to treat them accordingly.

In November 1998, a federal trial court in Montana handed down its decision in *Inter-Tribal Bison Cooperative v. Babbitt*,[19] in which it turned aside an effort by several dozen American Indian tribes and conservation organizations to prevent the continued killing of Yellowstone buffalo when they exited the park in search of winter forage. In 1985 the Montana legislature had authorized the issuance of buffalo hunting licenses to the public for the purpose of killing Yellowstone bison if they attempted winter migration; in a suit brought by a wildlife conservation group, a federal judge in Montana later upheld the state's power to do this.[20]

But "hunting" bison is hardly as romantic or challenging as it might sound. Given their size, approachability, and usually calm demeanor, hunting most bison requires little more skill than hunting a cow. What does require skill is to kill one quickly and cleanly, with one shot. One of the problems with the public bison hunts of the late 1980s was that many of the "hunters" did not have that skill, resulting in an even gorier public spectacle than the one televised in the winter of 1996–1997, when it was department of livestock marksmen rather than weekend sportsmen gunning down bison as they left the park.

In 1995, the State of Montana sued the federal government in an effort to compel control of the Yellowstone herd size and to prevent its winter migration out of the park. The two parties negotiated a settlement that allowed the state department of livestock to continue killing migrating buffalo in "emergency" situations,[21] and the following winter over one-third of the herd were killed. This prompted the suit by the Inter-Tribal Bison Cooperative (ITBC) and the Greater Yellowstone Coalition to enjoin continued implementation of the Interim Management Plan and continued killing of the Yellowstone herd.

Even though the state was unable to prove that brucellosis had ever actually been transmitted from a bison to a cow, the court nevertheless found that it was within the state's police powers to protect the public health and safety by "removing possibly infected YNP [Yellowstone National Park] bison that migrate into Montana."[22] The court also characterized the history of YNP herd as more domestic than wild, since it had been intensively ranched by federal wranglers within the park during its recovery period. Thus, the *ITBC v. Babbitt* decision framed the entire dispute as one of the federal government failing to comply with state estray and animal disease control statutes. In short, the trial court determined that the Park Service had been practicing negligent livestock management by allowing the YNP bison herd to follow its instincts down out of the high country to winter feed.

Another rationale this court offered for support of the continued destruction of YNP bison by the state was its repetition of the finding of a district court decision in 1991, to the effect that the carrying capacity of Yellowstone National Park for bison is approximately 2,400 animals. This finding made it possible to support the park superintendent's discretion to allow all animals in excess of that number to be destroyed on exiting the park, as YNP's interim management plan negotiated in settlement of the 1995 suit acknowledged the state's authority to do under emergency conditions.[23] However, a research report commissioned by the National Academy of Sciences and published in 1998 has determined the winter carrying capacity of Yellowstone to be "about 3,000 bison."[24] This report also found the risk of bison-to-cattle transmission of brucellosis to be so low as to be unquantifiable. In order for the *ITBC* court to find the destruction of "excess" animals a reasoned exercise of discretion, therefore, it had to rely on a seven-year-old court decision rather than the latest evidence from the most authoritative government source of scientific information.

Lastly, the *ITBC* court upheld the Yellowstone superintendent's finding of no significant [environmental] impact occasioned by the bison kill. Making this finding alleviated the park superintendent from having to prepare an environmental impact statement before agreeing to the kill, as would otherwise be required under the National Environmental Policy Act.

Just a week earlier, another federal trial court at the opposite end of the country had heard another case raising remarkably similar issues but had reached opposite conclusions on nearly every major point. In *Fund for Animals v. Clark*,[25] the U.S. District Court for the District of Columbia granted a preliminary injunction against implementation of a bison management plan on federal lands adjoining Grand Teton National Park, which would have allowed the Wyoming Game and Fish Department to kill buffalo to control herd size. Two important reasons the court gave for this action were that the U.S. Fish and Wildlife Service had failed to comply with the National Environmental Policy Act in authorizing the hunt and had likewise failed to demonstrate the likelihood of brucellosis transmission from the Grand Teton herd to neighboring cattle if the bison hunt was not allowed to go forward.

In reaching this latter conclusion, the court agreed with the position taken in the National Academy of Sciences study, holding that a remote and speculative possibility of brucellosis transmission was not enough to warrant the bison's destruction. This was in sharp contrast to the Montana U.S. District Court's finding in the *ITBC* decision that if the *state* concluded there was a brucellosis threat, that was all that was needed to justify killing bison if they migrated out of Yellowstone. The D.C. District Court in *Clark* also agreed with expert testimony that there was "virtually no risk" of human infection by the disease—again, a different conclusion from the *ITBC* decision.

In both the *ITBC* and the *Clark* cases, federal agencies were defendants, because in both cases these agencies had entered into intergovernmental agreements authorizing state agencies to kill members of federal wild bison herds on federal lands. At issue in both cases was whether the federal agency in question had adequately evaluated the environmental impacts of these kills (NEPA [National Environmental Policy Act] compliance), whether the scientific evidence pertaining to bison-borne brucellosis was sufficient to support the destruction of wild herd members, and the degree of state agency authority over the control of wild bison on federal lands. In both cases, the federal agencies sided with the states. For the plaintiff groups concerned with the future well-being of wild bison in the United States, both agencies failed and are continuing to fail in their responsibility to steward this resource.

Desacralizing the Bison: Law, Culture, and Identity

In the context of wildlife management in the Greater Yellowstone ecosystem, conflict over cultural beliefs is occurring in multiple dimensions. The most obvious is between the American Indian tribes in the region (who regard animal species such as the buffalo and the wolf as relatives and as sacred intermediaries to spiritual dimensions of their universe) and commercial livestock operators (who see these same animals as direct threats to their own economic survival and way of life). Largely unseen, because of the ways the issues have been framed, is the persistence of a powerful conflict between different groups within Euro-American society.

Customarily, conflicts between resource-extractive industries and environmental conservation groups in American society have been cast as struggles between competing political interest groups, because their contests are usually played out in political or legal arenas. But something far more fundamental is at stake. Environmental conservation groups and western ranching interests experience political and legal conflict in part because they are proceeding from profoundly different understandings of what the appropriate relationship between humankind and other living creatures ought to be.

In this dispute, different groups are seeking to conceptually construct and thus to treat wild bison in radically different ways. If, as cultural anthropologists such as Renato Rosaldo assert, culture "refers broadly to the forms through which people make sense of their lives" and "all human conduct is culturally mediated,"[26] one conclusion to be drawn from the research described here is that the variation in legal constructions of the bison as depicted in table 1 reflects differing cultural constructions of the same species of animal across these jurisdictions.

My own fieldwork in this area, as well as the study of other recent data-gathering on the role of culture in managing the YNP bison herd, has led me to conclude that among the three principal stakeholder groups featured in this study (American Indian tribes, conservationists, and ranchers), the perception of and relationship to the Yellowstone bison herd on the part of the conservation community more nearly resembles that of the tribes than it does that of the ranchers. This, in turn, is what has led to conservationists and the Inter-Tribal Bison Cooperative making common legal cause in this ongoing controversy.

This suggests that a much better grasp of the cultural complexities and variations in the bison management conflict is a necessary precondition to federal land managers' ability to make better decisions in the field and federal judges' ability to make better decisions in the courts when reviewing agency actions. "Better" in this context means tribes, ranchers, and conservationists all sensing that the survival of their respective cultural identities—as well as the respective herds of horned, hoofed animals they care about so deeply (albeit for different reasons)—will be met at a satisfactory threshold level.

A rich ethnographic tradition documents the centrality of the buffalo to the spiritual identity and practices of the Plains tribes,[27] just as, in contrast, a rich historical record documents nineteenth-century Anglo-American religious teachings depicting wilderness and the wildlife within it as made subordinate to man by God and subject to absolute human dominion. Only now are we gaining a better understanding of the spiritual (if not overtly religious) dimensions of the Euro-American conservation movement and the increasing frequency with which reverence for life arises in both the vision statements and the advocacy discourse of these groups.

Reflective of an interesting new direction in studies on the anthropology of religion, ethnographer Nurit Bird-David challenges head-on the modernist perspective of animism (i.e., the perception of the sacred or at least the venerable in nonhuman forms) as a "savage" religion and failed epistemology. Instead, she suggests that animism is a sophisticated system of relational knowing: humans and their behavior are integral (though not central) to the natural order rather than distinguishable and separate from it. Based on her own and others' historical and contemporary work in this area, she goes on to propose that such intuitive self-understanding, which includes seeing oneself as an intersection in a seamless relational network rather than a separate observer/manipulator of "nature"—may be a much more common human trait than has previously been acknowledged.[28]

While others have alternately lauded and derided some contemporary environmental discourse as the "new animism" or the "new anthropomorphism," Bird-David recommends study of this increasingly evident feature of the postmodern environmental movement as an emergent phenomenon that should be taken seriously. She suggests: "It would be interesting to compare hunter-gatherers' animism with some current environmental thought. Schools such as deep ecology, social ecology, and eco-feminism envisage an all-encompassing moral community constitutive of humans and non-humans. Some radical environmentalists even call for a paradigmatic shift in not only our view of nature but our view of the self, for example, from 'ego' to 'spirit,' understood as a self not split but differentiated from others within relationships."[29]

The contrast between contemplative (including animistic) and calculative ways of knowing our environment is one of the principal delineating features between the sacred and the secular in conventional constructions of Western thought, which is why it should come as no surprise that there is growing emphasis on spiritual affinity with nature as a motivating principle among several member organizations in the Greater Yellowstone Coalition. Relational knowledge also features prominently in ways they have described their relationship to the bison in ethnographic research on the subject, as well as in court. At around the same time coalition members were focusing public attention on the 1997 YNP bison herd slaughter, Sierra Club executive director Carl Pope, at a 1997 symposium on religion, science, and the environment, acknowledged that "we discovered a very large number of people in the Sierra Club who in church were closet environmentalists and in the Sierra Club were closet members of their churches. They felt they had to keep these two aspects of their souls separate." He went on to admit: "The environmental movement for the past quarter of a century has made no more profound error than to misunderstand the mission of religion and the churches in preserving the Creation."[30]

This focus on relational knowing, in combination with and in some ways indistinguishable from the environmental movement's rediscovery of its nineteenth-century spiritual origins (per the writings of Thoreau and Muir), has also begun to gain recognition in the institutions called on to translate the discourses of cultural self-identification into the language of the law. In *Fund for Animals v. Clark,* the federal judge granted plaintiff conservationists standing based in part on what he termed their desire to "commiserate" with the Grand Teton bison herd.[31] "Commiserate" was an interesting and important choice of words by this judge, in that its standard American English dictionary definition is "to feel or express sorrow or compassion for, to feel or express sympathy, to condole."[32] These are interpersonal terms, reflective of plaintiffs' assertion of a personal relationship with the Teton bison and of the court's willingness to recognize this extra-rational, relational status to the bison as a grounds for granting conservationists legal standing to advocate on the herd's behalf.

Nor is this emphasis on the need for renewed spiritual relationships with nature confined to what detractors have labeled the "new anthropomorphists" of the environmental movement. One of the more significant developments in contemporary American religious affairs has been the 1993 founding of the National Religious Partnership for the Environment, an umbrella organization of mainstream religious denominations that disseminates teaching materials on celebrating the divine in nature and lobbies Congress for more protective environmental legislation. Its member denominations are now beginning to appear as co-plaintiffs and amici in several major lawsuits mandating enforcement of the Endangered Species Act and supporting indigenous peoples in the preservation of sacred sites on public lands.

I am not arguing that all the conservation groups in the Greater Yellowstone Coalition are imbued with deep relational knowledge and motivated solely by spiritual affinity with the bison, just as I am also not maintaining that none of the ranchers in the Greater Yellowstone Ecosystem feel a personal affinity with and deep affection for the rural environments in which they live and work. These two groups are not monolithic, and there is a tenuous continuum of thought within as well as between them. Indeed, in his 1991 book *Community and the Politics of Place*, former Missoula, Montana, mayor Daniel Kemmis maintains that both groups have strong feelings about their relationship to their land and all it holds; they simply see that relationship quite differently and thus try to compel government institutions to act in accordance with their conflicting visions.

But in the words and deeds of advocacy organizations that these groups comprise and support, strikingly different constructions of their respective worldviews are clearly evident. The construct of the hierarchical Great Chain of Being western settlers inherited from neo-Platonists and early Christians, via the New England Calvinists and Latter Day Saints, still dominates much western rural thought and thus lawmaking in the legislatures of many western states (such as the ones that construct bison as livestock). For them, the purpose of creation is to serve the needs of man, and any other environmental policy goal must remain subordinate to that anthropocentric prime directive.

In equally clear distinction, among conservation groups in networks such as the Greater Yellowstone Coalition, the growing emphasis on a capacity for relational knowledge of self in nature, as well as a rediscovered appreciation for the divine in nature, is creating a strikingly different sense of self-identity among them, as well as a strikingly different moral vision of what ought to be humankind's relationship to the natural world. The Christians among the conservationists are reviewing and redefining their religion's teachings on the divine in nature, while others in the movement are just as intent on rediscovering and revitalizing the pre-Christian, Earthen traditions originated by their ancestors in ancient Europe.

Acknowledging or Ignoring Cultural Difference in the Courts

Whether this state-by-state effort in the American West to culturally and legally reconstruct the bison will succeed depends to a considerable extent on which federal court is handling the issue and what that court's views are on questions of federalism and cultural pluralism.

The *ITBC* and *Clark* cases discussed earlier provide some dramatically differing perspectives on whether this reconstruction effort is likely to succeed, growing out of their widely varying perspectives on the interests plaintiffs were trying to assert and the relative responsiveness of the federal agencies involved to the assertion of those interests.

In the *Clark* case, individual plaintiffs were seeking (and were granted) standing based simply on their desire to see and be among wild bison in their natural habitat. The court noted that the individual plaintiffs "enjoy observing, photographing, and generally commiserating with the animals" and that to allow a state-organized hunt outside Grand Teton National Park of the sort that had earlier been conducted outside Yellowstone "would cause them [the plaintiffs] to suffer an aesthetic injury."[33] This "aesthetic injury" (i.e., severance of connection with the environment's wilderness heritage experienced through contact with its wildlife) was an important enough interest in the view of this court to warrant a preliminary injunction against a state-administered bison "hunt," pending a trial on the issues of compliance with National Environmental Policy Act (through preparation of an environmental impact statement), and on the defendant agencies' ability to carry the burden of proof of demonstrating that the threat of bison-to-cattle brucellosis transmission was significant enough to justify the wild buffalo's destruction. In this decision, the judge was clearly unwilling to sacrifice the concerns of one community of interest for the sake of another's—at least not until all the facts were in.

Neither the plaintiffs nor the bison fared so well in the *ITBC* decision. Both the Inter-Tribal Bison Cooperative and the National Wildlife Federation are member organizations of the Greater Yellowstone Coalition (although the ITBC is always careful to distinguish its own cultural interests from other member organizations). While the two organizations' respective reasons for participating in this legal action differed in some important regards, they have acknowledged shared interest in one common outcome: that Yellowstone's wild bison herd be treated with respect in the way it is managed,[34] to the extent that some form of management is needed at all.

It was precisely this "aesthetic sensibility"—a cultural interest in conservation and management of the Yellowstone bison as free, wild animals—that the *ITBC* court went out of its way to declare as nonexistent. Two years before eventually dismissing the case, at the outset of this litigation the court denied preliminary injunctive relief to plaintiff Indian tribes and the Greater Yellowstone Coalition. It held that there were no "environmental, emotional, and aesthetic interests" on the plaintiffs' part that would be irreparably injured by allowing the state bison slaughter to continue until a trial could be held on the merits.[35] The judge went on to observe that even if the National Park Service decided to manage the bison within Yellowstone National Park exactly as if they were a herd of cattle, it was within that agency's discretion to do so, and there was little either the tribes or the conservationists could do about it.

Two years later, in dismissing the case by granting the defendant federal and state government agencies' motion for summary judgment, the same judge found that, to the extent that the tribes and conservationists actually had "aesthetic, emotional, religious, and cultural interests" at stake concerning Yellowstone's wild bison herd, they would be unaffected by the continued destruction of brucellosis-positive bison until such time as the National Park Service and the State of Montana came up with a different approach to the problem.[36] Thus, in this case, the court's failure to recognize the role of religious and cultural significance of wild bison to either First Natives or conservationists was an important and ultimately discriminatory act of cultural disregard, as well as an open-ended future death warrant for all brucellosis-positive bison in Yellowstone National Park who have the misfortune to follow their instincts down out of the high country in a winter migration.

In terms of cultural pluralism in American society, the federal courts clearly have the authority either to accommodate or to subordinate the culture-based interests being advocated before them. It is perhaps not surprising that a federal judge in the heart of cattle country and the American West's historic ranching-based aura of self-identity chose to subordinate, while another judge in the District of Columbia chose to accommodate. But as the concluding section of this chapter suggests, perhaps both the nation's remaining wild bison and the various groups affected by their status would benefit from a more comprehensive, culturally informed, and accommodative approach to the issue than simply depending on a roll of the dice as to which judges in which federal courts around the country will be called on to address these issues.

The Bison's Path, Part 2: Alternative Futures

At the beginning of the nineteenth century, there were sixty million buffalo in the United States; by its end, there were barely a thousand. As with so many species before, it seemed that human "progress" was inexorably herding them over the cliff of extinction. But their plight roused the conscience of Congress, and a federal poaching statute, in combination with wild herd augmentation by concerned stewards, opened up another path for the bison, away from the brink of oblivion. This rescue so thoroughly embodied the nation's newfound commitment to preserving its endangered natural heritage that the American bison's likeness became the centerpiece of the official emblem of the Department of the Interior. What irony, for a bureaucracy whose own icon celebrates it proudest conservation achievement to now be assenting to its degradation and possible destruction.

By the end of the twentieth century, multiple forces were once again herding America's wild bison to the edge of existence. The difference between the threats at either end of the twentieth century is that, in the new millennium, extinction may be accomplished not by exterminating the animal but by genetically and legally transforming it. Many (although not all) commercial livestock operators are doing this in three ways. The first is by selective breeding (and eventually, inevitably, artificial insemination) of captive herds, in combination with feed enhancement and various drug supplements. The second is by deliberately interbreeding buffalo with cattle (as in Texas). And the third is by doing everything possible to sharply limit the continued existence of wild herds on the federal lands.

If these interests have their way—in Congress, in the federal bureaucracy, and in the courts—by the end of the twenty-first century the American buffalo may well have gone the way of the aurochs. As with those creatures in the caves of Lascaux, the wild bison may linger on in the great seal of the Interior Department and in the remembered religious traditions of the Plains Indians, but it will no longer exist in the flesh anywhere on Earth.

But once again, just as at the end of the nineteenth century, another path for the bison may open up, away from oblivion and toward a future of more peaceful coexistence with cattle ranchers, government officials, and other wildlife on the public lands. And just as a hundred years ago, making way for survival of the wild bison will involve a combination of political will, cultural cooperation, and mindful wildlife management.

One possibility, admittedly remote in a Congress sharply divided over most federal land management issues, is passage of a federal statute granting wild bison herds the same protection from state slaughter on federal lands that Congress extended to wild horses and burros a generation ago. Surely this ancient icon, so central to the religions of America's indigenous peoples for the last ten thousand years, deserves the same measure of respect and protection as the imported feral livestock that got away from Spanish soldiers and gringo prospectors one to three hundred years ago.

Short of legislative protection, the same goal of assuring the continued viability of wild bison herds could be accomplished if federal agencies simply stewarded more assertively and protectively the wild bison entrusted to their care. There is no shortage of national public support for such an approach, even if there is sometimes intense local political opposition. In 1998, the Interior Department released its draft environmental impact statement on future management of the Yellowstone herd, several options within which included Montana's continued removal of bison from federal grazing lands outside Yellowstone National Park. The state's preferred option included the killing of bison within the park itself. By the fall of that year, however, the Interior department had received sixty-seven thousand comments on the DEIS, over forty-seven thousand of which rejected all of its options in favor of an alternative "Citizens' Plan to Save Yellowstone Buffalo." The plan was crafted under the leadership of the Greater Yellowstone Coalition, one of the unsuccessful plaintiffs in *ITBC v. Babbitt*, the Montana federal district court decision upholding the continued destruction of Yellowstone buffalo until the environmental impact statement and long-term management plan are finalized.

Whether or not the danger of brucellosis transmission to cattle is "remote and speculative," the fear of it among cattle ranchers grazing herds on lands bordering Yellowstone and Grand Teton National Parks is very real. Bison can harbor the brucellosis pathogen but generally are not as seriously affected by the disease, which can devastate whole herds of cattle. While there is no reliable vaccine against brucellosis in bison, an effective one does exist for the protection of cattle. Thus, in an effort to make their proposed management alternative more acceptable to ranchers, in the spring of 1999, the National Wildlife Federation started offering free brucellosis vaccinations to any of the cattle herds being grazed within fifty miles of the Yellowstone herd if they exit the park. Whether this gesture will be enough to build support for—or at least lessen opposition to—the citizens' alternative among Montana's political leaders, state agency officials, and ranchers remains to be seen.

In a different realm altogether, more attention must be devoted to the general cultural competence of the federal judiciary, whether it be by those on the trial bench reflecting on their intended actions, by higher courts reviewing trial court decision making, or by those members of the executive and legislative branches involved in the judicial appointment process. For a judge to rule that the religious interests of neighboring Indian tribes will be unaffected by the state slaughter of wild bison at Yellowstone's north gate is akin to telling orthodox Jews that their religious interests will be unaffected by the presence of anti-Semitic graffiti on Jerusalem's Wailing Wall. There is probably no more profound act of desecration to the living religion of the Plains Indians than the state actions the court condoned at Yellowstone; to pretend this is not the case is to ignore one of the American West's most enduring—if painful—cultural realities.

Many Indian leaders are now coming to see that their tribes' future cultural survival and the wild bison's physical survival are intimately related, which accounts in large part for the growing number of reservations now hosting their own wild bison populations. Herd size and management approach vary, depending on reservation conditions and tribal leadership decision making. In this effort, they have found common cause with the conservation community, which sees the survival of wild, free bison as essential to the ability of Euro-Americans to learn from their own environmental mistakes.

Archeological evidence suggests that pre-Christian Europeans once revered animals such as the aurochs in somewhat the same way that contemporary indigenous peoples of the United States still regard the bison. As ethnographers and paleobiologists alike are suggesting, if we look far enough back in time, we may discover that the deepest roots of Euro-American and indigenous American cultures are less different than we have traditionally been led to believe.

At a 1999 convocation of Inter-Tribal Bison Cooperative leadership, ITBC co-founder and Cheyenne River Sioux Tribe bison herd manager Fred DuBray emphasized the similarities between the historic treatment of his people by the Euro-American culture and the plans of some western ranchers for the future of the bison. He reflected on how Indian children had been taken from their families hundreds of miles away to missionary and government boarding schools, forbidden their own culture, and force-fed the dominant one. "They tried to kill the Indian while saving the red man," he observed. "Now they want to kill the buffalo while keeping the meat alive."[37] In that reflection, he was giving contemporary Sioux voice to views shared by American nature philosophers from Henry David Thoreau to Gary Snyder: a sense that the roots of our environmental crisis lie in the Euro-American culture's historic efforts to dissociate the spirit from the flesh, the scientific from the sacred, and the wise from the wild.

Perhaps that last aurochs did not actually die without purpose, and the lesson of its passing will not be lost after all. Perhaps all of us sharing stewardship of public lands and resources—our national commons—can come to understand that it is actually quite an honor to have in our midst an unbroken lineage of ten-thousand-year-old wild animals on whose existence the survival of entire human populations once depended. Preservation of wild bison is clearly and closely linked to the cultural survival of lineage descendants of those ancient indigenous peoples. Perhaps, in ways we are just now coming to appreciate, it is linked almost as closely to the cultural identity of Euro-American peoples as well.

9

Conservation and Cultural Renewal

Hunting, Gathering, and Cleansing the Waters

The place is a retreat center in the coastal hills of northern California, early in the year 2000. The gathering is a meditation retreat co-led by Joanna Macy, an internationally known author and meditation teacher who focuses on Buddhism and environmental care, and Wes Nisker, another Bay Area meditation teacher, writer, and poet.

At the retreat they teach methods for developing a more personal, relational, and contemplative knowledge of the natural environment. One is the practice of Vipassana (Insight) meditation, as taught within the tradition of Theravada Buddhism ("Theravada" being a Pali word meaning "Way of the Elders"). Practiced long enough and intensively enough, this method produces states of concentration deep enough first to perceive the mind in the process of literally creating the self and then to quiet the mind to the point where it is no longer doing even that. When this happens, the distinction between self and other vanishes, whether the "other" is another human, another life form, or the Earth itself; at which point a contemplative sense of unity with all creation can arise. During outdoor walking meditation, participants learn to bring this state of quiet, selfless, choiceless awareness to bear in taking in whatever is around them — to perceive both the essence and emptiness of all that is. It is from this insight that unity with all being can be realized in the Buddhist tradition.

Another technique Macy used in this retreat is featured in her writings on Buddhism and the environment, and which she regularly employs at retreats, workshops, and conferences such as this one. Known as the Council of All Beings, it is a convocation conducted in three stages:

1. *Mourning* the scope and intensity of harm done to other plant and animals species—including premature extinction—by reason of thoughtless human action
2. *Remembering* the continuity of evolutionary development that has made it possible for human beings to come into being
3. *Speaking for other life-forms*—a testimonial process in which participants speak in the first person on behalf of whatever plant or animal they may have developed an affinity with during the course of the retreat during walking meditations, illustrating how their existence benefits the ecosystem, and invoking the human mindfulness that will be necessary to make continued coexistence possible.[1]

The combined effect of these activities is to encourage a profound sense of interconnectedness with all life, both in the present and through all time (including the future). When the Dalai Lama asked how she was able to effectively share these teachings among non-Asians, who for the most part do not believe in rebirth, she gave this answer: "'For rebirth we substitute evolution' I said. And to illustrate I took his hand and led him on a two-minute evolutionary remembering. 'Each atom in each cell in this hand goes back to the beginning of time . . . and to the first explosion of light and energy, to the formation of the galaxies and solar systems, to the fires and rains that bathed our planet, and the life-forms that issued from its primordial seas. . . . We have met and been together many times.' 'Yes, of course,' he replied quietly. 'Very good.'"[2]

Most other well-known world religious traditions as well as myriad indigenous ones offer some such form of such "sacred technology" (as Mircea Eliade describes it) for inducing this state of mind.

Every Eastern and Western contemplative tradition teaches some method for softening, if not dissolving altogether (at least temporarily), the boundaries between self and the environment. In summarizing indigenous examples of this approach, Dennis and Barbara Tedlock write: "In this emptying of the everyday mind, the seeker humbles himself; in the words of Black Elk, he must see himself as 'lower than even the smallest ant.' This means that he must let go of the self, which belongs to the calculative world of ego and object. He experiences this letting go as death itself; as Lame Deer puts it, 'You go up on that hill to die.'"[3]

These Eastern, Western, and indigenous techniques for achieving unity with nature represent just a few of many contemplative means of heeding Barry Lopez's advice (given in at the beginning of this book) for entering into an ethical relationship with all around us. And it is the nature of this relationship that is the subject of this chapter, compared across intercultural membranes.

In the story of the bison told in chapter 8, the relational, ethical perspectives of some conservation group members in the Greater Yellowstone Coalition are closely attuned to those of the First Native groups comprising the Inter-Tribal Bison Cooperative, which is what makes it possible for them to work in close coordination. However, this kind of alignment is not always so easy to come by, as two of the case studies described in this chapter (concerning the Makah and the Hopi) make abundantly clear. For while contemporary Earth-friendly Christian teachings emphasize stewardship and care for all creation, and Asian traditions such as Buddhism and Hinduism teach the honoring of all life through *ahimsa* (i.e., "non-harming"), certain indigenous cultures throughout the world (including some in the Americas) honor their connectedness to spiritually significant animal species by incorporating them into rituals in which they kill them.

Moreover, some of these culture groups are now asserting rights under various sources of law discussed earlier in this book to take these animals from public lands such as national parks, monuments, and federally controlled ocean waters. For many people in mainstream American society, it's one thing when tribal members capture and ritually sacrifice an animal on their own reservations; but when the capturing and perhaps the killing takes place on public lands or waters administered by a federal agency on behalf of all the peoples of the United States, it's quite another matter.

The considerable contrast in this picture is that while both Euro-Americans attuned to issues of environmental ethics and traditionalists among First Native groups may hold these animals sacred, they express their reverence in radically different ways. As exploration of these cases will make clear (and as also demonstrated by the earlier story about the bison), on some occasions Euro-American ideas and ideals on the subject of biotic resource conservation go hand in hand with tribal efforts at cultural continuity, renewal, and revival; and sometimes they do not.

To provide some conceptual context, the following section briefly summarizes the range of thought in contemporary American society on questions of environmental ethics generally and the treatment of animals specifically—especially as reflected in public policy making. No one American Indian perspective is provided by contrast in this section since, as noted in chapter 2, there *is* no one American Indian perspective. Instead, each tribe brings to each environmental decision situation its own ethical orientation and its own reasons for wanting to hunt or gather on the public lands. As far as possible, in each of the cases described in this chapter I have tried to find statements in the tribes' own words as to why these rituals are important to them.

At the close of the twentieth century, the Makah and Hopi cases were among the higher profile examples of intercultural tension over the management of biota on public lands. Two reasons for including them here are that, in addition to their notoriety (and perhaps because of it), these cases are well documented and cast into sharp relief both the intercultural and the legal issues in play.

In some ways, however, they represent the exception rather than the norm, so to dwell on their particulars too much loses sight of the fact that in national parks and monuments, national forests, and other public lands throughout the United States, on a very regular basis indigenous peoples and federal land managers quietly and peaceably work out arrangements for harvesting various plant and animal species for ceremonial purposes, and they have been doing so for quite some time. One of these less contentious examples—that of cactus-fruit harvesting at Saguaro National Park—also gets some attention here, to reinforce the point that this kind of peaceable accommodation is much more common than general press coverage of these issues would have us believe, to the considerable credit of all parties involved.

The final two cases featured in this chapter are noteworthy for other reasons. The Idaho gray wolf reintroduction case represents the first instance of the U.S. Fish and Wildlife Service entering into a direct agreement with an American Indian tribe to comanage the reintroduction of an endangered species onto federal lands, following the refusal of the state in which these lands are located to cooperate in the reintroduction program. And the last case casts the First Amendment/trust responsibility rights talk into a different resource context altogether—that of major freshwater sources (in this instance, the Rio Grande) shared by all but used with very different spiritual connotations by different groups. Especially in the arid Southwest, nothing is more sacred to indigenous peoples or more sought after by everyone living there. The related issues of what duty of care we owe to one another regarding water-quality management and what level of respect is owed to the resource itself (a seldom-asked question) provide yet another example of how the coming together of culture, spirituality, and law in the management of natural resources creates a much more richly textured portrait of the western landscape than may first meet the eye.

The Rights of Nature in the Western Mind and in Public Policy

To even use a phrase such as "the rights of nature" frames the issues in ways that implicate both moral philosophy and public law, which themselves represent only two of several ways to think about these matters.[4] We are starting with these perspectives because to the extent that public land and resource management is informed by ethical considerations at all, it is usually within this framework. The approach will be to scan the range of received moral thought in the Euro-American tradition and then to seek out how this thinking relates to the creation of public policy.

At one end of this range or continuum is the point of view that ethical considerations have no role to play in managing the public estate. Essentially a market-based approach, this position holds that social need and consumer demand should be the only forces governing public lands and resource policy, whether the demand is for food, fiber, forest products, energy minerals, and precious metals or for outdoor recreation.[5] Rather than ethical analysis, all that is needed in this approach is market analysis, gauging consumer willingness to pay for these "commodities" as the basic guiding principle for public lands and resource management.

A related but different perspective, which does admit to ethical analysis of environmental decision making, is that of *ulitilitarianism* (originally associated most closely with the nineteenth-century British philosopher and political reformer Jeremy Bentham), which is commonly understood to involve parallel philosophical and political processes for determining what uses of the national commons will provide "the greatest good for the greatest number" of people. In this view, the value of things in the environment is still measured principally in terms of human need satisfaction (even if the need is to see a sunrise or sunset in an unspoiled wilderness or wildlife running free in public open space), but with the understanding that since *willingness* to pay and *ability* to pay are not the same thing, government forces (in the form of the policy process), as well as market forces, are needed to define what the greatest good for the greatest number will be and how the body politic ought to go about achieving it.

A quite different approach is suggested by the deontologists (drawn from the Greek word meaning "duty"), whose founding principles in modern Western thought can be traced back mostly to the writings of another nineteenth-century European philosopher, Immanuel Kant. In this view, people in society hold certain duties or obligations in relation to each other. The rights and duties may be defined through a political process, or they may be thought to be a natural or divinely bestowed birthright, such as the American revolutionaries' claim that we have all been endowed by our creator with inalienable rights to "life, liberty, and the pursuit of happiness."

In chapter 4 of this book, "Culture and Justice: Nature and the Rule of Law in the New World," I pointed out some natural tensions that occur when a majoritarian political process defines the greatest good for the greatest number in ways that severely impinge on the life, liberty, and pursuit of happiness rights of a social, ethnic, or religious minority. The situation is made more complex when treaty rights and the trust responsibility are factored in with other rights and liberties, as the following review of federal wildlife law suggests.

However, both the utilitarian and the deontological views described here and as traditionally understood concern only the rights, needs, and preferences of human beings. In the terminology of environmental ethics, these perspectives are classified as being *homocentric* (or anthropocentric) in nature; that is, the status of humans is the central focus of analysis in either of these approaches.

By contrast, some ethicists advocate instead a *biocentric* perspective—one that takes all life and living systems as the focus of analysis and concern. Applying utilitarian thought, the question then becomes not what action will provide the greatest good for the greatest number of humans but what action will provide the greatest good for the greatest number of living beings, or for a given ecosystem in its entirety. From the deontologists' viewpoint, the question is what duty of care human beings owe not just to each other but to other lifeforms and ecosystems also.

One important distinction within the biocentric perspective in terms of units of analysis is that of individual living beings versus ecosystems.[6] For example, some ecologists will argue that animal hunting by human beings plays an important role in maintaining wildlands ecosystem balance, because otherwise the game species population would grow to the point of exceeding its habitat carrying capacity, eat all the available food, and then starve. Thus, hunting is good for the ecosystem and the prey population as a whole, even if it does not seem to be beneficial for the individual animals that are killed. Some animal rights advocates dispute this argument, holding that we can substitute the reintroduction of natural predators (e.g., wolves and lions) for hunting, and achieve the same balance (this is also a better solution, they argue, because natural predators choose the easiest-to-kill herd members, thus improving herd quality overall). Furthermore, some First Native teachings on hunting hold that for a hunt to be successful, the prey must agree to be killed and must offer itself for this purpose.[7] As demonstrated in the Makah case that follows, different conservation organizations hold different views on the question of whether this indigenous perspective is defensible in terms of managing the federal wildlife estate.

Symbolism and Salvation in Federal Wildlife Law

Until passage of the Endangered Species Act in 1973, congressional measures to protect wildlife on federal lands emphasized more than anything else the symbolic importance of the animal whose existence was at stake. Among the first of these acts was the 1894 law making it a federal crime to kill bison grazing on public lands, which, when finally enforced, was instrumental in keeping the species from becoming extinct (see chapter 8). In taking this action, Congress realized that the disposition era's largely unregulated despoiling of the public domain was wiping out some of the very plant and animal species that had come to symbolize the American West. The buffalo was saved because of what its continued existence meant to the nation's image of itself and its heritage, just as its demise would have clearly shown the nation to be one that had no regard for either its past or (in terms of future generations of Americans) its future.

The United States' relations with Canada stimulated the next significant legal development in federal wildlife law, when in 1920 the Supreme Court ruled that a treaty entered into by the two countries for the protection of internationally migrating waterfowl superseded state law when the two came into conflict.[8] The sight of viable populations of these birds wending their way southward in winter and northward in summer was a living example of the peaceful and cooperative relationship between the two countries, which share the world's longest undefended international border.

In terms of indigenous wildlife, however, nothing more graphically symbolizes the national identity than the icon that appears on its money, the presidential seal, and the signs on federal property throughout the nation—the bald eagle. By the 1930s this animal, like the bison forty years earlier, was at the brink of extinction, owing to a combination of habitat destruction and killings by sheep ranchers, since these largest of all American raptors had discovered it was easier to make a living off of domestic lambs than wild prey.

So in 1940 Congress passed the Bald Eagle Protection Act, on a finding that "the bald eagle is no longer a mere bird of biological interest but a symbol of the American ideals of freedom; and ... the bald eagle is now threatened with extinction."[9] The act did not dwell on who was to blame for this threat to the national symbol, but it did make it a federal crime for anyone to take or possess an eagle, eagle feathers, or eagle parts without government permission to do so.

More "saving the symbol" legislation followed in 1971, in the form of the Wild Free-Roaming Horses and Burros Act. While by no means endangered, these animals—originally escapees from Spanish conquistadors, Indian tribes, and prospectors in the sixteenth through the nineteenth centuries—were being killed in large numbers on federal lands by ranchers who had leased federal range to feed and water their cattle and did not want these wild horses and burros consuming water and forage intended for their livestock. In passing this act, Congress found and declared "that wild free-roaming horses and burros are living symbols of the historic and pioneer spirit of the West; that they contribute to the diversity of life forms within the Nation and enrich the lives of the American people; and that these horses and burros are fast disappearing from the American scene."[10]

So once again, symbolism saved the species, although—unlike the bison and the bald eagle—these horses and burros were feral livestock rather than indigenous wildlife and were not in immediate danger of being wiped out. But as "living symbols of the historic and pioneer spirit of the West," they were able to get federal legislative protection essentially for that reason alone.

Passage of the Endangered Species Act of 1973 signaled a change in intentions within federal wildlife policy. During the "saving the symbols" era, it could be argued that Congress was more concerned about the self-image of the nation than about the animals whose survival was at stake. However, the purposes underlying the creation of the ESA are more diverse and complex.[11] From one perspective, the law can be seen as homocentric in nature, in its finding that "these species of [threatened and endangered] fish, wildlife, and plants are of esthetic, ecological, educational, historical, recreational, and scientific value to the Nation and its people" and in its belief that treaty obligations (duties to other nations) also require this legislation.

TVA v. Hill (concerning the little snail darter and the very big

Tellico Dam) was the first and perhaps is still the most famous case in which the U.S. Supreme Court tried to discern congressional intent underlying passage of the Endangered Species Act. Finding it necessary to dig more deeply than the preamble to the act cited above, the Court quoted extensively from the act's legislative history:

> As we homogenize the habitats in which these plants and animals evolved, and as we increase the pressure for products that they are in a position to supply (usually unwillingly), we threaten their—and our own—genetic heritage. *The value of this genetic heritage is, quite literally, incalculable.* ... From the most narrow possible point of view, *it is in the best interests of mankind to minimize the losses of genetic variations.* The reason is simple: they are potential resources. They are keys to puzzles which we cannot solve, and may provide answers to questions which we have not yet learned to ask.
>
> To take a homely, but apt, example: one of the critical chemicals in the regulation of ovulations in humans was found in a common plant. Once discovered, and analyzed, humans could duplicate it synthetically, but had it never existed—or had it been driven out of existence before we knew its potentialities—we would never have tried to synthesize it in the first place. Who knows, or can say, what potential cures for cancer or other scourges, present or future, may lie locked up in the structures of plants which may yet be undiscovered, much less analyzed? ... Sheer self-interest impels us to be cautious. *The institutionalization of that caution* lies at the heart of H. R. 37. ... (H. R. Rep. No. 93–412, pp. 4–5 [1973]) [Emphasis added.]
>
> As the examples cited here demonstrate, Congress was concerned about the *unknown* uses that endangered species might have and about the *unforeseeable* place such creatures may have in the chain of life on this planet.[12]

The "cure for cancer" rationale certainly played a significant role here; that is, we shouldn't thoughtlessly wipe out plant and animal species because one may contain within its genetic code the cure for some terrible human disease—clearly a homocentric "nature as drugstore" perspective. However, this passage also points out the need to preserve species just because they are there, since our understanding of how the world works is still so limited and so primitive—and thus our potential for doing harm is so great—that we must do what we can to *simply take care of* (i.e., steward) these many species over whom we hold the power of life and death. This comes as close to anything else in federal land and resource management policy to heeding Aldo Leopold's advice that we adopt an ethic equal to our awesome destructive power. Furthermore, he maintains, such an ethical perspective must be based on something more than a homocentric fear that we will ultimately destroy ourselves by destroying our environment, although both the modern science of ecology and the ancient teachings of indigenous elders assert that this is surely the case: "An ethic to supplement and guide the economic relation to land presupposes the existence of some mental image of land as a biotic mechanism. We can be ethical only in relation to something we can see, feel, understand, love, or otherwise have faith in."[13]

On the one hand, legislation such as the Bald Eagle Protection Act and the Endangered Species Act would seem to be in perfect harmony with indigenous perspectives on environmental care. And in principle, this is probably true. On the other hand, in practice, the situation has worked out somewhat differently.

The basic problem here from the ethical perspective is that while it was not the actions of indigenous peoples that drove the bison, the bald eagle, and numerous other threatened and endangered species to the brink of extinction, these people, along with the rest of the American population, are being prohibited from treating ESA-listed species and their habitats in any way that might further threaten their existence. In some unfortunate instances, the implementation of federal wildlife conservation law has pitted species survival against cultural survival.

For example, In *United States v. Dion* (appeal of the conviction of a member of the Yankton Sioux tribe for killing bald eagles on reservation lands), the Supreme Court made Indian rights subordinate to congressional policy on these matters:

Dion [the defendant/appellant] asserts that he is immune from Endangered Species Act prosecution because he possesses a treaty right to hunt and kill bald eagles. We have held, however, that Congress in passing and amending the Eagle Protection Act divested Dion of his treaty right to hunt bald eagles. He therefore has no treaty right to hunt bald eagles that he can assert as a defense to an Endangered Species Act charge.

We do not hold that when Congress passed and amended the Eagle Protection Act, it stripped away Indian treaty protection for conduct not expressly prohibited by that statute. But the Eagle Protection Act and the Endangered Species Act, in relevant part, prohibit exactly the same conduct, and for the same reasons. Dion here asserts a treaty right to engage in precisely the conduct that Congress, overriding Indian treaty rights, made criminal in the Eagle Protection Act. Dion's treaty shield for that conduct, we hold, was removed by that statute, and Congress' failure to discuss that shield in the context of the Endangered Species Act did not revive that treaty right.[14]

After *Dion* (which technically was a review of Bald Eagle Protection Act enforcement), the next year the federal trial courts also began to rule that Congress by implication did intend to abrogate treaty hunting rights when it enacted the Endangered Species Act. The case in point involved a member of the Seminole tribe prosecuted for killing an endangered Florida panther on reservation lands (the panther was not endangered when the treaty rights were established in 1855).[15]

Realizing the serious intergovernmental friction that implementation of the Endangered Species Act (ESA) was causing, in the mid-1990s Interior Secretary Bruce Babbitt initiated a consultation with tribal governments, with the intention of drawing up guidelines for the cooperative implementation of the ESA with Indian tribes.[16] These consultations resulted in a secretarial order jointly promulgated by the secretaries of Interior and Commerce (who share ESA implementation authority) calling for advance consultation.

At the height of the assimilation era in 1887, Congress ordered the executive branch to no longer enter into treaties with Indian tribes on behalf of the United States. At the signing ceremony for this measure, however, Secretary Babbitt offered the view that the order was "the equivalent of a treaty" because it was created out of a "mutuality" between the United States and "sovereign tribal governments." "It is my hope," he concluded, "that from this day on we will banish forever the traditional treaty process that has been one-sided, over-bearing and not infrequently unfair."[17]

Eagles in Two Worlds

What happens when two different cultures invest the same animal species with tremendous symbolic significance, yet as a result treat the animal in diametrically opposing and mutually incompatible ways? Such was the situation at Wupatki National Monument in northern Arizona in the closing days of the twentieth century.

As the Supreme Court acknowledged in *Dion:*

> Among the many birds held in superstitious and appreciative regard by the aborigines of North America, the eagle, by reason of its majestic, solitary, and mysterious nature, became an especial object of worship. This is expressed in the employment of the eagle by the Indian for religious and esthetic purposes only.
>
> There are frequent reports of the continued veneration of eagles and of the use of eagle feathers in religious ceremonies of tribal rites. The Hopi, Zuni, and several of the Pueblo groups of Indians in the Southwest have great interest in and strong feelings concerning eagles. In the circumstances, it is evident that the Indians are deeply interested in the preservation of both the golden and the bald eagle.[18]

This is especially true of the Hopi. Different clans within the tribe maintain a traditional ritual connection with specific eagle nesting sites in lands occupied by the Hopi before the coming of the Europeans, one of these sites being within the borders of Wupatki National Monument near Flagstaff, Arizona (other sites are within the Hopi reservation or on lands jointly occupied with the Navajo tribe, raising its own set of issues). One ritual practice involves taking eagle chicks and raising them in captivity on the reservation, and then, at maturity in the summer, releasing their spirits to travel back to join all eagle spirits by smothering them in cornmeal. The tribe holds a permit to collect about forty eaglets a year; but hunting is generally not allowed within national parks and monuments.[19] Although golden eagles are not endangered, their taking is subject to federal regulation because the chicks resemble bald eagle chicks.

According to a tribal press release, the Third Mesa Greasewood Clan (the one with a traditional affiliation to the Wupatki site) had been gathering eaglets there "for centuries," but when they formally sought access for that purpose in 1999 (when, for the first time, they officially requested Park Service permission to do so), park rangers would not allow them to collect the animals.[20] The reason they gave was a federal regulation that grants some discretion to park superintendents in authorizing hunting and gathering but also states that "this section shall not be construed as authorizing the taking, use or possession of fish, wildlife or plants for ceremonial or religious purposes, except where specifically authorized by Federal statutory law, treaty rights or [other applicable regulations]."[21]

On consultation with Interior Department attorneys, park officials were advised that they could not allow this capture of eaglets unless and until the regulation was modified to specifically allow the Hopi to engage in this practice at Wupatki.[22] In the closing days of the Clinton administration in January 2001, such a regulation was published in draft form, leaving it to the Bush administration's new Interior secretary to determine whether this exception to general Park Service policy ought to be adopted.

Among the conservation groups objecting to the Interior Department's proposed, Wupatki-specific rule amendment were the National Audubon Society and the Southwest Parks and Monument Association, exemplifying the tenuous nature of the relationship between American Indian tribes and some environmental organizations on the sensitive question of wildlife conservation and cultural survival.[23] The view expressed by some of these groups is that an exception such as that proposed at Wupatki sets a dangerous precedent in that it will now be necessary to honor all such requests from any tribe making them. At the end of the Clinton administration, however, Interior Department policy was that the general prohibition against hunting and gathering for ceremonial purposes should stand and that any tribe wanting an exception to the rule must carry the burden of proof of showing why an exception ought to be granted. And if the rule is waived, it must be by the secretary of the Interior rather than by the superintendent of the national park or monument at issue.[24]

Wake of the Gray Whale

Similar to the history of the bison and bald eagle, heedless and unregulated commercial whaling by the industrialized nations of the world drove the California gray whale to the brink of extinction early in the twentieth century. This was bad news for the Makah Indians of Washington's Olympic Peninsula, who had been hunting whales for fifteen hundred years, and whose continued right to do so was assured by an 1855 treaty with the United States.[25] In the treaty, "the Makah ceded most of their land on the Olympic Peninsula to the United States in exchange for 'the right of taking fish and of whaling or sealing at usual and accustomed grounds and stations' (Treaty of Neah Bay, 12 Stat. 939, 940 [1855])."[26]

The U.S. entered into another treaty in the 1940s—this time with the other nations who had contributed to the whale's demise—for the purpose of protecting the species and restoring the population. The whale was listed as endangered under the legislative predecessor to the Endangered Species Act in 1970. Benefiting from the whaling moratorium (which applied to the Makah along with everybody else), the California gray whale population rebounded to what was thought to be its original size—somewhere slightly in excess of twenty thousand animals. Accordingly, the whale was "de-listed" (determined to no longer be threatened or endangered) in 1994, and, in the interest of reviving their whaling-based way of life and culture, the Makah made plans to once again go to sea in search of both the gray whale and their former way of life.[27]

Since the whale had nearly become extinct seventy years earlier, no living member of the Makah tribe had any experience whaling in the traditional manner. Therefore, some members of Makah clans historically associated with whaling culture trained in these methods with culturally similar tribes, and they formulated a whale hunting plan in consultation with the Commerce Department's National Oceanic and Atmospheric Administration (NOAA). In keeping with the 1855 treaty, the federal government supported the Makah's request to resume whaling, which was presented to the International Whaling Commission (IWC). NOAA asked the IWC to establish a "quota of gray whales for subsistence and ceremonial use by the Makah Tribe"; it was approved in 1997.[28]

As eventually implemented, the plan includes a mixture of traditional and modern methods. Makah whalers were to set out into the open ocean paddling hand-carved canoes, followed by two motor-powered chase boats. If a whale "presents itself for sacrifice," a crew member in the canoe first harpoons it; then a Makah marksman in one of the chase boats quickly finishes the kill with a high-powered rifle (specifically designed for this purpose by a marine veterinarian).[29]

Using this approach, in May 1999 the Makah took their first whale in over seventy years. But while the Makah celebrated the revival of their cultural traditions, some environmental groups decried what they saw as unwarranted cruelty to animals. The Humane Society of the United States opposed the hunt, although it has not objected to subsistence hunting by some other indigenous groups. The distinction the Humane Society made was that since the Makah whaling tradition had been interrupted, their situation was not analogous to Alaska natives, whose cultural and physical survival depend entirely on whaling.[30]

A Los Angeles–based environmental activist group—the Sea Shepherd Society—took a much more aggressive and high-profile approach, sending its own chase boats out to sea and attempting to physically disrupt the hunt (apparently running over a surfacing whale in the process), only to be arrested by the Coast Guard.[31] However, Greenpeace, a larger environmental group (some of whose dissident members formed the Sea Shepherds), which has used such tactics to try to protect more immediately threatened species from commercial whalers, did not oppose the Makah hunt. Along with the Audobon Society and the Wilderness Society, Greenpeace took the position that the problem is not with cultural revival of subsistence whaling by groups such as the Makah, whose quota is no more than twenty whales over a five-year period. According to a spokesperson, "We're not going to oppose the Makah hunt because we think the real threat is commercial whaling."[32]

At one point the tenor of protests and the rhetoric on local talk shows and op-ed newspaper pages became so extreme that Seattle-area religious leaders publicly beseeched disputants not to allow the strength of their feelings to become an excuse for fomenting overt racial hostility. As so often happens in disputes of this intensity, the issue eventually wound up in the courts. U.S. representative Jack Metcalf (Republican from the state of Washington), the Fund for Animals, a whale-watching tourism company, and a dissident Makah family filed suit against NOAA to enjoin further whaling by the Makah, charging that, among other things, the federal government had failed to adequately assess the environmental impact of its decision to support the Makah's IWC request and subsequent cooperate in the reinstitution of Makah whaling. In June 2000 the Ninth Circuit Court of Appeals agreed, ordering a temporary halt until NOAA had done a better job of documenting the likely effects of the Makah whale hunt.[33]

In this case, neither environmental organizations on one side nor members of the Makah tribe on the other were unanimous in either opposing or supporting the resumption of whaling. According to the chairman of the Makah Whaling Commission, 85 percent of the tribe supported the return to whaling to restore their "traditional sea food and sea mammal diet" and "to fulfill the legacy of our forefathers and restore a part of our culture," which is also the position of the tribal government.[34]

As asserted in chapter 1, if cultures are to survive and thrive, they cannot remain static. Knowing what is important to bring forward and what is best to leave behind is key to charting a wise future course for all culture groups. Whether it is the Plains tribes and the bison, the Hopi and the eagles, or the Makah and the California gray whale, these tribes in their own internal deliberations have concluded that instrumental to the survival of their cultures are rituals for maintaining sacred relationships with various animal species—rituals that may include taking the life of individual animals. The problem is that in so doing, they are also making a claim on the national commons, which some other members of the commons believe ought to be managed in dramatically different ways.

Although not exactly analogous, I have heard in discourse on these matters the view that in some ways these rituals are not all that different from the taking of communion in Christian churches, in terms of symbolic connection. The difference, of course, is that when an indigenous hunter understands a prey animal to be "offering itself" for the kill, the animal is saying "Take; eat; this is my body" quite literally, as distinguished from Jesus of Nazareth's more figurative use of the expression at the Last Supper.

Within their own frame of reference and worldview, First Natives see the taking of wildlife in a ritually approved way and for cultural continuity purposes as a profoundly moral act, reaffirming the sense of connection with the animal clan on which the survival of both the species and the culture are thought to depend. Whether environmental ethicists in Euro-American society will ever come to fully understand and accept that view remains an unanswered question.

Plants as Friends and Neighbors

It is hard to imagine an environment more different from the open ocean of the Pacific Northwest than the upper Sonoran Desert of southern Arizona or a culture as traditionally dependent on the plant harvest of this arid landscape as the Makah were on the marine mammals of the northern Pacific Ocean. And yet, the ancient Hohokam and their contemporary descendants—the O'odham—have survived just as successfully in this setting over the last two millennia as have the indigenous whalers of the Olympic Peninsula.

Formerly known as the Papago (a Spanish colonial name for the tribe, meaning "bean eaters") the tribe has always referred to itself as the O'odham, which in their own language means "Desert People" and is now the tribe's official name.[35] A very laterally organized culture group, the main reservation is at Sells, Arizona, about sixty miles southwest of Tucson, with affiliate reservations near San Xavier del Bac mission in the (now) southwestern suburbs of Tucson; they also have a site to the west of Tucson, and another to the north.

As reflected in practices such as the placental burial ceremony described in chapter 2, various O'odham clans and families have relationships with very specific locations in the tribe's traditional range in the Sonoran Desert—especially in regard to stands of the giant saguaro cactus, which in all the world grows only in this landscape. Growing to heights of sometimes fifty feet and living for well in excess of one hundred years, the saguaro is revered by the O'odham, for one reason, because "the appearance of fruit on this cactus comes during a period of food scarcity due to the absence of rain. The fruit was processed into syrup, jam, dehydrated pulp, chicken feed, seed flour, oil, pinole, atole, snack foods, soft drinks, wine and vinegar, only the outer husk of the fruit going to waste. And even in discarding the fruit husk, a good result is thought to inure to these agricultural people, as it is always laid on the ground with the inner red part point upward 'to hasten the rains.'"[36]

When the city of Tucson, Arizona, began its explosive post–World War II growth in every direction from the center of the "Old Pueblo," the only effective conservation measures for the desert environment was (and continues to be) federal reservation, in the form of the Coronado National Forest in the Catalina Mountains, to the north and east of Tucson, and of the Saguaro National Monument, to the immediate east and west on the desert floor, established in 1954. In 1994, Congress upgraded the monument to national park status.[37] As more and more of the desert environment was destroyed by urban and suburban development, the principal remaining saguaro stands were on these federal lands, either on the O'odham reservation itself, in the lower reaches of the national forest, or in Saguaro National Park.

Inasmuch as saguaro fruit harvesting and processing was a well-established traditional use of the ecosystem by the O'odham at the time the monument and then the park was established, the approach of Park Service personnel has always been that the association between specific sites in the park (in the western annex) and specific families among the Tohono O'odham having a historical relationship with those sites ought to be maintained. So at the ritual harvest time (summer, in advance of the monsoon season), these families are given permitted access to certain sites for the purpose of setting up "cactus camps" to harvest and process saguaro fruit, as their ancestors have been doing for at least the last two thousand years.

The permitting and harvesting process occurs under the same regulations that caused a problem for the Hopi at Wupatki National

Monument, which granted discretion to park superintendents to allow modest levels of harvesting for "personal" although not "ceremonial" purposes. In the half-century history of this arrangement, the only problem that has arisen is one time when some harvesting family members tried selling some saguaro fruit product at a roadside stand within the park, which—as a commercial exploitation of the harvest—Park Service regulations preclude.[38]

The legal relationship between specific tribes and specific national parks, monuments, and forests can vary considerably, depending on the legislation or executive order that brought these federal reservations into being and the kinds of agreements that may or may not have been created between the tribes and the federal government (such as the Makah's 1855 whaling rights treaty). In other words, the claims of all tribes are not necessarily equal. Moreover, there are some evident conflicts at law between the language of congressional enactments such as the American Indian Religious Freedom Act and the Park Service regulations that preclude hunting and gathering for ceremonial purposes.

Of course, the Supreme Court's 1988 *Lyng* decision also made clear that federal land managers need take AIRFA into account only to the extent they deem appropriate in the management of the federal estate. This gives administrators such as park superintendents a lot of discretion, but relatively little guidance.

Species Restoration, Cultural Renewal, and Protective Partnership

The variables of wildlife management, culture, policy, and environmental ethics come together in a wide variety of configurations on the public lands and waters of the West. In the Makah and Hopi cases, some environmental and animal rights groups are in opposition to indigenous ritual claims on the resource; in the bison case featured in chapter 8, conservation groups and the Inter-Tribal Bison Cooperative joined together in opposition to both federal and state policies that govern treatment of the Yellowstone bison herd. Yet another variation is occurring in Idaho, where the Nez Perce tribe has taken on responsibility for comanagement of the U.S. Fish and Wildlife Service's program for reintroduction of gray wolves on federal lands there.

Idaho reintroduction was one element of a three-part plan that also included federal lands in Montana and Yellowstone National Park, most of which is in Wyoming. Immediately on its promulgation, livestock operator organizations in all three states sued the Interior secretary to enjoin its implementation. One measure of their local political strength was that—inasmuch as the plan called for coordination with the fish and game departments in all three states (since these departments customarily manage wildlife populations on federal as well as other lands, subject to federal permission)—the Idaho legislature took the unusual step of legislatively prohibiting its fish and game department from cooperating with the federal government in reintroducing the wolf.[39]

The Fish and Wildlife Service plan also made provision for entering into cooperative agreements with American Indian tribes for its implementation, so when the state of Idaho refused to participate, the Nez Perce tribe (whose reservation is located there) volunteered to do it, and the Fish and Wildlife Service agreed. Several factors informed this history-making decision—the first known instance of the federal government entering into a comanagement agreement with a tribal government for endangered species protection and reintroduction:

> The Tribe was able to bring important attributes to the table as they "lived in the area and understood local sensitivities" regarding the reintroduction of wolves. In addition, like most Indian tribes, wolves hold cultural and religious importance for the Nez Perce....
>
> The Nez Perce Tribe's wildlife management blends traditional wisdom with modern science. When the wolves were first brought to central Idaho, a tribal elder sang a religious song to welcome them, and later said that the experience had been "like meeting an old friend."[40]

Just as the tribe was preparing to put this history-making agreement into effect, however, the Wyoming Farm Federation Bureau convinced a federal judge (the same one who would later hand down the trial court ruling in the Devils Tower case) to enjoin implementation of the gray wolf recovery plan in all three states and to have all the wolves either removed from the field or destroyed.[41] The judge did stay enforcement of his death sentence against the wolves and the reintroduction program pending appeal of his decision. In January 2000 the Tenth Circuit Court of Appeals in Denver reversed the trial court ruling and reinstated the recovery program, including the Nez Perce agreement with the Fish and Wildlife Service.[42]

This is probably as good an example as any in this book of what is described in chapter 1 as *cultural coevolution*—two culture groups (Euro-American and Nez Perce government officials) affecting each other's perceptions and behaviors in a mutual effort to reach a common goal. And as was the case with the bison, it stimulated a powerful, culturally rooted backlash on the part of ranching and farming interests in these agrarian states.

If such mutually protective partnerships (that is, protective of indigenous cultural integrity, protective of endangered species, and protective of Endangered Species Act reintroduction programs) are to flourish in Idaho and elsewhere in the rural West in the future, additional attention must be devoted to the problem of livestock losses occasioned by wolf predation since ranchers are just as interested in preserving their way of life as are tribes such as the Nez Perce.

Of Sewage and Holy Water

In terms of conflicting sacred and secular uses of the same resource, another graphic example is that between the city of Albuquerque and the downstream Isleta Pueblo along the Rio Grande River in central New Mexico. Congress amended the Clean Water Act (CWA) in 1987 to grant American Indian reservations roughly the same legal authority as states, insofar as implementation of the CWA by the Environmental Protection Agency (EPA) was concerned. In 1992, the Isleta Pueblo Indian Reservation, situated on the Rio Grande downstream from Albuquerque, adopted water-quality standards for the Rio Grande as it flowed through the reservation that were more stringent than the state standards (as allowed under the CWA), which the EPA subsequently approved. The agency then amended Albuquerque's effluent discharge permit to bring it into conformance with the Isleta Pueblo's water-quality standards.[43]

In suing the EPA to enjoin enforcement of its revised permit requirements, which forced the city of Albuquerque to clean its wastewater discharges into the Rio Grande to a higher level of purity than it would otherwise have had to do, the city charged that since one of the reasons the pueblo wanted the water to be cleaner was for ceremonial purposes, in approving the Isleta standards the EPA was impermissibly entangling itself in the establishment of Indian religion, in violation of the religion clauses of the First Amendment.

The tribe's water-quality standard states that one of its uses of the Rio Grande is for "primary contact ceremonial use": "The tribe defines 'Primary Contact Ceremonial Use' as 'the use of a stream, reach, lake, or impoundment for religious or traditional purposes by members of the Pueblo of Isleta; such use involves immersion and intentional or incidental ingestion of water.'"[44] In other words, the Isleta Puebloans wanted to enter the river for ceremonial purposes (somewhat akin to rites of immersion baptism among rural southern evangelical denominations), and they wanted the water to be free enough of Albuquerque's sewage effluent to keep them from getting sick when they did so.

As with many of the other cases discussed here, the First Amendment issue came down to the question of whether the EPA was impermissibly colluding in the establishment of Indian religion in approving the Isleta water-quality standards or was, instead, permissibly accommodating the free exercise of tribal religion under both AIRFA and the free exercise clause of the First Amendment.

The Tenth Circuit Court of Appeals decided that it was the latter.[45] In its view, congressional intent in enacting the Clean Water Act was to clean up the nation's waterways, and the EPA was acting in accordance with that secular purpose when it approved the Isleta plan. That one of the reasons the pueblo wanted the water cleaner was for ceremonial purposes was incidental to the intent of the act and EPA's implementation of it.

For many years, western state governments have decried what they saw as tribal government laxity in environmental protection matters, and sometimes with good reason. Now that tribal governments are on an equal footing with states in terms of federal environmental law enforcement, and some tribal governments are beginning to incorporate their own cultural values into the environmental protection process as well as developing administrative infrastructures to translate those values into enforceable environmental standards, it will be an interesting turn of events if tribal jurisdictions—like the Isleta Pueblo—begin to use this enhanced status to enhance the environmental quality of the west.

As the case studies described in this chapter have demonstrated, there is no clearly emerging pattern in terms of political alignments or the harmonizing of ethical perspectives on the question of religion and the management of biotic and water resources on federal lands. In some cases the tribes are in natural alliance with environmental groups; in others they clearly are not. All these cases do tend to demonstrate that, as suggested in chapter 1, Euro-American and indigenous culture groups seem to be coevolving on the question of spiritual uses of the resources of our national commons. Each group is learning more about the worldview of the other (whether they generally find themselves in agreement or not), and each is gradually coming to the conclusion that continued coexistence requires that this learning continue, if this coexistence is to be durable and peaceful rather than an ongoing, tenuous, and uneasy truce.

10

Pacific Rim Variations

Between East and West

Looking at a continental map of North America or Asia, we see north at the top, south at the bottom, west to the left, and east to the right. But looking at a map of the Pacific Ocean, framed by the continental coasts, the picture is not so simple. North is still up and south is still down, but over on the left edge is the shoreline of the landmass Europeans call the Far East, and over on the right is the shoreline of the Far West.

To further confuse matters, running down the middle of my map of the Pacific from top to bottom is a thin dashed line that looks a little like a sewing seam, which is actually a pretty good simile. When British cartographers during their nation's age of empire went about mapping the world, they placed their own country on the meridian at the exact mid-point between the left and right edges of the picture they were sketching (which in their calculations was also the spot from which time is measured) and then wrapped their picture around a big ball and stitched it up the backside. For eighteenth- and nineteenth-century British imperialists, the mid-Pacific was literally the backside of their world—as far away from their own center of the universe as one could get.

If they did find themselves out there, standing on the deck of a ship just east of this "international dateline" and pointed west, they were actually looking into tomorrow and the Far East; if the ship was just west of this mythic seam in space and time, pointed east, they were actually looking into yesterday and toward the Far West. And these were the same people who sailed around the Pacific belittling the quaint, nonsensical myths of indigenous islanders.

Because of their vastness, their remoteness, and what was initially thought to be their relative lack of lack of marketable riches (with the important exception of gateways to the wealth of Asia, such as Hong Kong), lands of the Pacific Rim were among the last places the British added to their string of colonies. The Crown didn't assert military-backed colonial claims to Australia and New Zealand until early in the nineteenth century, and by the time they decided to claim title to as much land in the Northwest Pacific coast as possible, the United States was willing to go to war to hold them at bay. (Two small historic national parks at either end of the State of Washington's San Juan Island—one the American camp and the other the British— mark the place where these two nations nearly entered into a shooting war over where the international boundary between the United States and Canada was to be drawn.)

These four former ex-colonial common law nation-states of the Pacific Rim—Australia, Canada, New Zealand, and the United States— all share more than the same language and cultural and legal heritage. They also share a history of conquest of indigenous peoples and the imposition of their legal traditions upon them. In the hopes of learning from each other's experience, this chapter presents case studies intended to provide some comparative perspective on how culture, religion, and law combine to affect the management of public lands and resources in these other nation-states around the Pacific Rim. The focus is particularly on comanagement or cooperative management of lands and resources.

Beginning with Canada, we move counterclockwise around the circle to Australia and New Zealand, and then back by way of the highest mountains and thus some of the holiest sites of the Pacific— the volcanoes on the Big Island of Hawaii. The federal law governing management of the national parks and monuments in this western-most of the United States may be the same as cases on the mainland described earlier, but the indigenous cultural context is quite different, indeed, as is the legal status of Hawaiian peoples.

Despite the very wide variations in climate, topography, indigenous cultures, and history, there are some similarities that make case studies in these four countries worth comparative study. The first is the reason the British founded these colonies in the first place: to extract material wealth. Especially when they encountered varying degrees of indigenous resistance, resource extraction required establishing and enforcing a set of rules that facilitated achieving this primary goal. And within the common law tradition, this entailed enforcing colonial variations on the doctrines of property and contract.

With the exception of Australia, the first step in this process usually involved drawing up a treaty with representatives of indigenous groups, whereby each side reserved sovereignty over the internal governance of their respective culture groups, but fashioned agreements for trade that inevitably took on the form and flavor of British property and contract law. This is an important point, since these doctrines are among the principal legal concepts by which individuals and corporate entities in British society amass and defend private wealth, so the key to the first step in colonial resource exploitation among the British was privatization of the resource base.

For indigenous peoples throughout the Pacific Basin, this approach was antithetical to their own relationship to land and resources, which was highly collective in nature. Although some of these culture groups were (and are) very lateral and egalitarian in structure while others are quite hierarchical, land and resources were nonetheless held and managed tribally. Not surprisingly, then, a continuing source of intercultural friction from the outset of colonization to the present day has been the conflict between collective and individual rights.

But the most enduring single source of intercultural conflict has been and remains the conditions under which indigenous peoples lost control over lands and resources in the first place, and the contested legitimacy of ex-colonial nation-state government assertions of authority over these places and resources. And that, finally, is another reason that a comparative look at these cases is instructive. For each of them in one way or another exemplifies experimentation, with the culture groups involved trying to fashion new forms of intercultural governance over sacred sites and resources that ameliorate rather than perpetuate the wounding effects of colonial domination.

Reconstituting North Canada

In the two closing decades of the twentieth century, Canada underwent some extensive rebuilding of its constitutional infrastructure. For the most part, this was good news for Canada's First Nations, the indigenous peoples inhabiting the North American landmass that was to become Canada. Most (although not all) First Native groups signed treaties with the Crown as first Britain and then the Canadian government itself asserted national authority over their homelands.

Since the late nineteenth century, Canadian courts had held that lands and resources not specifically retained by tribes entering into treaties with the national government should be considered as available for non-Indian access and development. However, in 1973, in *Calder v. Attorney General of British Columbia*,[1] Canada's highest court reversed eight decades of precedent by ruling that aboriginal title to land and resources should be considered as not extinguished, except as a result of an affirmative gesture to do so by the Crown. Twelve years later, the same court affirmed that this unextinguished residual title inhered not only in individual Indian claimants to land and resources, but also in tribal governments.[2]

Reflecting this shift in judicial attitudes, when Canada reformulated its constitution in 1982, it included language that reaffirmed existing aboriginal treaty rights.[3] Emanating from the constitution itself, these rights—as in the United States—are considered the supreme law of the land, and they prevail when found to be in conflict with either subordinate legislation from the Canadian Parliament or lawmaking at the provincial level. This continuing shift in the negotiated relationship between Canadian national government, provincial governments, and First Nations has in some cases actually exacerbated already existing tensions over activities such as logging in the forests of British Columbia; but it has also resulted in some remarkable experiments in reconstituting the very political identities of lands in which indigenous peoples comprise the majority populations.

What of those indigenous peoples who never entered into treaties with either the British or Canadian governments, either because they did not recognize colonizing forces as legitimate or because there were no tribal leaders authorized to negotiate with the colonizers (or both)? This is the situation with the Inuit (who, along with neighboring groups, were formerly referred to collectively as "Eskimos"). Although only about twenty-two thousand in number at the time of this writing, Inuit peoples live in an area of far northern Canada above the province of Manitoba—the Nunavut territory (the name means "Our Land" in the Inuit language)—which at nearly two million square kilometers comprises about 20 percent of the total land mass of Canada. As Inuit leader John Amagoalik pointed out, "Our luck was to inhabit a land that no one coveted."[4] The reasons the area is so sparsely populated are that the conditions are so harsh that no one except a native has a good sense of how to survive there, and there was nothing of sufficient value to outside colonizing interests to make it worthwhile to venture into this forbidding landscape.

This is no longer true. Even as the historic negotiations described in this chapter were drawing toward a successful conclusion, "members of the mining industry and Inuit negotiators began settling deals to mine copper, zinc, gold and other base metals, and to a lesser extent, diamonds from Arctic mineral fields."[5]

The Supreme Court's *Calder* decision created the necessary incentive for the national government to reach a land settlement deal with the Inuit, especially as reinforced by the Constitution Act (even though the Inuit were not a treaty tribe). Negotiations concluded in 1992 in the Nunavut Land Claims Agreement, in which the Inuit "acquired title to the largest land claim in Canada's history in addition to the creation of the political entity, Nunavut."[6]

In some ways, this agreement parallels the Alaska Native Land Claims Settlement Act, which codified a land and resource settlement between the United States government and most of the indigenous peoples of Alaska. For in the Nunavut Agreement, the tribe relinquished all unextinguished aboriginal claims created by *Calder* in return for clear title to about 15 percent of the total Nunavut Territory land mass, mineral rights and royalties, and hunting rights.[7] But just as important, rather than creating a self-governing ethnic enclave (like an American Indian reservation), what the agreement did instead was to establish "public government"—that is, a territorial government subject to the same constitutional powers and limitations as other such entities within the Canadian national government framework. As expressed in the national government report summarizing the agreement, the public government model "expresses self-determination through an Aboriginal-controlled public government rather than an Aboriginal-exclusive form of self-government."[8]

Comprising about 85 percent of the population of Nunavut Territory, the Inuit people evidently concluded that they would ultimately gain more authority over their traditional homelands by establishing a nonethnic government structure within the federal constitutional framework (somewhat like a state within the United States) rather than an Inuit-only ethnic homeland subject to national government policies regarding indigenous peoples (somewhat like an American Indian reservation). The trade-off here is that while they probably get more real immediate political power and more direct control over the entire territory (in addition to the 15 percent they hold title to), they do not get the semi-sovereign nation status accorded to Canadian Indian tribes.

Whether this was a wise agreement only time will tell. As long as Inuit remain such an overwhelming majority within the territory's population and as long as they vote as a bloc (assuming, of course, that they turn out to vote), the tribe can clearly maintain more political control over their own destiny as well as their lands and resources than had formerly been the case. But if any of these variables changes significantly, their future relationship to their land and resources is much less certain.

In addition to extractive-resource agreements, the other principal component of the Inuit's environmental management plan is ecotourism. For the Nunavut agreement also created three new national parks: "the Auyuittuq National Park Reserve on northeastern Baffin Island; Ellesmere Island National Park Reserve just south of the North Pole; and a third area on northeastern Baffin Island. The types of tourism will include back country hiking, wildlife watching (beluga whales, walruses, seals, polar bears, . . . caribou, and over 40 species of birds. Tourists will also get an opportunity to meet with and observe the Inuit "carrying out traditional hunting of marine mammals and caribou," as well as learn about Inuit culture in nearby communities."[9] To say the very least, this represents a bold new experiment in interethnic relations between indigenous peoples and a common law nation-state of the Pacific Rim. Unlike national parks in the United States, this one will allow self-regulated indigenous hunting and fishing (for the right price, some tourists will be allowed to do so as well),[10] as well as a permanent indigenous residential presence.

Like some western states in the United States, the two principal land and resource uses the Inuit will be managing are minerals extraction (historically the most environmentally destructive) and national parks–based ecotourism (historically among the most environmentally protective). It will be interesting to see whether the additional variable of Inuit land-based cultural values will result in their achieving a balance between these two that is qualitatively different from similar management efforts either elsewhere in Canada or in other Pacific Rim nations.

Regaining the Summit "Down Under": Australia

For Imperial English cartographers holding a globe in their hands with their home country squarely in front of them, the Australian continent was not just on the backside of the world; it was also on the underside. The nineteenth-century British government further reinforced this image of the place by colonizing it first with people from English society's own underworld—its criminal convicts. Thus, in the Anglo construction of the world, Australia was doubly "down under"—as the British colony furthest south of the equator and as deliberately populated by those on the lowest rungs of the social ladder. But as with every other common law nation-state discussed here, as colonial society was organized, yet another rung was added to the bottom of the ladder: its indigenous peoples.

Of these four nation-states, first British colonial and then Australian national courts legally constructed Aborigines in ways that were clearly the most disadvantageous to their interests. In Canada, New Zealand, and the United States, colonial and national governments generally recognized indigenous tribes as legitimate political entities with whom agreements for land and resource use should be fashioned by the treaty-making process. In Australia, however, the courts adopted the common law doctrine of *terra nullius* ("empty land"), holding that all lands not already permanently occupied by other people was open for acquisition by European colonists. Since Australian Aborigines appeared to the European eye to be nomadic hunting tribes not permanently settled in any one place, the terra nullius doctrine construed them as having no legitimate ownership rights in land.[11]

In 1975 the Australian Parliament moved to put an end to overt social discrimination against Australian aborigines (and other people of color) with passage of the Racial Discrimination Act. However, the measure did not address land and resource rights. As with the *Calder* and *Guerin* decisions in Canada, this crucial aspect of law and policy reform was instead instigated by the courts. In Australia, it would be the *Mabo* decision.

As of this writing, the most dramatic single legal event affirming Aboriginal rights to land and resources is still the Australian High Court's 1992 decision in *Mabo v. Queensland* (called *Mabo II* in this text).[12] Recognizing the profound injustice done to the nomadic and essentially defenseless Aboriginal tribes of nineteenth-century Australia, the *Mabo* decision invalidated the terra nullius doctrine and held that when the government did not take affirmative steps to extinguish Aboriginal ownership rights, all such lands are susceptible to claims of residual Aboriginal title.[13] The same court earlier also struck down state legislative efforts to retroactively assert intent to wipe out all Aboriginal title as violative of the nation's Racial Discrimination Act.[14]

One symbol of just how far Aborigenes have come in their long march toward reestablishment of sovereign status and a land and resource base on which to exercise that status is the change in management structure and approach at one of Australia's most spiritually significant natural landmarks. The following story also symbolizes how much Australian society itself has changed in its regard for the indigenous peoples of its country.

The site in question was formerly known to most of the English-speaking world (and certainly to both tourists and the tourist business) as Ayres Rock, named for the then–South Australian premier Henry Ayres by the European explorer who "discovered" it in 1872. But to the Anangu peoples with the closest cultural affiliation with the place, it is Uluru, the world's largest monolith (one single piece of stone). Located in Uluru-Kata Tjuta National Park, it rises about 350 yards above the plains of Australia's remote Northern Territory, and its oblong shape is nearly six miles in total circumference.[15] As at other giant monoliths such as Bear's Lodge/Devils Tower in the United States, the color of Uluru's sandstone surface changes with the weather and the angle of the sun. Sunrises and sunsets in particular have a transformative visual effect.

Beginning with the 1975 antidiscrimination act, the Australian government entered its own "era of atonement" with Aboriginal peoples. In the 1980s the atonement grew to include relinquishing management authority over several national parks, especially those located in the historical homelands of tribes that had direct cultural affiliation with them. This shift in policy has had mixed results. In some instances it has engendered fresh conflict, from some Aboriginal groups on one side, who do not see the devolution process going quickly enough or being comprehensive enough, to some Anglo-Australian groups who do not believe Aboriginals can be trusted to manage lands and resources in an environmentally protective way.

In the mid-1990s several trouble spots in Queensland erupted, such as the occupation of Lawn Hill National Park by representatives of an Aboriginal tribe demanding a role in its management. Paralleling the situation in the United States regarding the Makah Indians' resumption of whaling, some Anglo-Australians resent the permission given to Aboriginals alone to hunt and fish in comanaged national parks.[16] And as with the Makah case, different conservation organizations hold different views about the appropriateness of this practice. The mainstream Wildlife Preservation Society of Queensland supports Aboriginal hunting, in part because in the past they have formed effective alliances with local Aboriginal tribes to oppose mining and other resource development schemes; but a splinter group from that organization (like the Sea Shepherds who broke off from Greenpeace in the Makah case) has organized to oppose Aboriginal ceremonial and subsistence hunting.[17]

By contrast, one of the widely perceived success stories in the realm of negotiated comanagement is Uluru-Kata Tjuta National Park. The Pitjantjatjara and Yankunytjatjara peoples (also collectively known as the Anangu) negotiated an agreement with the national government in 1985, under which the Uluru-Kata Tjuta Aboriginal Land Trust (representing the traditional owners) assumed ownership of the park and then leased it back for ninety-nine years to Parks Australia to manage the area as a national park. Under the comanagement agreement, many of the sacred sites and shrines on the monolith are not open to the public.[18]

On the tenth anniversary of Anangu assumption of ownership and initiation of comanagement with Australia's national park service, the United Nations Educational, Scientific, and Cultural Organization (UNESCO) jointly awarded the Aboriginals' board of management for the park and the Australian national government its Picasso Gold Medal. The award "recognized that Australia had set new international standards for World Heritage management by indigenous peoples through the management arrangements at Uluru-Kata Tjuta National Park.[19]

This agreement's implementation demonstrates that such successful comanagement is indeed possible—when there is common intention to preserve both physical and cultural heritage for the use and appreciation of multiple cultural groups and when those intentions are matched by a commitment of staff expertise and other resources necessary to ensure that the purposes of the agreement are fulfilled. While political, legal, cultural, and financial circumstances certainly vary from country to country on these matters, there may be still be much to learn from the history, as well as the ongoing implementation of the management partnership for this bicultural, intergovernmental sacred site.

Rhetoric and Reality in the "Land of the Long White Cloud": New Zealand

About a millennium ago a small fleet of Polynesians in large outrigger canoes set out from the present-day Cook Islands, or perhaps the Society Islands, on a voyage of discovery that carried them westward over more than a thousand miles of unknown, uncharted open ocean. Their journey ended with landfall on the two largest islands in the Pacific Ocean. So massive were these volcanic islands that the winds and humidity caused perpetual condensation around their peaks.

The name their Polynesian discoverers gave them collectively was Aotearoa, one English translation of which is "the land of the long white cloud."

These people called themselves by their respective clan names and eventually by the collective name Maori. Aotearoa was the only collective name for their homelands until Dutch and English navigators came upon the place in the eighteenth century and named it New Zealand. Captain Cook first dropped anchor off the north island in 1769, and soon thereafter whaling ships started making landfall there to replenish supplies, as they had already begun to do throughout Polynesia. But the reception both whalers and British explorers received from the Maori was a little unlike what they had encountered in either Hawaii or further to the west in Australia.

In stark contrast to the nomadic and basically unarmed Aboriginals of sparsely populated Australia, the Maori were a warrior culture in an already well-populated, somewhat mountainous, rain-forested land. The major tribes of both islands were in a state of intermittent ongoing conflict with each other over control of the adjoining valleys fanning out from the bases of the huge volcanoes that formed the islands. Well armed with their own effective handmade weapons, as soon as they acquired firearms from European traders and whalers these tribes became formidable opponents to any European visitors seeking to exploit Maori resources without permission.

As far as British colonists were concerned, the Maori granted that permission to the Crown in the 1840 Treaty of Waitangi. Although only a handful of local chieftans originally signed the treaty, the British thereafter took it to be enforceable law governing trade relationships between the Crown and Aotearoa/New Zealand's indigenous peoples. When colonial government representatives later took the treaty into the field trying to secure the signatures of leaders from the roughly four dozen *iwi* (tribes) comprising the Maori world, it was often with the assistance of Christian missionaries, whom Maori leaders had grown to trust.[20]

One term used in the treaty, *rangatiratanga* (variously translated as "chieftanship," "authority," or sometimes "sovereignty"), has as much importance in contemporary New Zealand environmental law as it did when this agreement was first fashioned. Maori signatories to the treaty in all likelihood thought the treaty was guaranteeing them continued control over their lands and peoples, leaving to Great Britain the external defense of the country and governance of trade with foreign nations (the French had also been trying to take by force some New Zealand real estate, and the Maori feared they might soon be invaded by additional European powers with colonial ambitions).[21] But the British government representatives had instructions to make clear that sovereignty meant British sovereignty over all of New Zealand, with residual tribal powers to be held at the discretion of the Crown. So, in 1840 were sown the seeds of confusion (deliberately, some historians believe) that have since sprouted into continued ambiguity and dissonance in treaty interpretation today.

Along with rangatiratanga, another important concept in New Zealand environmental law is that of *kaitiakitanga*, which is usually translated as "the exercise of guardianship; and, in relation to a resource, includes the ethic of stewardship based on the nature of the resource itself."[22] In Maori culture, certain iwi are thought to bear a stewardship responsibility for the care of certain resources, such as a specific river, forest, or plant or animal species. Upholding an iwi's kaitiakitanga is believed to be crucial to maintaining both environmental harmony and the iwi's cultural integrity.

The New Zealand courts first recognized kaitiakitanga as a possibly controlling principle in environmental law in *Huakina Development Trust v. Waikato Valley Authority*,[23] a high court decision finding that this stewardship principle required Maori involvement in managing the nation's longest river (which, like most long rivers in most nations of the world, gets progressively more polluted the closer it gets to its rendezvous with the ocean). Disturbed at this empowering precedent, a higher appeals court later ruled that granting this kind of authority to the Maori could not simply be implied by the courts via Treaty of Waitangi interpretation but, instead, could only be done by affirmative action of the New Zealand Parliament.[24] In 1991 Parliament did just that, in adopting its remarkable Resource Management Act. Part 2 of the act requires as national policy the sustainable management of natural resources, which the act defines as managing the use, development, and protection of natural and physical resources in a way, or at a rate, which enables people and communities to provide for their social, economic, and cultural well-being, and for their health and safety while

(a) sustaining the potential of natural and physical resources (excluding minerals) to meet the reasonably foreseeable needs of future generations; and

(b) safeguarding the life-supporting capacity of air, water, soil, and ecosystems; and

(c) avoiding, remedying, or mitigating any adverse effects of activities on the environment.[25]

In addition to alluding generally to "cultural well-being" as an aspect of sustainable environmental management, in section 7 the act also specifically refers to kaitiakitanga as a matter that government officials charged with implementing this act must have "particular regard to."[26]

So it would seem that at least in the rhetoric and language of the law, the Maori have a very significant role to play in implementing this, the nation's most important piece of environmental legislation. As the act has been implemented, however, just how meaningful the involvement has been seems to vary from one part of the country to another and from one resource to another. In comparative case study research done in the mid-1990s on Maori participation in regional government decision making on major water withdrawals from large rivers in which the respective iwi had a demonstrable kaitiakitanga relationship, a New Zealand colleague and I found that Maori concerns were all but ignored in a case involving relatively impoverished and politically disorganized iwi in rural northern New Zealand, before a regional council dominated by ranching and farming interests. But in applying the same law to the same water resource management issue in an urban water supply situation near metropolitan Auckland (and involving some of the same Maori whose kaitiakitanga was vindicated in the *Huakina* Trust case), Maori views figured very prominently in resource management decision making, with the result that decisions made were far less environmentally damaging than they might have been otherwise.[27]

So absent definitive guidelines from national government and policy clarification from Parliament, the actual meaning of the act's requirement that environmental decision makers must "have regard for" kaitiakitanga remains nebulous and somewhat uneven across the nation. Likewise, the role of the Maori in the actual comanagement of lands and resources—while at least contemplated by the act, as well as by the tribunal set up to adjudicate claims arising under the Treaty of Waitangi—is a concept that is just now beginning to be implemented in a significant way.

In 1994 the New Zealand Department of Conservation worked out an agreement with the Maori in the North Island's Northland region for management of the government-owned Motatau Scenic Reserve (national forest). Elsewhere, the prodevelopment national government of the mid-1990s offered back to the Maori some lands that were being held in a conservation estate, in return for iwi assurances that they would allow logging and other forms of resource development and extraction. One particularly outspoken New Zealand environmental group thereupon accused the Maori of abandoning their own traditions of reverence for nature in order to make a fast dollar, while more mainstream Anglo conservation organizations have generally supported intercultural comanagement, as long as enforceable environmental protective mechanisms are also in place.[28] So once again, as in other Pacific Rim nation-states, Anglo environmental organizations have diverging views on the wisdom of devolving significant management authority back to indigenous peoples, although on the whole the weight of opinion and judgment seems to lie mostly on the side of support for increased shared management efforts.

As this book was going to press, a draft report was circulating within New Zealand administrative government summarizing efforts to date with bicultural comanagement of lands and resources in Aotearoa/New Zealand. While noting that significant progress has been made at several sites around the country in at least preparing agreements on issues such as water quality in large bodies of fresh water, the report also observes: "Local communities in many cases are unable to take on resource management roles without some assistance and encouragement. In order to work effectively, collaborative management has to be strengthened by building the capacity of iwi, local institutions, and community groups to help make management decisions. . . . One of the biggest challenges facing resource managers is how to fund collaborative arrangements between iwi and councils [regional councils of government]."[29]

It was a little disheartening to come across this particular passage, in that my New Zealand colleague and I came to just the same conclusion and rendered just the same advice in reporting our own research on the role and status of the Maori in Resource Management Act implementation several years earlier.[30] What this situation seems to demonstrate is that it is one thing to adopt foresightful, progressive policies that seek to ensure both environmental and cultural sustainability, along with ensuring that the spiritual values of indigenous peoples will play a significant role in environmental decision making, but it is quite another to actually expend the public funds necessary to make sure that the rhetoric becomes a reality. In this regard, this is a story whose end has not yet been written.

Who Is Hawaiian, and Whose Is Hawaii?

Each of these case studies from around the Pacific begins with a short summary of the evolving legal status of indigenous peoples. The reason for this is that how they are seen in the eyes of the (dominant culture's) law has been crucial to their ability to assure varying degrees of influence over the management of sacred sites and publicly held resources. And it is for this reason that this case study of sacred site management in Hawaii—specifically, the volcanoes on the Big Island—begins with the tortured history of the related legal issues of what constitutes the Hawaiian commons and what constitutes being Hawaiian.

The archaeologists' current best guess seems to be that the first human inhabitants of Hawaii sailed there from Tahiti sometime in the eighth century C.E. During the ensuing thousand years until Captain Cook first dropped anchor off the southwest coast of the Big Island in 1778, the indigenous population grew to an estimated size of 200,000 to 300,000 persons, inhabited all the major islands in the chain, and practiced a polytheistic spiritual tradition whose deities resided both at specific places and in the spirits of specific plant and animal species.[31]

Cook's "discovery" presaged a continuous influx of European and American explorers, traders, and whalers—and, later, missionaries. They arrived during a turbulent time. In a succession of intertribal wars, King Kamehameha I eventually succeeded in uniting all Hawaii under his rule in 1810, by which time there was also some intermarriage between indigenous Hawaiians and European and American settlers. And thus began the friction between the collective (if hierarchical) land ownership pattern imposed by Kamehameha and his successors and the thirst for private property imported by Anglo immigrants.

Later Hawaiian monarchs ceded some of their land to other Hawaiian royalty and sold or gave some to Anglo settlers. Further, international competition for control of Hawaii mounted throughout the nineteenth century, with the monarchs trying to play off one power against another while maintaining their own sovereignty. American settlers, capital, and military presence became the dominant forces on the islands late in the century, at which time the little independent nation's last monarch, Queen Liliuokalani, attempted to reassert her authority by promulgating a new constitution restoring some monarchical power while vesting most governmental authority in a Parliament whose representatives could be elected only by Hawaiian subjects.

What happened next, as acknowledged by both Congress and an important Supreme Court decision on this matter, is that American businessmen and the U.S. minister to Hawaii, with the military support of a contingent of U.S. Marines acting at the minister's request, staged a coup and overthrew the monarchy in December 1893.[32]

Alarmed and angered that American government representatives and armed forces had seized the little country and abolished its government without authorization to do so, President Grover Cleveland denounced their actions before Congress and refused to recognize the provisional government the American corporate vigilantes had cobbled together. But this was the age of empire, for the United States as well as for European powers (at least insofar as the Caribbean and the Pacific were concerned), and American business interests had no trouble convincing a later Congress and Cleveland's successor, President William McKinley, to recognize Hawaii's corporate "republic" and annex the Hawaiian Islands as a territory of the United States.[33] In this measure, Hawaii's "provisional" government ceded to the United States all the monarchical lands they had seized after their coup. Two years later, in 1900, Congress passed the Hawaiian Organic Act establishing the Territory of Hawaii and providing for a territorial government,[34] to which it gave control of the ceded lands except for reserves that Congress might establish for other purposes (such as national parks, monuments, and military bases, as it would turn out).

Within two decades of the United States' seizure of Hawaii, native Hawaiians had fallen into a desperate state. Their population had been decimated by disease and material deprivation: from an estimated 200,000 to 300,000 at the time of the first European contact in 1778, it had fallen to less than forty-eight thousand some one-hundred years later.[35] And loss of land meant loss of wealth; native Hawaiians as a group were to become among the poorest citizens of their own former country.

In response to these circumstances, Congress in 1921 passed the Hawaiian Homes Commission Act, which "set aside about 200,000 acres of the ceded public lands and created a program of loans and long-term leases for the benefit of native Hawaiians."[36] When Hawaii achieved statehood in 1959, it adopted the act as part of its state constitution, thereby agreeing to implement congressional intent through state law. On statehood, Congress also ceded back to the state over a million additional acres of land, with the understanding that proceeds from the use or sale of this land would be used to support public education, public improvements, and public land uses such as parks; for the diffusion of private property (most of the land in Hawaii is owned by very few persons and interests); and "for the betterment of the conditions of Native Hawaiians." To further implement this purpose, in 1978 Hawaii amended its constitution to create the Office of Hawaiian Affairs.[37]

Since the United States acquired Hawaii by means of an unauthorized covert corporate/military coup instead of through a military conflict authorized by Congress and followed by a peace treaty (as was the case with some American Indian tribes), native Hawaiians did not automatically fall under the "ward–guardian" and "domestic dependent nation" status Justice Marshall had declared to be the United States' constitutional relationship to Indian tribes early in the nineteenth century.[38] In an effort to remedy this lesser status of indigenous Hawaiians, the 1978 Hawaii constitutional amendment also set up a nine-member trust board to be made up of and elected by indigenous Hawaiians, the purpose of the board being to manage the trust lands and accounts for the benefit of indigenous peoples. In this way, the 1978 constitutional convention and the voters who adopted its proposed amendments (the vast majority of whom are not indigenous Hawaiians) were trying to elevate the status of indigenous Hawaiians to something approximating that of American Indians, by creating an internal government authority which could function in a manner similar to the tribal council of an American Indian tribe, insofar as the management of tribal lands, resources, and financial trusts is concerned.

But in 1999 the U.S. Supreme Court determined that the Hawaiian constitutional convention and a majority of the state's voting populace did not possess this authority. A descendant of pre-annexation white settlers (not indigenous Hawaiians) had sued the state for not allowing him to vote in the elections for the board of trustees in the Office of Hawaiian Affairs (OHA). A federal trial court in Hawaii and the Ninth Circuit Court of Appeals in San Francisco both upheld the state's restriction of voting rights to indigenous Hawaiians as reasonably related to congressional intent in managing the trust estate as originally authorized under the 1921 Hawaiian Homes Act. But the Supreme Court chose instead to find that the OHA trustee election statute restricting voting rights to indigenous Hawaiians violated the post–Civil War Fifteenth Amendment to the U.S. Constitution, which prohibits states from using race as a basis for barring participation in elections.

To achieve this result, the five members of the court who signed the majority opinion (two more concurred in the outcome but not for the same reasons) chose to ignore the entire constitutional history of the United States' relationship with its indigenous peoples, holding that it was inapplicable because indigenous Hawaiians as a group had never been recognized as a *political* entity as distinguished from an *ethnic* entity by the United States government.[39] The terrible irony here is that the very reason Hawaiian voters established OHA in the first place was to make up for the fact that since indigenous Hawaiians as a nation had been destroyed by a covert American corporate coup, they never had a chance to be recognized as a political entity. The government of the land Congress annexed in 1898 and declared a territory in 1900 represented the coup leaders, and not indigenous Hawaiians.

In sum, the very wrong Hawaiian voters were trying to right in setting up OHA and its board of trustees provided the Supreme Court majority's rationale for not allowing the state of Hawaii to recognize its indigenous peoples as empowered to govern the estate that Congress had established for them. In 1993, Congress itself had acknowledged the terrible injustice indigenous Hawaiians had suffered as a result of American imperialist greed and apologized to them for it in writing.[40] In the wake of *Rice v. Cayetano*, it now seems that the only way Congress will be able to make good on that apology is to legislatively reverse this decision, by voting to accord indigenous Hawaiians as a group the same status as an American Indian tribe.

Technically, the Supreme Court's decision in this case directly affects only the question of who may vote in an OHA trustees election. But the broader implication is that it also restricts the state's authority to grant indigenous Hawaiians a greater measure of autonomy over the governance of the estate that has been set aside on their behalf (at least until either the state or the Congress can come up with a voting scheme that, in the view of the current Supreme Court, does not violate the Fifteenth Amendment). How great a say indigenous Hawaiians as individuals or as a group may have in the management of publicly held lands and resources that they hold sacred therefore depends considerably on what government agency or institution has management responsibility, as well as the degree to which that agency or institution has been instructed to take indigenous Hawaiian views into account. And at least insofar as the volcanoes on the Big Island (i.e., the Island of Hawaii within the Hawaiian Island chain) are concerned, it turns out that a great deal depends on whether they are under federal or state management, as the two contrasting case studies make clear.

Congress originally established the present-day Hawaii Volcanoes National Park in 1916. Of the Big Island's three major volcanoes, the park contains the two active ones: Mauna Loa and Kilauea, as well as numerous other steam vents and lava tubes. Standing at the edge of one of these calderas, one gets an unmistakable sense of being present at the continuing creation of the Earth. It is therefore no surprise that for indigenous Hawaiians, these are among the most sacred sites in all the islands. And also because of this indigenous Hawaiian linkage to place, Congress specified in both the 1978 American Indian Religious Freedom Act and the 1992 Historic Preservation Act amendments that the provisions of both of those laws would apply to native Hawaiians as well as American Indians, Eskimos, and Aleuts.

In balancing preservation with access, Park Service staff have developed a working relationship with several Native Hawaiian consultants whose families or clans are known to have a traditional cultural affiliation with various sites within the park. This consultation network is an ongoing aspect of park management.[41] Consultants advise on the permitting process for the gathering of certain plants and for a limited amount of sea life harvesting on the park's shoreline, which is normally prohibited but specifically provided for by act of Congress for certain indigenous families having affiliation with the site. This parallels in some respects the permitted collecting that takes place in Saguaro National Park.

One of the more interesting management issues park staff must deal with on a continuing basis is the leaving of ritual objects and the building of rock cairns in and around the calderas, which raises the question of when a gift to Pele (the Hawaiian goddess of volcanoes, whose principal residence is thought to be the Kilauea caldera) actually becomes littering. Although the practice of leaving an offering near one of the steam vents in the Kilauea caldera is well established among indigenous Hawaiians, it has also been taken up by non-Hawaiian tourists, and staff regularly collect an amazing array of objects left in these places. This practice caught Comanche author Paul Smith's attention when he visited the park in the 1990s, at a time when the management of sacred sites was very much on his mind:

> In the fall of 1995, while on honeymoon in Hawaii, my wife and I peered into a volcano. It was somewhat active, but said not to be too dangerous at the moment. The volcano was a mountain that rose from the rain forest, and to get there you drove across a moonscape of black and gray rock. Just beyond the guardrail that kept us from stumbling through the lunar rocks into the lava fields below, I noticed a small bottle of Jack Daniels attached to a note. Next to the flask were cigarettes and loose tobacco.
>
> On the way down I read a Park Service sign explaining that the volcano has religious significance for many native Hawaiians. One way they demonstrate this, the sign explained, is by leaving offerings. Without saying so exactly, the park authorities made clear that if you were not a native Hawaiian they would not look kindly on any offerings you might want to offer. This solution seemed as perfect as could be hoped for. Common sense prevailed.[42]

Over time and through conversations with native Hawaiian consultants, park staff have come to develop a working understanding of what kinds of gifts are traditionally left by indigenous Hawaiians and what kinds are not. They leave in place those thought to be indigenous in origin out of respect for the practice, but not others. This represents an interesting judgment call, since it does involve the Park Service in making decisions as to what does and does not constitute an allowable religious practice at the site.

The same holds true for the building of rock cairns, which according to park staff seems to be particularly popular among Asian tourists. As higher and higher numbers of them began to engage in this practice, a park ranger asked them why they did this (since at the end of the day park staff dissemble them). The answer was "The tour bus driver told us to." When park staff took up the matter with the tour bus driver, he said that passengers had asked him what was an appropriate ritual gesture to make at this obviously auspicious site, and he replied, "Whatever you do in your home country." More directly First Amendment–related issues have arisen with Asia-Pacific immigrants who now live in Hawaii and when they visit the park want to make some gesture reflective of their own culture's relationship with sites of volcanic activity, which generally are sacred to many culture groups around the Pacific Rim.

Because of both its location between East and West and the cultural diversity within the state, Hawaii Volcanoes National Park (HVNP) is even more of an international, intercultural crossroads than other national parks and monuments. To this end, consultation with indigenous Hawaiians having a cultural affiliation with the site is a continuous and ongoing process, rather than something resorted to only when a particular problem or high-profile management decision is called for. And in this regard HVNP is probably riding the forward crest of a wave of national park, monument, and forest management practices that will in some form or other move through the structure of every federal land management agency in the years to come.

Away to the north of the park in the center of the Big Island is the biggest mountain in the Pacific—Mauna Kea. Rising nearly fourteen thousand feet about the ocean, the volcano is thought to have last erupted about forty-five hundred years ago. All of the higher elevation land mass of the volcano (including the summit) is public land owned by the state of Hawaii and managed by its Department of Land and Natural Resources. In 1968 the State Board of Land and Natural Resources leased several thousand acres of the mountain including the summit) to the University of Hawaii for a period of sixty-five years, for the purpose of creating an observatory complex at its peak.[43]

Construction on the summit began immediately, with the placement of telescopes by the National Aeronautics and Space Administration (NASA) and the U.S. Air Force. This was soon followed by the Canada-France-Hawaii telescope, another NASA facility, and an infrared telescope built by the United Kingdom. In 1983 the University of Hawaii's Institute for Astronomy built a mid-level facility at the nine-thousand-foot level to house astronomers and construction crews, so that once acclimated to working at the fourteen-thousand-foot level, they would not have to daily make the physically punishing journey all the way back down to sea-level lodging. The Institute for Astronomy also encouraged the proliferation of additional telescope installations on the summit, built by various international partnerships of countries such as Taiwan, Japan, Chile, Australia, Argentina, and Brazil. Later both the University of California and Caltech built their own facilities. By the end of 1999 there were twelve different observatories on Mauna Kea's summit, with five more planned.[44] The place had become an astronomical subdivision.

In 1983 the University of Hawaii published a master plan for the future of the facility, including a proposal for the building of additional telescopes, which was done. However, the plan also called for (1) building a telescope at the mid-level facility for the public to use; (2) hiring rangers to prevent damage to flora, fauna, and archeological sites; (3) creating a visitors' parking area and trash control receptacles on the summit; and (4) establishing a multijurisdictional management committee (the Hawaii Departments of Land and Natural Resources and Transportation, as well as the University of Hawaii (UH), all have management authority at the site). By the end of 1999, none of these four plan elements had been implemented. The reason the university gave for failing to do so was "budget cuts."[45]

One reason for the university's reticence to manage the summit as anything other than an international science colony at which the presence of the public is grudgingly tolerated but in no way encouraged may be found in the 1968 lease language under which the university acquired control of the site: "The land hereby leased shall be used by the leassee [UH] as a scientific complex, including without limitation thereof an observatory, and as a scientific reserve being more specifically a buffer zone to prevent the intrusion of activities inimical to said scientific complex."[46]

However, the relentless pace of observatory construction and a seeming disregard for the physical and cultural effects this activity was having began to arouse public resistance to the way the university was so single-purposedly managing the site—especially its failure to implement aspects of the 1983 master plan not having to do directly with the furtherance of astronomy. So in the late 1990s the university initiated yet another master planning process, which again documented many of the same increasingly serious management problems

UH had failed to address in the previous fifteen years. These problems include:

- Jurisdictional overlaps and gaps between state agencies, and a resulting lack of unified, coordinated management of the site
- Lack of meaningful consultation with and involvement of local populations directly affected by Mauna Kea management decisions, particularly (but not exclusively) regarding native Hawaiian peoples having a particular connection with the place, such as a site the resident deity of which is a certain group's *aumakua* ("family or personal god")
- Ambiguities and conflicts regarding access: although public visitation beyond the mid-level facility is not encouraged, it is also not forbidden, resulting in considerable damage caused by off-road four-wheel drive vehicle use, accidents on the steep, unbanked, unrailed roadway. Yet proposals to restrict vehicular access have alarmed the local population, especially families with an aumakua relationship to sites on the mountain
- Harm to archeological resources, some of which happened during early construction before adequate archeological surveying, and some of which has occurred due to unrestricted access.
- Population decline in a rare species of insect—the Wekiu bug—known to exist only on Mauna Kea (above the twelve-thousand-foot level) and Mauna Loa.
- Potential future harm to both the physical environment and the sacred character of the site for indigenous Hawaiians occasioned by planned expansion of the observatory facilities on the summit.[47]

In 1999 and 2000 the university circulated successive drafts of its master plan for public review and comment, seeking a management balance point among various competing objectives. As of this writing, there are several major issues in the plan as adopted by the University of Hawaii regents that remain substantially unresolved in the view of some participants in the planning process—particularly local environmental organizations and native Hawaiians.[48]

One of these issues is that observatory construction activities will continue to expand, including the installation in the already cramped area at the summit of a gigantic new instrument, the lens diameter of which will be twenty-five to fifty meters (half a football field) wide. Another concerns the financing of better management. Mainland universities, NASA, the Smithsonian Institution, and a host of foreign countries have installed hundreds of millions of dollars worth of telescopic equipment at the Mauna Kea summit and are planning to continue to do so; yet the university failed to implement the management reforms promised in the 1983 master plan due to budget constraints.

The university refused then and in its latest management plan continues to refuse to charge its astronomer tenants user fees to cover the cost of managing the reserve lands it has leased. Locals have no more confidence that the university will implement any element of the new master plan—other than allowing more telescopes to be built—than it did the last one. Responsibly implementing its new master plan will be expensive. If the university is unwilling to charge the users whose presence is largely responsible for these problems the costs of remedying them, it will either need to use state education funds that could have been devoted to other purposes to implement the plan or again default on the promises made in this document.

One of the reasons this is a sensitive point is that the Mauna Kea Science Reserve is on ceded lands (Hawaiian monarchical lands that eventually became public after the overthrow of the monarchy). A claim has been made that these lands should be considered part of the trust estate and that 20 percent of any revenues accruing from use of these lands should go to the Office of Hawaiian Affairs. Thus native Hawaiians feel trebly wronged in this case: one of their most sacred sites has been thoroughly desecrated and their ability to practice their religion accordingly impaired; this was done on lands that may rightly be a part of their estate but without their permission or consultation; and if the prior point can be sustained by law, they have also therefore been deprived of revenue the university has been refusing to obtain from the resident observatories.

In some ways, administrators at the University of Hawaii's Institute for Astronomy face a far greater challenge than simply determining the origins of the universe or the future of the sun. They have been looking up for so long that they have neglected to look as carefully down and around them. This is unfortunate, for around them circumstances have changed—on the ground, in the culture, and in the law. Inevitably, their management of the Mauna Kea Reserve suffers badly by comparison with the National Park Service's care of Hawaii Volcanoes National Park in terms of environmental preservation, public access, and respect for traditional cultural practices. The two were established for dramatically different purposes, but the university is now being held to a much higher standard than it is comfortable trying to meet—or to charge its tenants to help it meet.

When the university negotiated its lease for the exclusive occupancy of the upper four thousand feet of Mauna Kea in 1968, Hawaii had been a state for less than a decade. As essentially a colony of the United States, residents of territorial Hawaii had been accustomed to if not pleased at having great swaths of their land set aside for military bases and other similar uses that precluded public access, without their having much say in the matter. And the 1968 lease has similar-sounding language: it provides for a scientific complex at the summit and "a buffer zone to prevent the intrusion of activities inimical to said scientific complex"—an explicitly single-use mandate. So over the years the university has understandably read this as permission to keep the world at bay and to treat the site in any way that in its view best met the needs of astrophysical science.

But times have changed, and upper Mauna Kea is severely contested space. Despite the university's consistent efforts to the contrary and the language of its anachronistic lease, Mauna Kea is gradually being reconstructed in the eyes of everyone who holds some personal relationship to the mountain—indigenous Hawaiians and *haoles* (Anglos, "white folks") alike—into a commons rather than an exclusive preserve. To manage this site well will require constructing a shared vision of what Mauna Kea is and how it should therefore be treated.

Constructing Mauna Kea

The place was Hale Pohaku, the visitor center and staff dorm facility at the nine-thousand-foot- level entrance to the Mauna Kea Reserve, on a sunny summer morning. A mutual friend on the Big Island had introduced me to a native Hawaiian cultural consultant who has been advising the drafters of the university master plan on the specifics of the spiritual significance of the place to the indigenous peoples who hold it sacred. When he learned that I was planning to visit the summit for the first time, he offered to meet me here, to provide a ritual introduction to the mountain, and to explain during a journey to the summit why native Hawaiians care so deeply about how this place is treated.

The visitor center features some literature and displays that try to convey why this is such a coveted place for astronomers from around the world. Away from major light-emitting and air-polluting population centers (hooded street lights in towns around the island cast a dim amber glow that minimizes light pollution), and above the fair-weather cloud level, the Mauna Kea summit offers some of the best night-viewing conditions of any observatory site in the world. It is also less than two hours' drive to an international airport and seaport, unlike high-altitude sites in the Andes or central Asia.

The descriptions of research goals and activities as given at the center and in the University of Hawaii's master plan are certainly philosophical if not spiritual in nature: "Astronomers come to Mauna Kea in search of scientific answers to some of humanity's most fundamental questions: How and when did the stars, planets, and galaxies form? What threats do we face from the Sun and other celestial bodies? What will be the ultimate fate of the universe?"[49] The clear message in these presentations is that Mauna Kea is one of the best astronomical viewing sites in the world; that some of the best viewing equipment in the world is installed on its summit (with more to come—count on it); and that several national and international institutes have sent some of the best astronomers in the world here to use it. As an academic, I could appreciate the University of Hawaii's efforts here to tell the world it is trying to do its best to fulfill its public trust responsibility to further human understanding of the universe.

Then my native Hawaiian host (who was also to become a friend) and I began our venture to the summit, and I realized that competing constructed visions of Mauna Kea were forming one after the other in my mind. The first was the university's portrayal at the visitor center and in its master plan. The second began to take shape at a stopping place on our way to the summit: a stone altar in an out of the way location. After some meditation, my host left an offering and said a prayer to the mountain, introducing us and conveying our intentions in making this journey.[50]

Our next stop in the ascent was Pu'u Lilinoe, a cinder cone a little below the summit which is identified with the deity Lilinoe, goddess of the mist, and regarded by many as one of the four most sacred sites on the mountain. Again, offerings at an altar, a few moments of "receiving and being received by" the place, and a prayer to Lilinoe, explaining our intentions and apologizing for the desecratory placement of a nearby VLBA radio telescope. These stops also allowed us to gradually acclimate to the altitude (rather the opposite of staged descent in deep scuba diving).

Below and to one side of the cinder cone are the fields to which ancient adze makers came both to pray and to quarry the exceptionally hard basalt created when molten lava erupted below a glacier ice cap and pressed against the thick ice and cooled. The priests and craftsmen who came here also erected many upright stone shrines. When I asked about the larger shrine sites on the mountain, my host acknowledged that there are several, but then went on to explain that in the way he was introduced to it and was taught to regard it, the entirety of Mauna Kea—this highest and most massive of Hawaii's volcanic mountains—is a *heiau*, or place of worship. More specifically, in the way he was taught, the upper regions of Mauna Kea comprise a naturally occurring *lana nu'u mamao,* a three-tiered oracle tower Hawaiian priests would construct at some sacred sites. Most lana nu'u mamao are man-made three-level platforms, usually constructed of timbers lashed together and covered with bark cloth, perhaps twenty to thirty feet in height. The ground floor, or *lana*, is the first level; and the second floor is a sacred level where offerings are made to make amends or requests to the various deities. The third floor is the highest level, the *mamao,* into which only the priesthood had access. Replicas of these prayer towers may be found at some of the major *heiau* in the islands.

As he explained it to me, in understanding upper Mauna Kea itself to be a gigantic naturally occurring prayer tower, the area above Hale Pohaku (the visitor center area where we met) up to the lower edge of the adze quarry is the lana, the first level of transition into the realm of the gods and goddesses. The second level where we made our stop at Puʻu Lilinoe is the nuʻu where many clusters of rock shrines were placed around the mountain at this elevation to honor the various deities representing specific family groups. The third level at the summit is the mamao, or highest pinnacle of the heiau. This is the place where only the priesthood ventured, and then only to conduct ceremonies and leave. It was a place too sacred for the constructs of man, which explains the prehistoric lack of altars or heiau on the summit: this was not and was never intended to be a place of continuous habitation.

This vision, this understanding, of all of upper Mauna Kea as a lana nuʻu mamao stayed with me until we reached the summit, when the visual impact of the observatory sites abruptly reconstructed Mauna Kea for me once again. The place looks like a cross between a military radar installation and one of Colorado's high-altitude mines—all sheet metal, machinery, and technological function. Contractors simply cut the top off the mountain, flattened it into a construction site, and built as many telescope enclosures as the limited space could accommodate. It is an industrial worksite. It is about the production of scientific knowledge, and obviously nothing else.

It is here amid the many telescope structures that Puʻu Kukahauʻula rises above all else This highest cinder cone at the summit, I am told by my host, is the most sacred of sacred places on the mountain. This highest point is the mamao, where ancient priests and prophets stood to give prayers of thanks and acknowledgment.

The only nonastronomical structure in view is an *ahu* or stone altar built by a native Hawaiian woman whose family's aumakua is Poliahu, the deity residing at the summit. Shortly after this structure was first built, a staff worker at the observatories destroyed it. The woman rebuilt it, and the staff destroyed it again. When public attention was drawn to this contest, after she built it again University of Hawaii administrators allowed it to remain. The entire incident only served to demonstrate how contested a place the upper reaches of Mauna Kea has become.

Looking around this observatory village, the two competing constructions of Mauna Kea—the lana nuʻu mamao and the science factory—started switching back and forth in my mind's eye like alternating current, until they began to merge into one image. This is when it dawned on me that what we were seeing is a haole science version of a lana nuʻu mamao.

The astronomer/administrators instinctively knew exactly how the ancient kahunas (priests) managed the site hundreds of years ago, and they are doing exactly the same thing. As enshrined in their lease and to the extent possible in the master plan, these new kahunas of science encourage the supplicants and other commoners to stay down at the lana—the visitor center at Hale Pohaku on the first level. Archeologists and others seriously interested in studying what this incredibly rich site has to offer can proceed to the second level (nuʻu)—the adze quarry and the uprighted stone shrines. But under the current management plan, the mamao—the summit, the pinnacle, the place of transference—is reserved for the kahunas of astronomy from around the world.

This insight struck with considerable force and lingered for a long time. But on reflection, I also remembered that in the latest version of the master plan, UH abandoned an earlier position and moved to assure native Hawaiian access to sacred sites (including the summit) in much the same way the Park Service has at Hawaii Volcanoes National Park. In the latest version of the plan the university also promised to do what it can to find the same fulcrum the Park Service endlessly seeks, trying to balance access to with preservation of Mauna Kea's treasures for future generations—future generations of native Hawaiians and of all the peoples for whom this site has been entrusted to the university's care.

In consultation with their faculties and with the communities of which they are a part, university administrators are coming to realize that there are many kinds of valuable knowledge that Mauna Kea has to offer. Like the little Wekiu bug, the social sciences and the humanities, the native Hawaiians, and the environmentalists are all trying to find a niche in which they may be able to survive in the rarified atmosphere—the nuʻu and the mamao—of Mauna Kea.

Our last stop on this odyssey was Puʻu Poliahu—the mound at the summit that is the place of Poliahu: sister to Lilinoe, guardian of the summit, another of the sacred sites on the mountain. And from this place we looked down on yet another: the little lake called Wai`au. According to both the ethnographic studies done for the master plan and the teachings of my host, Mauna Kea is the point of origin—the *piko*—of the island of Hawaii (*piko* being a Hawaiian word variously translated as "origin point," "navel," and "umbilicus"). And just as Mauna Kea is the piko of the Big Island, so is Lake Wai`au the piko of Mauna Kea—the water-filled navel of the mountain. For this reason, according to the master plan's ethnographic research, several native Hawaiian families bring the umbilicus of their newborn children to plant near Pu`u Wai`au. For these families, there is no more powerful way to connect their children with their culture and with the land where they were born.

So to be above and look down into the center of Wai`au is to look down into the birthplace of Mauna Kea, which is to look down into the birthplace of the island of Hawaii, which in the understanding of many native Hawaiians—as in being with the goddess Pele at the Kilauea caldera—is to look down into the place of the continuing creation of all that is.

And that, finally, is where my two competing constructions of Mauna Kea came to rest, side by side. Standing atop Pu`u Poliahu my friend and I saw below us—on one side of this geographic and cultural divide—the observatory cluster from which haole science looks up into the heavens, seeking the source of all creation. And on the other side was Pu`u Wai`au, where native Hawaiians look down into the womb of the Earth to find the same thing.

PART FOUR

Charting a Common Course

11

Coming Home

Euro-Americans and Contemplative Rediscovery of the "New World"

> We shall not cease from exploration
> And the end of all our exploring
> Will be to arrive where we started
> And know the place for the first time.
> — T. S. Eliot, " Little Gidding V,"
> *Four Quartets* (1943)

In 1808 Gabriel Moraga led a party of explorers up the northern half of California's Central Valley. There they found wetlands teeming with all manner of aquatic life, huge herds of tule elk, and flocks of migratory waterfowl blanketing the lowland marshes. In addition to alluvial soils and mild climate, what made this abundance of life possible was the majestic watercourse defining the valley's center. Understanding it to be the entire region's fountain of life, the name Moraga gave this great river was the Spanish Catholic term for the sacred expressed in material form: the Sacramento.

A little earlier, Lewis and Clark's "Corps of Discovery" had worked its way up the Missouri River and over the northern ranges of the mountain west in their historic if unsuccessful search for a northwest (waterway) passage from the Great Plains to the Pacific Ocean. On the day they found the headwaters of the river they had followed up into the mountains, Meriwether Lewis wrote: "At the distance of 4 miles further the road took us to the most distant fountain of the waters of the mighty Missouri in search of which we have spent so many toilsome days and restless nights. Two miles below McNeal had exultingly stood with a foot on each side of this little rivulet and thanked his god that he had lived to bestride the mighty & heretofore deemed endless Missouri."[1]

If only the worshipful spirit the wilderness aroused in these explorers had endured down through the years. But this was not to be. Today we can only imagine what these landscapes looked like when Euro-Americans first saw them. The waterways they navigated have long since been dammed, drowned, diverted, riprapped, channeled, and otherwise transformed into servants of agriculture and industry. One thing we do know about both groups of explorers is that everywhere they went they found human occupation; they were sojourners in First Native homelands.

As reflected in writing as disparate as that of Aldo Leopold and Jack Kerouac, since the middle years of the twentieth century Euro-Americans have been rediscovering these wild places—or what is left of them (their original indigenous inhabitants having been long since evicted and confined to reservations). Conservation interests had managed to preserve at least some of the more visually stunning and soul-stirring landscapes by mid-century; and with the post–World War II growth in the popularity of outdoor recreation there came the possibility for those who went to these places for the same kind of inspirational connection the earlier explorers had expressed in their journals.

Leopold writes that his real rediscovery of the wild happened in the national forests of New Mexico, when as a Forest Service timber cruiser (one who estimates the board-feet of lumber that could be logged out of a given forest tract), he and coworkers shot one of the few wolves still trying to make a living in those recently acquired federal lands. Avid deer hunters, Leopold and his friends relished the chance to wipe out a natural competitor for their own favorite prey. But on approaching the wolf as she died, something in the way he saw the natural world changed forever:

> We reached the old wolf in time to watch a fierce green fire dying in her eyes. I realized then, and have known ever since, that there was something new to me in those eyes—something known only to her and to the

mountain. I was young then, and full of trigger itch; I thought that because fewer wolves meant more deer, that no wolves would mean hunter's paradise. But after seeing the green fire die, I sensed that neither the wolf nor the mountain agreed with such a view.

Since then I have lived to see state after state extirpate its wolves. . . . I have seen every edible tree defoliated to the height of a saddlehorn. . . . I now suspect that just as a deer lives in mortal fear of its wolves, so does a mountain live in mortal fear of its deer. And perhaps with better cause, for while a buck pulled down by wolves can be replaced in two or three years, a range pulled down by too many deer may fail of replacement in as many decades.[2]

In this passage, Leopold made the case as eloquently as anyone since Thoreau for shifting from a homocentric to a biocentric perspective on how we should view, understand, and interact with the world around us. And in addition to writing about this perspective, he and other conservationists such as Bob Marshall had successfully advocated the establishment of wilderness areas within the public domain by mid-century. Later the postwar baby boom generation would form what could be called a "corps of spiritual rediscovery" and would enter these wild spaces in unprecedented numbers.

As early as 1958, Kerouac envisioned what the American wilderness would soon experience, and in committing what he imagined to writing perhaps he helped bring it about: "I see a vision of a great rucksack revolution thousands or even millions of young Americans wandering around with rucksacks, going up to the mountains to pray, making children laugh and old men glad . . . all of 'em Zen Lunatics who go about writing poems that happen to appear in their heads for no reason and also by strange unexpected acts keep giving visions of eternal freedom to everybody and to all living creatures."[3] That Kerouac was personally transformed by his own wilderness experience—as arranged by his friend, poet and Zen student Gary Snyder— he freely admitted in his fictionalized account of a summer spent alone as a forest fire spotter in the Cascades: "Standing on Desolation Peak . . . I said out loud 'I don't know when we'll meet again or what'll happen in the future, but Desolation, Desolation, I owe so much to Desolation, thank you forever for guiding me to the place where I learned all.' . . . Down on the lake rosy reflections of celestial vapor appeared, and I said 'God, I love you' and looked up to the sky and really meant it. 'I have fallen in love with you, God. Take care of us all, one way or the other.'"[4]

If such a late-night urbanite and drunken reprobate as Kerouac described himself to be could develop a love of God in the wilderness, it was a stirring testament to the wilderness's spiritually healing power. And so his rucksack revolution did indeed come about, and—at least insofar as wilderness use is concerned—it showed no signs of abating at the end of the century, as the post–World War II baby boom generation's grown children headed for the back country in numbers at least equal to their parents'.

In returning to these places that had been "discovered" by Euro-American explorers two centuries ago, millions of annual visitors to national parks and forests and the smaller but still significant numbers who travel by foot and pack animal deeper into wilderness areas are, to use T. S. Eliot's phrase, "arriving where we started." And we have ample evidence that in the sense of contemplative knowledge, Euro-American society is just now coming "to know the place for the first time."

In terms of calculative knowledge, we have learned with great precision how to measure and gauge nature's material value—in board-feet of timber, acre-feet of water, tonnage of precious metals, and barrels of fossil fuels. But Euro-Americans as a culture group are now coming to better "know the place" contemplatively, as First Natives have from time immemorial. And in coming to know these places in this way, in a very real sense we are also *coming home* to them. In 1830 de Tocqueville found that quality of connection to place largely lacking in the American character; today it has emerged and is continuing to grow. How to rightly own being born of this place without displacing or diminishing the continuous, ancient, elder status of the continent's indigenous cultures is at least as great a challenge for the dominant culture of Euro-America as is the sustainable stewardship of our natural heritage.

This chapter provides some examples of how contemplative knowledge of the sacred in nature is being made manifest in the diverse spiritual practices of Euro-American society; how it is being expressed politically and legally; and how it is providing a new and different set of challenges to managers of federal lands, who now must pay attention to the fact that—for better or worse—more and more Euro-Americans, as well as First Natives, are coming to see park and forest rangers as stewards of holy lands.

Eastward into the Woods

The "rucksack revolution" Kerouac foresaw was probably fueled as much by opposition to the war in Vietnam as it was a positive vision of what our world might look like if we were to take better care of it. Lynn White's indictment of Western religion for at least complicity if not moral culpability in the despoiling of nature stimulated some serious doctrinal rethinking among the Christian faithful. But in Euro-American society, this disaffection with Western religious institutions no doubt did at least as much to encourage exploration into completely different spiritual and cultural constructions of the relationship between humans and the natural environment.

Although Taoism and Buddhism had come to Gold Mountain (the nineteenth-century Chinese immigrant name for America) over a century earlier, they tended to stay within the cultural enclaves of Chinese and Japanese immigrants who brought them here.[5] It was not until the 1960s that fully accomplished traditional Buddhist meditation teachers such as Zen master Shunryu Suzuki Roshi founded centers in the United States for the authentic transmission of these ancient Eastern teachings to Western students. While many other teachers and traditions from the Indian subcontinent and East Asia would come and go during the turbulent, culturally reinventive times of late-twentieth-century America, this is one that would endure.

While Aldo Leopold advised "thinking like a mountain," he offered no detailed advice on just how to go about doing so, and certainly not in contemplative terms. The Zen masters did. They provided the "cutting-through" technology of mind that, through contemplative experience, makes it easier to see things from the mountain's point of view. As Robert Aitken put it:

How do we actualize the oneness of all beings? Through responsibility, the ability to respond—like that of the clover. When the clover is cut, its roots die and release their nitrogen, and the soil is enriched. Earthworms flourish in the rich soil and deposit more nutrients. New seeds fall, take root, mature, and feed other organisms.....

Thus the place of the human being is a matter of choice. We can destroy the gene pool of the earth organism and eliminate all choices, or we can discipline ourselves and find the source of responsibility. That source is the mind of clover. There you are nurtured; there you nurture. Settle there, at least once in your life.[6]

As this tradition and this point of view gradually began to make their way into public discourse on human relationships to nature in America, it would be Jack Kerouac's friend Gary Snyder who most effectively synthesized this perspective into an Earth ethic that paid homage both to his own Zen training and to some indigenous teachings imparted by friends in the upper Rio Grande pueblos. He did it through the medium of poetry, perhaps most famously in *Turtle Island,* which won the Pulitzer prize for poetry in 1975.

In stressing Buddhism's affinity with nature, Snyder was tapping into historical roots traceable to the very founding of this particular spiritual tradition. When the Buddha first began to teach meditation subsequent to deciding that he had something to teach (i.e., after his enlightenment), step one in the first method he taught was for the student to go "to the forest or to the root of a tree or to an empty hut,"[7] sit down in a comfortable but wakeful position, and patiently begin to establishment mindfulness of all existence (the mind's knowing of the inner and outer world). Later he gave more specific, step-by-step instructions on how to literally expand one's consciousness beyond the borders of the self and into the concentric surrounding realms of the forest, the earth, the sky, and infinite space.[8] Thus it was no accident that when Buddhism first began to take hold as an established spiritual tradition in Euro-American society, each urban meditation group or center quickly established a rural counterpart in or in as close a proximity as possible to preserved open space. Soon after Suzuki founded the very urban San Francisco Zen Center in the 1960s, he also established the very rural Tassahara retreat center, in a narrow canyon adjoining Big Sur's Ventana Wilderness in the Los Padres National Forest.

After students of the Tibetan teacher Chögyam Trungpa Rinpoche founded the urban Naropa Institute in Boulder, Colorado, he established the five-hundred-acre Rocky Mountain Shambhala Center on former ranch land near a national forest high in the Rockies. The first Vipassana—or Insight Meditation—retreat held in California in 1974 was based in a campground in Sequoia National Park in the Sierra Nevada. When American practitioners in this Southeast Asian Buddhist tradition later built east and west coast meditation centers, it was on rural land surrounded by hundreds of acres of open space. As in the Asian forest monastery tradition, establishing the rural centers emphasized building on as little of the land as possible (usually less than 10 percent of holdings) and managing the surrounding open space (most of which had formerly been either heavily grazed ranch land or previously logged forests) in a way that fostered as complete a restoration as possible to environmental conditions before resource extraction. Among Insight Meditation practitioners, a tradition has also been established of holding small retreats that take the form of backpacking trips into wilderness areas in some western states.

Taoist teachings on unity with nature also enjoyed a surge in popularity in the late twentieth century. Its outward manifestations are in practices such as the martial arts (t'ai chi and xi gong), acupuncture and herbal medicine, and feng shui (geomancy), but the same inward principle governs them all. This is the Tao, the Great Way, the unseen ordering of the universe that when recognized and understood makes all things possible, and when ignored or controverted leads to conflict, destruction, and sorrow. It is to be known simply by carefully observing nature itself and acting in accordance with its ways. Additionally, advises the twenty-five-hundred-year-old *Tao-te Ching* (Laotzu's prose poems, and perhaps Taoism's principal text), one can learn this teaching by observing those who understand it. And who were these sages? "They were careful as someone crossing an iced-over stream.... Fluid as melting ice. Shapable as a block of wood. Receptive as a valley. Clear as a glass of water. Do you have the patience to wait till your mud settles and the water is clear? Can you remain unmoving till the right action arises by itself? The Master doesn't seek fulfillment. Not seeking, not expecting, she is present, and can welcome all things."[9]

Nature as teacher. Surrender of self and unity with nature as a path to understanding and to freedom. Doing contemplative practices in natural settings. Although Asian in origin, for Americans familiar with the writings of New England's nineteenth-century transcendentalists or with First Native spiritual traditions, these words and practices have a familiar ring to them. The similarities begin to appear as significant as the differences. And the possibility begins to suggest itself that somewhere in the Judeo-Christian tradition there might also lie parallel teachings. That is just what a good deal of contemporary theology on the subject has come to conclude.

The Greening of (Judeo-Christian) Faith

Is the Judeo-Christian tradition inherently antienvironmental, or have its teachings merely been interpreted this way down through the ages to rationalize and justify Western civilization's generally rapacious treatment of the earth? That is a question theologians and church leaders wrestled with seriously for the last three decades of the twentieth century. And at least insofar as their resulting policy statements are concerned, it appears that during this period a quiet doctrinal revolution has been under way, in terms of reclaiming and emphasizing teachings on the moral relationship between humans and the natural environment.

One scholar of this "green reformation" within the Judeo-Christian tradition classifies the teachings on Earth–human relations in the book of Genesis as falling into one of three broad categories.[10] First is the "despotic interpretation" the Calvinist immigrants brought to New England in the early seventeenth century (discussed here in chapter 3). In this view, wilderness is the abode of evil; its conquest and subordination to yield material wealth is literally commanded by God.

Second is the "stewardship" interpretation, emphasizing not the "overcome and subdue" language of Genesis 1:28 but, instead, God's instructions to Adam in Genesis 2 to "dress and keep" the Garden of Eden—the Garden (all nature) being God's gift to humanity. As

Callicott points out, these terms—from the first English translation of the Old Testament as commissioned by King James—are the same ones used to describe the responsibilities of groundskeepers and gamekeepers to the lord of a manor. In this stewardship formulation, humans are therefore caretakers rather than owners.

Third is the "citizenship" interpretation, which sees humanity as fully embedded in the web of life rather than above and separate from it. Noting that the very name "Adam" is derived from *adamah*, the ancient Hebrew term for Earth, this interpretation holds that man's "original sin" was in coming to perceive the world dualistically, as categorizable into good and evil, based exclusively on nature's usefulness to man:

> In this interpretation ... of the oldest biblical creation myth, anthropocentrism itself is man's original sin and is responsible for the famous Fall. God presumably cared for the whole of His creation and for each of its parts equally. When man—originally just one part of creation— acquired divine knowledge of good and evil, he began to size up the rest of creation as it pertained to himself.... Man nurtured and cultivated the anthropocentrically "good" parts of nature, domesticating the tractable animals and edible plants, and attempting to destroy the anthropocentrically "evil" parts—the "pests," "vermin," "varmints," and "weeds." This, we may suppose, upset the balance and order of nature as a whole—as God had created it and as, surely, He wished it to remain.[11]

Given the policy statements many mainstream Christian denominations have produced as a result of this theological inquiry, the stewardship interpretation (with some intimations of the citizenship view) seems to have carried the day. The American Baptist Churches U.S.A. state that their congregations have an obligation to "promote an attitude affirming that all nature has intrinsic value and that all life is to be honored and reverenced."[12] In a similar vein, the Evangelical Lutherans have declared as a result of their own study and reflection on these matters that "humans are a part of nature, but with a special role on behalf of the whole.... Other creatures ... have a value apart from what we give them."[13]

This appreciation for nature as a manifestation of divine intelligence and grace is not a teaching fabricated by latter-day apologists for religious complicity in environmental degradation. As alluded to in chapter 3, simply doing a content analysis of Old and New Testament texts yields far more nature-friendly and nature-positive statements than the "overcome, subdue, and dominate" rhetoric that is found only in Genesis 1. As is true in the history of any well-established religious tradition with an extensive canon, different features of its teachings are emphasized and understood in different ways at different times. But contemporary church leaders are finding far more support in original texts, as well as in current scholarship, to support the stewardship and citizenship perspectives than their "despotic" alternative; and they are acting on those views.

When the western United States began to become more urbanized early in the twentieth century, mainstream Christian denominations and organizations such as the YMCA all built church camps and retreat centers, similar to the Buddhist centers, in or near national forests in the high country throughout the west. As a Christian religious leader at one of these camps once remarked, "It's a little easier to hear God's voice in the breeze in the pines than in the roar of a cross-town bus."

For nearly as long as there have been national parks, there have also been Sunday morning Christian worship services held in them. In the larger, older parks, these usually take place in chapels built for just that purpose with private donations and government permission early in the twentieth century. While the Park Service does not sponsor, plan, or play a direct role in conducting these services, it does coordinate with park-based ministries to accommodate this form of religious expression by national park visitors, as the First Amendment requires. Thus, the spiritual linkage between mainstream Christian denominations and the public open spaces of the rural west has a history dating back nearly to the time when Congress decided that our natural heritage should be preserved.

Within American Judaism, there has been a good deal of activity paralleling the serious reinvestigation of traditional teachings on God and nature in the Christian church—much of it coordinated through the Coalition on Environment and Jewish Life. An interesting turn of

events in this regard has been a revival of and reemphasis on the celebration of Tu B'Shvat, the New Year of the Trees. As explained by the
Coalition: "In recent years, Jewish communities around the world
have begun to celebrate Tu B'Shvat as a 'Jewish Earth Day' — organizing *seders*, tree-plantings, ecological restoration activities, and educational events, all of which provide an opportunity to express a Jewish
commitment to protecting the earth."[14] And as with Christianity's
green reformation, rabbinical scholars have also begun to shift their
emphasis to scriptural teachings that affirm human responsibility
for care of the earth: "The Holy Blessed One took the first human,
and passing before all the trees of the Garden of Eden, said, 'See my
works, how fine and excellent they are! All that I created, I created
for you. Reflect on this, and do not corrupt or desolate my world; for
if you do, there will be no one to repair it after you.'"[15]

Euro-American and Indigenous Religions on Common (Shaky) Legal Ground

The 1988 Supreme Court decision in *Lyng* represented one of the first
instances in which Euro-American religious organizations advocated
support for tribal arguments for free exercise.[16] Both the American
Jewish Congress and the Christian Legal Society filed amicus briefs
on behalf of the northern California tribes, trying to prevent the
construction of a logging access road through the center of their traditional ceremonial/burial grounds. Two years later the American
Jewish Congress and the Council on Religious Freedom supported
an unsuccessful effort before the Supreme Court to defend against
state drug control laws the use of peyote by two American Indians as
a religious sacrament.

But the real reason the Supreme Court's 1990 decision in *Employment Division, Oregon Dept. Of Human Resources v. Smith* thoroughly captured the attention of the American religious establishment
had less to do with its attack on the use of a well-established tribal
sacrament than it did a fundamental weakening in the level of protection the majority in *Smith* was willing to extend to *any* religious
organization or practice.[17] The five-member majority determined that
the state need only show that it had enacted a "valid and neutral law

of general applicability," the impact of which on the free exercise of religion was "incidental." In the majority opinion, Justice Antonin Scalia acknowledged that "leaving [religious] accommodation to the political process will place at a relative disadvantage those religious practices that are not widely engaged in." But he found the potential for such majoritarian discrimination greatly preferable to "courting anarchy" by more searching judicial scrutiny of religious practice restrictions, which in his view would result in a "system in which each conscience is a law unto itself or in which judges weigh the social importance of all laws against the centrality of all religious beliefs." He therefore found the need for judicial restraint and deference to state law sufficiently strong to defeat the free exercise claim.[18]

As a result of a concerted and highly unified lobbying effort by every major interdenominational religious organization in the country, two years later Congress legislatively reversed the Supreme Court's degraded protection for free exercise claims in passing the Religious Freedom Restoration Act (RFRA),[19] which again directed that any governmention burdening the free exercise of religion could be deemed constitutional only if it served a compelling government interest and served this interest by means that are least restrictive of the free exercise right. However, in 1997 the High Court lobbed another volley in this particular congressional–judicial constitutional tennis match, declaring that in legislatively reinstating the strict scrutiny standard of review on free exercise claims, Congress was impermissibly encroaching on the police powers of state and local government and was also creating separation of powers problems by trying to reverse judicial precedent by legislativeion rather than by rearguing the constitutional principles at stake before the Court.[20]

Although RFRA may not have had its ultimate intended effect, its advocacy and its congressional adoption created much closer conceptual and political bonds between First Native and Euro-American religious leaders and organizations than has perhaps ever before existed in American history. The year after Congress passed RFRA, it also amended the American Indian Religious Freedom Act to reinstate the legality of peyote use by American Indians for ceremonial purposes,[21] again referencing RFRA as the appropriate level of constitutional deference that should be accorded this practice.

A review of case law on tribal free exercise claims on nonreservation public lands over the last two decades reveals very little involvement of religious organizations (with the notable and consistent exception of the American Jewish Congress), as either cocounsel or amici. However, this, too, appears to be changing. For example, when commercial rock-climbing guides appealed the trial court's decision in the Devils Tower case to the Tenth Circuit Court of Appeals, the following religious *amici curiae* joined the tribes and the Park Service in defense of the climbing management plan:

- Baptist Joint Committee on Public Affairs
- Becket Fund for Religious Liberty
- Bureau of Catholic Indian Missions
- Dakota Presbytery in the Synod of Lakes and Prairies and the Presbyterian Church (U.S.A.)
- Evangelical Lutheran Church in America
- Friends Committee on National Legislation
- General Assembly, Presbyterian Church (U.S.A.)
- General Conference of Seventh-Day Adventists
- National Jewish Commission on Law and Public Affairs
- Prison Fellowship Ministries
- Union of American Hebrew Congregations
- Union of Orthodox Jewish Congregations of America.

Although the Tenth Circuit panel unanimously rejected the commercial climbers' appeal for lack of standing, in extensive dicta it did make clear its view that the Park Service was acting well within its statutory discretion in thus accommodating tribal religious observances in its climbing management plan for the site.[22] Arguments on behalf of the tribes and the Park Service took the position that sacred sites such as the one in question should be understood as having a spiritual significance similar to that of the Sistine Chapel for Catholics and should be managed with the same respect. Accommodating the tribes' free exercise rights and preserving the physical integrity of the site by seeking to limit human intrusion onto it were seen as one and the same.

In New Mexico, the National Religious Partnership for the Environment allied itself with Pueblo tribes in the upper Rio Grande Valley, trying to prevent construction of a suburban thoroughfare right through the Petroglyph National Monument to an exclusive residential subdivision near Albuquerque.[23] The monument had been established to preserve some of the most remarkable rock art ancient Puebloans had ever produced; and the site thus has tremendous contemporary significance as a contact point with ancestral spirituality for the contemporary Puebloans living nearby.

Lobbying Congress proved unsuccessful in this instance: New Mexico Senator Pete Domenici attached a rider to a supplemental appropriations measure taking land away from the monument and deeding right of way to the city of Albuquerque. He also advised Pueblo Indian leaders to ignore the counsel of their own spiritual advisors, and impliedly threatened them economically as well, since he sits on the Senate Budget Committee that influences spending on programs of benefit to the tribes.[24]

Faith in Action: Religious Organizations and Environmental Advocacy

Most Americans are understandably ambivalent about religious organizations getting too involved in politics and policy-making processes, which is why the Internal Revenue Service has rules about such matters. As described in chapter 3, the themes of religious dissent, sectarian conflict, and the efforts of one denomination to seize the reins of political power to impose its own religious views on others were formative influences in the founding of the colonies that produced the authors of the Declaration of Independence, the Constitution, and the Bill of Rights.

The playing out of sectarian prejudices has occasionally made for some altogether ignoble American history, such as murderous vigilante assaults on eastern Mormon colonies in the nineteenth century and the stoking of anti-Catholic sentiments to prevent Al Smith's nomination as a Democratic presidential candidate in the early twentieth century. By contrast, northern white churches played a crucial leadership role in the pre–Civil War Abolition movement, just as black southern churches orchestrated and spearheaded the mid-twentieth-century Civil Rights movement. And just as the more historically liberal denominations among white congregations also played a significant role in these equal rights struggles, so have some of the more conservative denominations been organized and active on policy issues such as prayer in schools, curriculum content in public education, and human procreation.

The closing decade of the twentieth century saw some unprecedented developments in environmental advocacy by mainstream religious organizations, and these movements continued to gather momentum even as this book was being written. The difference is that this time, the political demarcations between denominations are not nearly as clear-cut. This is very much a broadly interdenominational—and, for the most part, politically multipartisan effort—which is one of the characteristics that makes it a movement worth watching.

One history-making event that stimulated this relatively high level of nonpartisan cooperative faith-based action on behalf of the environment was an entreaty from some of the world's leading scientists to world religious leaders, asking them, first, to recognize human-caused environmental destruction as a profoundly moral and religious issue and, second, to use their influence to encourage more caring attitudes toward the natural environment.[25] In response, in 1993 American religious leaders established the National Religious Partnership for the Environment (NRPE), which is itself an environmental umbrella organization for other organizations, including the U.S. Catholic Conference, the National Council of Churches of Christ, the Coalition on Environment and Jewish Life, and the Evangelical Environmental Network.[26]

Since its formation, both the NRPE and its affiliates have grown more active in political and legal efforts at environmental conservation. Examples include filing lawsuits forcing compliance with the Endangered Species Act, lobbying the White House and Congress on national forest management policy, and—perhaps most interestingly for the purposes of this book—advocating on behalf of the free exercise of Earthen religion by American Indian tribes on the public lands of the United States.[27] Recognizing the growth and power of this movement, in 1997 the leader of one of the nation's highest profile environmental organizations conceded that "the environmental

movement for the past quarter of a century has made no more profound error than to misunderstand the mission of religion and the
churches in preserving the Creation."[28]

By the beginning of the twenty-first century, the rapid growth and
increasing social influence of this interdenominational movement to
take on stewardship of the environment as a religious cause became a
matter of serious concern to resource-extractive industries and their
friends within President George W. Bush's administration. During
the year 2000 a religious "brownlash" group arose in an effort to
rhetorically counter NRPE's growing influence and to provide moral
cover for Bush candidacy (and, later, Bush administration) stands on
aggressive exploitation of natural resources on public lands.

As described in one of the nation's most widely read outdoor
recreation magazines in 2001, this newly formed Interfaith Council
on Environmental Stewardship (ICES) "avows that it is a politically
centrist effort, but its ICES roster reads like a who's who of the religious right.... What's more, ICES's positions tilt unerringly to the
right. Global warming? Overblown, says ICES. Population crisis?
What population crisis? asks ICES. Rampant species loss? Not our
problem."[29]

Thus environmental care as a religious cause has also become the-
ologically more multidimensional. One telling difference, however, is
that the ICES might not actually be a countercoalition or denomina-
tional council at all. For while the NRPE's membership is comprised
of some of the nation's largest mainstream religious denominations,
as of this writing the ICES was not listing an institutional membership
at all, only an advisory committee made up of a few well-known
spokespersons for the politically active religious right (along with a
disavowal that these individuals were representing the views of organizations with which they are affiliated).

As one of the most significant immigrant religious institutions of
the Americas, the Catholic Church has over time played varied and
sometimes frankly conflicting roles in the realm of environmental
advocacy. Two cases in point exemplify this ambivalence. One concerns its ongoing half-millennium-old effort to integrate its teachings with those of the indigenous cultures of the Americas. In the late
twentieth century, one form this took in areas such as the state of

Chiapas in southern Mexico was that of "Indian theology." What this represents is a conjoining of some traditional Catholic doctrines with Mayan teachings on the sanctity of nature. According to Mayan theologian Petul Cut Chab: "In Mayan thought, the land is never seen as merchandise that can be exploited. It is capitalism that makes land an object to be sold, destroyed, poisoned. Socialism, meanwhile, maintains that land, instead of humans, must be exploited.... In the vision of the Indians, land must be respected: it is our mother. We Indians care for the land because we live in communion with her. If land is sold or damaged, we are hurting one of our family. It is like selling off God; it is that which gives us life."[30]

A leading church proponent and architect of this integrated Indian theology for the last third of the twentieth century was Samuel Ruiz García, whom Pope John XXIII named bishop of the diocese of San Cristóbal de las Casas in the state of Chiapas in 1959. In helping bring this new form of culturally integrated theology into being, Bishop Ruiz's efforts closely paralleled and in many ways informed teachings on Christianity and the environment expressed by the National Conference of Catholic Bishops/U.S. Catholic Conference. In its 1991 missive *Renewing the Earth,* the Bishops' Conference stated: "We seek to explore the links between concern for the person and the earth, between natural ecology and social ecology. The web of life is one. Our mistreatment of the natural world diminishes our own dignity and sacredness, not only because we are destroying resources that future generations of humans need, but because we are engaging in actions that contradict what it means to be human. Our tradition calls us to protect the life and dignity of the human person, and it is increasingly clear that this task cannot be separated from the care and defense of all of creation."[31]

In Bishop Ruiz's case, such doctrinal integration had implications that went far beyond scholarly discourse on matters of theological innovation: "Teachings of catechists in Chiapas include things like a tiny, white booklet that analyzes the changes made in Article 27 of the Mexican Constitution as part of preparations for the signing of the North American Free Trade Agreement.... In very simple terms, it aims to help the Indians understand complicated legislative maneuvers that erased their legal rights to communal lands that belonged originally to the Mayans. It tells them these changes were made to appease private foreign companies that, through free trade, want to invest in the Mexican countryside. In this sense, the church helped the indigenous communities to understand that free trade meant a threat to their land, which in Mayan theology is a threat to God and to life itself."[32]

The bishop's advocacy for both the land rights of his indigenous parishioners and their Catholicized Earthen theology came at a heavy price. Both he and his protégé (and presumptive institutional heir), Bishop Raul Vera López, were detained and had their lives threatened by the same right-wing paramilitary groups that had been periodically attacking Mayan settlements in the area. And at least partly in response to intensive lobbying by the Mexican government, the Vatican declined to appoint Vera bishop of Chiapas upon Ruiz's retirement at the end of 1999. In the words of Mexico's highest-ranking cleric, Cardinal Norberto Rivera, the Vatican had decided to appoint someone "who attends everyone and not just the Indians."[33] Pope John Paul had earlier on made no secret of his views on the subject; in January of 1999 he told reporters during a trip to Mexico that "the 'Indian theology' promoted by some Mexican Catholic leaders— particularly in the troubled region of Chiapas—is also a matter of concern, because it involves 'another version of Marxism.'"[34]

The Vatican has also demonstrated no sympathy for indigenous peoples trying to protect their place-based cultures elsewhere in the Americas. When the San Carlos Apaches and some environmental organizations objected to the construction of a large telescope complex on Mt. Graham in southeastern Arizona, the director of the Vatican observatory (which was a coinvestor in use rights at the proposed facility) wrote: "We are not convinced . . . that Mt. Graham possesses a sacred character which precludes responsible and legitimate use of the land. . . . We believe that responsible and legitimate use of the land enhances its sacred character. Land is a gift of God to be used with reason and to be respected."[35]

This Vatican scientist's opinion—that he is in a better position to tell the world what God wants done with Mt. Graham than are the indigenous peoples whose deities are thought to inhabit the place— raises some interesting if unsettling questions regarding the future management of public lands in the United States for spiritual and religious purposes. As with the treatment of wild animals, what is a manager of public lands to do when different religious groups want to use the same site for different purposes?

In this case, the Vatican and the San Carlos Apaches made diametrically conflicting spiritual claims on the same piece of real estate. To achieve its ends, the Vatican had no problem declaring that God had no problem with building the world's largest telescope atop Mt. Graham (it would, in fact, enhance its "sacred character"), while the Apaches were equally insistent that the planned construction would desecrate one of their holiest sites and would make impossible the perpetuation of some of their religious practices by driving away a divine presence they believed inhabited that place. Similar if less strident management dilemmas are beginning to crop up at other sacred sites on public lands in the west and will probably continue to do so.

As this book goes to press, Catholic bishops in the Pacific Northwest are circulating a rough draft of a pastoral letter entitled "The Columbia River Watershed: Realities and Possibilities."[36] Echoing Gabriel Moraga's sentiments some two hundred years ago, the document declares the entire Columbia River watershed to be a "sacramental commons." In setting forth the rationale for issuance of this teaching, the bishops observe that "there are problems and injustices in the watershed. Salmon, the indicator species of the life community, are becoming extinct, endangered or threatened. Greed, ignorance, irresponsibility and abuse of economic and political power cause problems and injustices."[37]

The letter's words are carefully chosen, and use of the term "sacrament" is not to be taken lightly. Prof. John Hart, a Catholic scholar who contributed to its preparation, described it thus:

> A sacrament in the Catholic definition is something that allows humans to connect with the divine. It is "a visible sign of an inward grace" according to one dictionary. Hart calls it "a moment of encounter with God." ...
>
> "To say the river is a sacramental commons means people can experience the Creator in creation, outside the formal church settings," he

continues. It's also an important departure for the church, because it implies that a sacrament does not need to be mediated by a priest. It moves the church closer to the beliefs Native Americans in the West practiced until the Europeans—with the help of the Catholic Church—outlawed them.[38]

As reflected in this passage and as suggested at the beginning of this book, it does indeed appear that Western religious institutions are beginning to come full circle, aligning to an ever greater extent with the proenvironment teachings in their own sacred texts, with the pre-Christian Earthen traditions of Europe, and with the indigenous ones of North America.

The Coming out of the Wiccans

In retrospect, the resurgence of interest in pre-Christian European Earthen religious traditions will probably come to be seen as one of the more significant developments in the modern religious history of the United States. Although beginning in England early in the twentieth century, in the United States it coincided roughly with the parallel interest in the rediscovery of spiritual connections with nature arising within mainstream Christian and Jewish congregations and with the importation of Eastern traditions such as Buddhism and Taoism in the late 1960s and 1970s. Without going into detail concerning the multifarious variations on a theme that different Wiccan groups around the United States exemplify, suffice it to say that at its core it represents a concerted effort to revive both the teachings and the rituals thought to embody the Earthen religions pre-dating Christianity in western Europe. As its "creation myth" is described in Margot Adler's comprehensive work on Earthen spirituality in contemporary American society: "Witchcraft is a religion that dates back to paleolithic times, to the worship of the god of the hunt and the goddess of fertility. One can see remnants of it in cave paintings and in the figurines of goddesses that are many thousands of years old. The early religion was universal. The names changed from place to place but the basic deities were the same."[39]

For reasons having to do largely with the pejorative connotation the words "witch" and "witchcraft" have acquired over the Christian history of Western civilization, adherents to this particular Earthen tradition generally prefer use of the term *wicca*, from a root word in Old English that conjoins "religion" and "magic"; another interpretation of the root meaning is to bend or turn, as to bend reality.[40]

This quest for historically rooted teachings and rituals for reconnecting Euro-Americans with their own pre-Christian heritage, as well as with nature itself, eventually led to the creation of religious organizations based on these teachings. But as filings for church status with the Internal Revenue Service began to grow in the early 1980s, the movement stimulated a conservative backlash within the Congress. In 1986, North Carolina senator Jesse Helms and Pennsylvania representative Robert Walker introduced amendments to Treasury Department funding legislation that would have categorically denied the tax-exempt status available to other religious organizations to any applicant group that was "substantially interested in the promotion of witchcraft."[41]

In response to a congressional inquiry on the matter, then–Treasury secretary James Baker informed Senator Helms: "Several organizations have been recognized as tax-exempt that espouse a system of beliefs, rituals, and practices derived in part from pre-Christian Celtic and Welsh traditions, which they label as 'witchcraft.' We have no evidence that any of the organizations have either engaged in or promoted any illegal activity."[42] This amendment, which appeared on its face to be wholly unconstitutional, actually passed the Senate, but was eliminated in a House–Senate conference committee working on compromise legislation. Whenever the issue has come before them, the federal courts have regularly determined Wicca to be a religion and its adherents due the same free exercise rights as those of more mainstream, populous religious denominations.[43]

In its earlier developmental stages, Wiccan ritual observances happened mostly on a relatively small scale and often indoors. As the movement grew and various groups had more and more interaction with each other, however, the size and scope of their gatherings began to grow also. And as this happened, they also began to move out of doors, usually gathering in large encampments in natural settings on May Day or around the time of the summer solstice.[44] On private lands, in city and state parks, and in federally managed public lands around the country, open spaces are increasingly becoming places of worship for these rediscoverers (or reinventors, depending on one's point of view) of Europe's pre-Christian, Earth-based spiritual heritage.

Ceremonies may include a processional, forming into a circle, chanting, drumming, singing, and the invocation of various Earth-based deities. Certain ritual objects may also be handled as a way of maintaining a focus on the symbolic significance of the ceremony. All this is by way of establishing conditions making it possible to induce contemplative states of consciousness insofar as how participants relate to each other and their environment. As one acknowledged authority (and sometimes participant/observer in outdoor Wiccan rituals) has put it: "[Ritual] allows us to feel biological connectedness with ancestors who regulated their lives and activities according to seasonal observances. Just as ecological theory explains how we are interrelated with all other forms of life, rituals allow us to re-create that unity in an explosive, non-abstract, gut-level way. Rituals have the power to reset the terms of our universe until we find ourselves suddenly and truly 'at home.'"[45] Coming home; returning to the source. For all the Earthen spiritual perspectives reviewed up to this point, this is the nexus—whether it be the Asian tradition in which it has always been a core value or the rediscovery of those aspects of Western traditions.

Of course, it is seldom the benign, Earth-loving celebrants in these ceremonies—who seem to constitute the vast majority of those acknowledging participation in the Wiccan revival—who draw most of the news media's attention. Instead, it tends to be that small minority professing adherence to forms of Satanism that preach moral justification for harming or even killing other persons considered a threat, and those who have overlaid the rediscovery of ethnic European roots with a thick layer of white supremacy ideology and, occasionally, overtly racist rhetoric. As mediagenic as these derivatives might be, they bear little resemblance in either their teachings or their practices to the mainstream Wiccan revival discussed in most credible contemporary literature on the subject or in the mission statements of the vast majority of Wiccan organizations.

It is also because of their potential for social disruption that prison authorities have been most skeptical of either Satanist or white supremacy Wiccan-related assertions of religious practice rights by inmates. While acknowledging both of these variations on a cultural theme as colorably religious in nature, prison administrators have sharply curtailed practice opportunities and possession of ritual objects among these groups, and the courts have regularly upheld their exercise of that discretion.

Ancient Settings in a New Age

Of all the Earth-based spiritual movements spiraling upward in America as the second millennium was winding down, none has proved more culturally agitating or has provoked more ire, irritation, and ridicule than an amorphous and incompletely defined array of beliefs and practices collectively referred to as "New Age" spirituality. One Euro-American anthropologist who has written extensively on the Hopi has gone so far as to label New Agers as "spiritual imperialists" for, in his view, appropriating the bits and pieces of indigenous cultures that suit their philosophical needs and weaving them into something altogether different and inauthentic.[46]

Not all writers and scholars are so unforgiving or so quickly dismissive of what the arising of the New Age phenomenon might mean. In *The Aquarian Conspiracy*, the first and perhaps still best-known effort to provide a coherent explanation of what the New Age movement is all about, Marilyn Ferguson writes:

> For the first time in history, humankind has come upon the control of change—an understanding of how transformation occurs. We are living in the change of change, the time in which we can intentionally align ourselves with nature for rapid remaking of ourselves and our collapsing institutions.
>
> The paradigm of the Aquarian Conspiracy sees humankind embedded in nature. It promotes the autonomous individual in a decentralized society. It sees us as stewards of all our resources, inner and outer. It says

that we are not victims, not pawns, not limited by conditions or conditioning. Heirs to evolutionary niches, we are capable of imagination, invention, and experiences we have only glimpsed.[47]

In differentiating the New Age movement from social and religious reforms efforts of bygone times, one student of this social phenomenon observes the following: "New Agers are neither nostalgic nor despairing. Quite the contrary, they are bullish millennialists. They welcome the death of the old as the necessary, if painful, prelude to a major cultural realignment. They see themselves as bearers of a paradigm shift in medicine, psychology, science, politics, business, and education—and thus as the messianic vanguard of a cultural reawakening that will lead, not just to a mending of society, but to its remaking. Something big and new is about to be born, they claim, out of our social crisis."[48] In some of their outward forms of ritual worship, such as chanting, drumming, invocation of various spirits, and other efforts to stimulate affective connections with each other and with the environment, they may appear to be not all that different from the Wiccans, as described above (and as described to me by park rangers around the Southwest who have been witness to some of their rituals, who don't commonly differentiate between the two groups). However, to lump them together on the basis of outward appearance would be misleading.

The ways they tend to use public open spaces may be similar, as may be the hoped-for effects of these rituals (contemplative connection with sacred sites and natural environments). There may be some discernible differences in motivation and in the underlying philosophies that give rise to those motivations, however. At the risk of oversimplification, it appears that the Wiccan revival is focused on contemplative linkage with nature and the spirits it is thought to embody principally by reference to the *past:* to the pre-Christian teachings and rituals of ancient Europe that constituted indigenous religion before the invasion of Roman Christians. By contrast, although contemplative connection to natural (including cosmic) forces is very much a part of New Age belief and ritual practice, its temporal orientation is much more toward the *future*—toward what the world and human consciousness are about to become by virtue of deliberate self-transformation. Additionally, for some New Age aficionados, there is a considerable amount of emphasis on the calling down of or connection with spirit beings from other galaxies and other time dimensions—a science fiction aspect that is lacking in the Wiccan revival. In some ways, this intergalactic spin is the New Age movement's counterpart to the Satanism and white supremacy sub-cults that are linked to Wicca, becoming the penumbral features that draw most of the media attention and, in the process, significantly distort the overall image of the movement.

In its frank incorporation of some First Native teachings, rituals, and practices into their own spiritual amalgam, the New Age move-ment also tends to be a little more place-based than Wicca, with more emphasis on doing certain rituals at specific sites—often ones already recognized as having spiritual import by First Native culture groups. For that reason, at least during the 1990s, New Age rituals conducted at sacred sites on public lands have occasionally engendered more conflict with American Indian tribes than have encounters with some other spiritual groups.

Some First Native groups and individuals view New Age ritualists at sacred sites as spiritual and cultural claim-jumpers. Conversely, some New Agers in these conflicts have pointed out that simply because their beliefs and rituals are unorthodox and syncretic, they should not be disqualified from having their First Amendment rights honored also.

Cultural Appropriation, "Playing Indian," and the Politics of Sacred Site Management

The kinds of reactions New Agers have provoked in other Euro-Americans, First Natives, and managers of public lands who were interviewed during the course of this research made it obvious that this topic was worth further investigation. For as "weird," "far-out," and "just plain goofy" as this movement has been portrayed by those who for whatever reason do not approve of it (including quite a few people in federal service), in some ways it is a quintessentially Ameri-can religious reform movement, with clearly recognizable anteced-ents in the spiritual history of the United States. Commenting on the phrase quoted above from the *Aquarian Conspiracy*, one religion scholar has advised:

> You will not be far off if you detect more than a whiff of Ralph Waldo Emerson here, updated with a dose of Teilhard de Chardin—and mixed with Mary Baker Eddy's mental healing and Norman Vincent Peale's "power of positive thinking." For good measure, salt with a bit of Joachim of Fiore's New Age of the Spirit as well. Ironically, New Agers may be throwbacks, the only Americans left who wholeheartedly sub-scribe to the nation's mission to create a . . . new world order. Crystal gazers and psychic channelers are the lunatic fringe, the easy targets. One may want to rain on the New Age parade, sober it up with some St. Augustine and Karl Barth—or with Hawthorne and Melville—but one cannot dismiss this crowd without thereby denying something in the human soul that demands historical movement, a new world.[49]

One of the reasons New Age presence at sacred sites has created some friction with First Native tribal governments and tribal members is that the New Age movement is frankly inventive. It readily admits to synthesizing a creative and original new spiritual vision out of what observants consider to be Earth-based sources of wisdom from other culture groups—especially indigenous ones. But while Aquarian ritual makers may consider it a gesture of respect to First Native peoples to incorporate their teachings into "spirituality for a new age," most indigenous peoples do not seem to appreciate the gesture very much. Lakota elder and Catholic catechist Black Elk's granddaughter Charlotte, who has led summer solstice Sun Dances at Bear's Lodge/Devils Tower, comments:

> As for New Agers, you have people who are on a genuine search for ful-fillment, but they don't want to take the time to learn their own tra-ditions, or they're totally fascinated with Native American religion. They're seeking power now, like the weight loss pills. . . .
>
> One of the dividing lines has been when I tell the New Age practi-tioners, "Go prepare for seven years." Most of them want a hodgepodge of things without embracing the total culture. Those people treat Native American ceremonies like they would a diving vacation to the Bahamas.

In reality, if you participate in these ceremonies, you have to give up a lot of things. You have to be accessible to the community, maybe even take foster kids in. Things like that. . . . In white America, they're able to buy their place in society. They can't understand why they can't buy a place in a Native American community. Indians judge you by your actions.[50]

Here Charlotte Black Elk is referring to a tendency toward cultural appropriation—the process whereby "primal religions are being adopted or recommended by those who historically belong to quite another tradition."[51] Another way this phenomenon has been described is as "playing Indian" —the adult version.[52] The awkward and painful communication problem here is that while New Age adherents may sincerely believe they are honoring indigenous traditions by incorporating their symbols and transcribed rhetoric into their rituals, some tribal spiritual and political leaders view such gestures as cultural hijacking—using these images in ways not intended or approved by their originators.

This is a distinction regarded with some care by the more institutionally organized Wiccans, especially among acknowledged leaders with some schooling and experience in the ritual expression of spiritual experience. In a conversation with an ordained Unitarian Universalist minister who hosts a Covenant of Unitarian Universalist Pagans at her church, she emphasized that Wicca in general is more focused on rediscovering and reviving the pre-Christian indigenous Earthen religious traditions of Europe rather than trying to explicitly incorporate American Indian symbols and rhetoric for just this reason: the Wiccans don't have permission, and they don't want to create the illusion that they are owning and transmitting a tradition not their own.

To complicate matters further, some American Indian tribal members have begun to offer ritual experiences such as Sun Dances and sweat lodge ceremonies to non-Indians, which many Euro-American participants find deeply moving and from which some also draw what they feel to be a sense of empowerment if not entitlement to share these experiences. The motives of First Natives who choose to share their traditions with non-Indians seem to vary widely. Author and Comanche tribal member, Paul Smith summarizes the situation:

Definitions of traditional Indian spirituality are many. Take sweat lodges. I know lots of Indians and right-thinking white people who believe it is terribly wrong for non-Indians to take part in sweat lodges, and have contempt for the New Agers who do so. It is true there are lots of fakes and sellouts who open ceremonies to whites for money, but there are also many Indians who genuinely believe the sweat lodge is for everyone. Others invite only members of their tribe....

What uniformity exists rarely resembles the popular image of the Traditionals vs. the Sellouts. It is rather a far more nuanced tapestry of traditional leaders deeply influenced by Christianity, as well as by Christians who attend sweat lodges, and lots of Indians who don't take part in any organized religion.[53]

What this raises is a question as old as the history of human religion itself: "Who is legitimately authorized to transmit what teachings to whom?" And the companion question: "Who authorizes the legitimators?" Puebloan tribes in particular tend to be highly secretive about their spiritual traditions, in part because of the unauthorized loss of secret knowledge they suffered at the hands of anthropologists in the early twentieth century and partly because of the cultural appropriation problems they are suffering now. And yet, other leaders (those from various tribes who have chosen to share at least some of their teachings) are so alarmed at the environmentally destructive behavior of Euro-American society, they want to offer whatever spiritual guidance they can to help the dominant culture learn from the past and reform its dangerous, short-sighted, and ecologically and culturally harmful ways.

Moreover, as Smith observes, "the management of sacred sites is also complicated by the fact that non-Indians also revere these sites."[54] All this creates quite a dilemma for managers of public lands who are entrusted with the care of sacred sites. New Agers are not devoid of First Amendment rights simply because First Natives don't approve of their cut-and-paste theology or because the press and some federal land managers find them easy to ridicule. If they choose to regard a natural formation or ancestral Puebloan structure on public land as sacred to their belief system, under our constitutional form of government, who is to tell them that they may not?

Certainly not park and forest rangers. In First Amendment cases on these matters, the courts have no sympathy for administrators who take it upon themselves to independently decide what does and does not constitute a legitimate religion or religious practice in public spaces. But the courts have been willing to uphold public land manager authority to govern public behavior in ways that strike a reasonable balance between their need to accomplish their agency's mission and the ability of First Natives and Euro-Americans to exercise their respective religious freedoms.

Most of the case law on this point derives from repeated constitutional challenges to Forest Service efforts at regulating the behavior of a group known as the Rainbow Family. During the 1980s and 1990s, ten thousand to twenty thousand members of this self-described (mostly) Euro-American "tribe" would suddenly materialize at a national forest campground for several days of encampment, socializing, and Earth-oriented ritual—all without benefit of a group camping permit. After repeated First Amendment challenges (based mostly on the grounds of free association rather than free exercise of religion) to Forest Service authority, the federal appellate courts eventually ruled that authority over group activity needed to be grounded in one of three rationales: "the need to address concerns of public health and safety, to minimize damage to National Forest System resources, and to allocate space among actual or potential uses and activities."[55]

In implementing criteria such as these (in addition to those mandated by various single-use statutes and the First Amendment itself), park and forest rangers and their supervisors must continuously make judgment calls. One poignant case I learned of concerned an Earthen-based group of Euro-Americans (most of whom worked in the entertainment industry in southern California) who make an annual pilgrimage to an ancestral Puebloan site in the Southwest that has within it the remains of several kivas (round, subterranean ceremonial enclosures built and used by both ancient and contemporary Puebloans). During a drumming and chanting ceremony in one of the large open kivas (originally they were roofed, but most archeological remains now consist only of walls) the group leader fell strangely immobile. At first thinking him to be in a trance, group members soon discovered that he was actually dead. Emergency medical efforts to revive him proved unsuccessful, and the local medical examiner concluded he had suffered a fatal heart attack.

A few weeks later, archeological restoration workers found a pile of ashes at the spot where the person had died. Rangers suspected what they were, and checking with a local mortuary confirmed that a friend had picked up the deceased's ashes a day earlier. Navajo workers at the site abandoned the premises immediately and refused to return until the place had been properly purified, since their religious beliefs have very strict teachings concerning the avoidance of places of death and the physical remains of the dead. Nearby Puebloan tribes having a direct cultural affiliation with this place were incensed to learn that the site had been desecrated and dishonored in this way.

So what seemed a fitting ceremonial gesture honoring completion of a friend's life cycle by a member of a marginal Euro-American spiritual group proved to be an extraordinary act of desecration and insult to two different American Indian cultures. As a result of this and similar incidents, the superintendent of this facility eventually decided that in the interests of preserving the physical resource as well as intercultural peace, no one would be allowed to enter that particular kiva in the future except archeological restoration workers.

Knowing the Place

The place is a federal reserve in the southwestern United States managed by the National Park Service. Early on a clear winter morning at opening time, as the first and so far the only visitor, I am hiking into a canyon, headed for a remote site open to the public that workers here told me was well worth the visit.

Walking through this place of natural beauty and multicultural human history, the issues and viewpoints described in this chapter are very much on my mind. Who owns history? Whose place is this, anyway? Can this site be fairly regarded as an intercultural spiritual commons, as well as an open national history book? Or does it intrude on and insult indigenous cultures for Euro-Americans of any spiritual orientation to also regard these places as sacred and treat them accordingly?

About a mile into the canyon I begin a 140-foot climb up a near-vertical sandstone cliff face, with the aid of niches carved into the rock face a millennium ago and strategically placed ladders made of tree trunks and branches—a partial re-creation of the old way. Like Samuel Johnson's remark about the knowledge one is to be hanged the next day, the ascent (with no hand rails and no soft landing spots) has a way of "wondrously focusing the mind." No past, no future, just hand over hand and foot over foot up the cliff face to a large, shallow, south-facing cave. It turns out to be good mental preparation for approaching what lies at the end of the climb. Up in this remote spot is a large shallow cave, with a small kiva in its earth and sandstone floor.

In the southwestern states comprising the Four Corners area, the federal government has established more than two dozen national parks and monuments to preserve pre-Columbian structural remains and rock art[56] and to provide opportunities for all the peoples of the United States, as well as large numbers of international travelers, to visit and learn from these places. Most of these parks and monuments were founded by either acts of Congress or presidential proclamation in the late nineteenth and early twentieth centuries, after indigenous peoples had been removed to reservations and at a time when these recently acquired federal lands were open to Euro-American homesteading, farming and ranching, mining, and logging.

As these sites were "discovered" by Euro-Americans in the nineteenth century, many of these places suffered vandalism to their structural remains and rock art and the pillaging of their artifacts. Park and monument designation was probably all that kept them from being destroyed entirely. In managing these sites over the course of the twentieth century, the National Park Service sought a continuously adjusted balance point between the *preservation* of these treasured places and the *provision* for their use and appreciation by the visiting public.

In most instances, the Park Service has done what it can to keep these sites from further deterioration (by reason of both natural elements and human presence), but has done relatively little in the way of extensive restoration, since a rebuilt structure would be as much an example of modern restorative building technique as of ancient culture. But of the many kivas to be found at the federal reserve I was visiting, the Park Service had decided to fully restore the one in this cave, using the same visible materials as the ancients who had created it. About twenty feet in diameter, it had a solid clay and timber roof. On the south side of the circle nearest the cliff's edge was a square opening in the roof, with a tree-trunk ladder leading down into the subterranean room.

Climbing down in, the interior of the kiva was empty, cold, and dark—the only light coming through the ladder hole in the ceiling. It was also very silent. After deliberating a moment, I sat down with my back against the north wall. Although I was quite alone in the cold and dark, instead of fear I had a distinct sense of being held, contained, and sheltered. Closing my eyes, I began to do a meditation in the Buddhist tradition that has been my sole spiritual path for the last quarter-century. Although staying awake and alert, the level of stillness and concentration became progressively deeper as the mind gradually ceased to construct the self, the final realization being that there was "no one" to "become one" with that place.

After what turned out to be quite a long time, I heard the approach of other hikers climbing up the cliff face ladders. Not wanting to frighten them or have them disturb me, I stood up and began to climb out of the kiva. The sensation was like feeling a gravitational pull in two directions. I knew it was time to go up and out into the sunlit world above, yet this round subterranean container was a difficult place to leave. It had been a place of refuge *in* and *of* the Earth, and in climbing out into the sunlight—in seeing with dazzling clarity the trees, rocks, and stream in the canyon below and the birds flying above—there was an unmistakable feeling of having been born anew into the world.

Since my childhood days growing up in Arizona I had known that some traditional Pueblo peoples regard the kiva as a womb in the earth, and in anthropology and religion classes later on I had been taught that emergence from it especially for ceremonial dances constituted transformation or rebirth into the mindset of the personage or spirit being danced. But this was the first time I felt I actually, experientially, *knew* what it meant to be in and of the Earth and to emerge from it.

Back on the canyon floor on the return path to park headquarters, still seeing the world as fresh and new, the sense of contemplative connection to place was still strong, but calculative thoughts reflecting on the nature of this experience also began to come up. Had I been "playing Indian," I wondered. Had I or my culture group—which now controlled the use of this place—taken something that was not rightfully mine or ours and that was not meant to be shared? Was there something intrinsically disrespectful or inappropriate about doing a contemplative practice from one spiritual tradition in a sacred space created long ago for other purposes by members of another tradition?

I do not know how you might answer these questions. I suppose for all of us it depends on our respective ethnic lineage and heritage, on our sense of what is right or just, and our understanding of what constitutes the sacred and how it should be regarded. On the question of taking what was not given, in my view there is little or no justice to be found in how explorers and immigrants from Great Britain, France, and Spain first conquered the indigenous peoples of the Americas and then evicted them from most of their homelands. In agreement with de Tocqueville, I believe the two greatest self-inflicted social traumas in the history of the United States are the enslavement of African peoples and the attempted extermination of indigenous peoples.

And as with posttraumatic stress disorder on a personal scale, the path to healing beyond these social traumas lies not in trying to forget they ever occurred but in coming into full realization of just what happened, why it happened, and how to live in the present in a way that will keep it from happening again. If the federal government had allowed all evidence of pre-Columbian life in the United States to be erased by vandals and treasure hunters in the late nineteenth century, denial of our collective past and some of its terrible injustices would have been easier. In physically preserving these sites for the use and appreciation of all the peoples of the United States, as well as visitors from abroad, agencies such as the National Park Service and the U.S. Forest Service are also maintaining a national intercultural commons within which our collective history is held, and therefore at which our collective intercultural destiny will continue to be mediated.

On reflection, I do not think the Park Service did wrong in reconstructing the kiva I visited and making it available for public visitation; nor do I think I did wrong in treating it as sacred space, even if expressed within the context of another tradition. In material terms, I sought to treat this constructed space and its natural surroundings with respect; I neither took nor left anything, and I altered it only in terms of the subtle effect of my coming and going. I also made an effort to come to the place with a clear enough mind to learn what the space had to teach.

Whether Christian or not, anyone standing inside a large stained-glass cathedral on a sunny day cannot help but get some sense of what its designers thought the Bible means when it speaks of Heaven. Sacred architecture teaches through form—through the experience one has within its constructed space. This is just as true of the ancient Puebloans who built that kiva. Whatever the specifics of their tradition when they created it a thousand years ago, they continue to teach through their creation today. For others, it might hold a different lesson. But for me, these ancient architects continue to teach what it means to be literally in and of the Earth and to emerge from it while remaining connected to it. It gives experiential meaning to the stated belief of indigenous peoples throughout the world that the Earth is the mother of us all.

Benito Juarez, a Mexican Indian who rose to become first a supreme court justice and then president of his country in the nineteenth century, once observed that "peace is respect for the rights of others." If sacred sites on public lands throughout the United States are to be places of intercultural peace rather than continuous conflict, perhaps the teaching of this multicultural leader is a good place to begin.

12

The National Commons as Sacred Space

Making Peace in the Field and Defending It in Court

A promise is a promise. In chapter 1 I issued an invitation to come on a journey of exploration into how culture, spirituality, and law combine to influence management of public lands and resources in the western United States. I also promised that, based on what was discovered, there would be some reflections and recommendations on how we might think about and work through these issues in the future. This is what appears in this chapter, beginning with a review of where we have been and ending with some thoughts on where we might be headed.

How We Are Alike and How We Are Not

On questions of intercultural difference, the news media seem to like nothing better than a good fight. In part for this reason, intercultural differences over public land and resource management that might have been peaceably and consensually resolved all to often get recharacterized and reframed in ways that make consensual outcomes more difficult, if not impossible, to achieve.

This is one reason that it seemed important to focus on the often-overlooked similarities between Euro-American and indigenous cultures in this study of spirituality and the public lands. For those similarities do indeed exist. The animistic, Earthern spiritual heritage pre-dating the Christianization of Europe is well documented in the archeological literature, and Europe's Earthen religious legacy has far more in common with the nature-based spiritual practices of the indigenous peoples of the Americas than it does with the Christianity that was to displace it.

Christian and Jewish theologians are now studying with renewed interest their received traditions to determine whether there is something inherently antienvironmental in the core teachings of their faiths or if, instead, they have simply been interpreted during periods of aggressive nation-building to condone a pillaging of the Earth, the basis for which in scripture is far outweighed by teachings of nature's sanctity. So far, the weight of scholarship and modern church doctrine seem to be settling ever more solidly on the latter interpretation. And this, in turn, is one reason that, more and more, mainstream Euro-American religious organizations are coming to the defense of American Indian tribes when the rights to free exercise of their place-based, nature-based religions are under attack.

Similar teachings, of unity with nature and the importance of treating all life with the same respect as we accord ourselves and each other, are central to the spiritual traditions of East Asia, such as Taoism and Buddhism. And even the New Age religious experimentation that has become an established fixture in the modern religious history of the West shares this same nature-based trait.

The one feature all these diverse ways of expressing human spirituality share is recognition of the sanctity of all life, accompanied by the related recognition that to harm the life-sustaining capacity of the Earth is ultimately to harm ourselves. This is central to the spiritual teachings of every indigenous culture group featured in this writing, and it is becoming an increasingly important doctrinal feature of mainstream Western religions as well.

Why is this happening? Why do these world religious traditions seem to be gravitating more and more toward teachings that have been at the center of indigenous spirituality from time immemorial? One possible answer may lie in evolutionary biology. Harvard professor, evolutionary field zoologist, and philosopher of science E. O. Wilson understands this propensity to recognize a spiritual affinity with other life forms and with nature as a whole to be an innate species survival mechanism. He theorizes: "We are inextricably part of nature, but human uniqueness is not negated thereby. 'Nothing but' an animal is as fallacious a statement as 'created in God's own image.' . . . To explore and affiliate with life is a deep and complicated process in mental development. Our existence depends on this propensity, our spirit is woven from it, hope rises on its currents."[1]

If Wilson is correct—and the ethnographic knowledge presented here strongly suggests that he is—our best strategy as a country of many different cultural lineages and beliefs is to do whatever we can to support and encourage this "exploration of and affiliation with" life in the way we manage our collectively held public lands and resources. But this is also where the differences begin to arise, since each culture has its own teachings about what it means to honor the life principle. Revering life and staying intimately connected with it does not take the same form among the Hopi or the Makah as it does among vegetarian Buddhists or members of the Humane Society.

Implications for Public Land and Resource Management

And so the basis for building consensus on the management of public lands and resources in ways that take diverse spiritual values and practices into account begins with developing a nucleus of first understanding where the similarities lie and then working outward toward accommodating difference. That is just the process used at Devils Tower National Monument and is similar to the one used at the Big Horn Medicine Wheel. In developing the final climbing management plan for Bear's Lodge/Devils Tower, indigenous and Euro-American stakeholder groups spent eighteen months educating each other on the relationship each has with this sacred site, and it was on this shared understanding that a basis for agreement grew.

At national parks, monuments, and forests throughout the western United States (including Hawaii), what I learned is that best practices in terms of reasonable accommodation of religious diversity in sacred site management involve key management staff maintaining an ongoing consultative relationship with the indigenous peoples having the closest cultural (and therefore) spiritual affiliation with the lands and resources entrusted to his or her agency's care. If the only time there is contact is when there is conflict, such circumstances make it difficult to develop the kind of mutual trust and respect that are necessary for genuinely accommodative planning and management to occur. In short, it may be time for a serious reconsideration of how land and resource management agencies at the federal level interact with all constituent groups wanting to use those resources for spiritual purposes.

Three factors contribute to the need for this reconsideration. First, existing legislation and agency regulations focus primarily on properties of "historic" value. This generally translates into policies that protect important archeological sites or historic structures. But often, lands that are considered religiously important to American Indians may not contain such "fabric"—no archaeological remains or historic architecture. In fact, places of religious importance to Indian peoples may be an entire mountain or a valley—landscapes that exhibit no obvious remnant of human activity as viewed by non-Indian observers. While there are provisions for considering these places for protection as "Traditional Cultural Properties" under the National Historic Preservation Act (NHPA),[2] and its recent amendments, the criteria used to classify these properties are largely if not entirely derived from the NHPA itself, and not necessarily from the perspective of the communities that define these places as important. An atonement-era executive order directs federal agencies to protect Indian sacred sites to the extent possible under existing law,[3] but leaves to each agency the task of designing procedures to ensure this protection. However, existing federal law does not directly address these kinds of cultural properties, and as yet unresolved First Amendment issues such as those implicated in the Devils Tower case continue to cast a shadow of legal uncertainty over multicultural consultations. Without clear provisions in law, agencies are left to craft creative solutions from legislation that may not be directly applicable.

Second, the internal procedures used by agencies to make planning and resource use decisions do not normally take into consideration the special relationship the agencies have with federally recognized Indian tribes. Too often, Indian tribes are viewed as just another set of special interest groups, when, in fact, their unique relationship with the federal government under the trust responsibility doctrine (and in some cases as a result of specific treaty language) gives them a legal status apart from the general public. To date, this special status has not translated into a set of consistent agency procedures (outside of the Bureau of Indian Affairs) that recognizes this legal relationship and affords consideration of tribal requests for sacred site protection on non-Indian federal lands.

Third, quite apart from any special legal relationship agencies may have with tribal peoples, the Devils Tower and the Bighorn Medicine Wheel cases point to the need for agencies to consider how resources are managed and how decisions are reached in a climate of cultural pluralism. To what extent should (or can) agencies be "blind" to the ethnic or heritage differences of their constituent publics? Aside from American Indian tribes, other ethnic groups in the United States do not enjoy any unique set of the rights or privileges that are not shared by the general population. Alternatively, agency planners and decision makers who are not knowledgeable and sensitive to the cultural differences of groups may be unable to avoid conflict that results from the clash of differing cultural values. While agencies should act in accordance with law and design procedures that are judged to be fair, the Devils Tower and Medicine Wheel planning processes suggest that it is possible to take cultural differences into consideration in ways that do not conflict with federal obligations under law. While the Devils Tower plan was subsequently (and for the most part unsuccessfully) challenged as unconstitutional, the Park Service procedures for reaching that decision in a multicultural environment were not.

One useful approach to applying theories of conflict management and dispute resolution to the actual settlement of disputes categorizes the framing of issues and the choice of disputing processes in terms of power, rights, and interests. Power-based contests may range from public relations efforts to voting, to public nonviolent or violent protests, to armed conflict; they focus more on a party's ability to mobilize brute force than on appeals to principle or moral authority. Rights-based contests usually involve the use of some forum for the vindication of rights, such as an administrative hearing or a courtroom, and usually invoke concepts of justice, equity, and fair play; moral authority and cultural norms play a much more dominant role here. Interest-based contests more often take the form of negotiated or facilitated dispute resolution and focus on the underlying interests that motivate a party to resort either to force or to legal rhetoric and process.[4] While acknowledging both the power and the rights claims that various stakeholders may bring to a given dispute, interest-based negotiation focuses on finding places of both agreement and divergence in the positions of various stakeholder groups in a conflict situation, to begin to construct a possible basis for consensus. By keeping all parties focused on the interests that underlie both rights and power-based strategies, facilitators and the negotiators use this beginning emphasis on similarity or sameness—emphasizing what all parties hold in common—as a way of building a foundation upon which just and durable agreements may be built.

As Forest Service negotiators at the Bighorn Medicine Wheel and Park Service facilitators at Bear's Lodge/Devils Tower both learned, no matter how much good faith effort is put into the quest for a negotiated resolution of competing demands on sacred site use, there is wide diversity of views on these matters among both indigenous peoples and Euro-American society. Some advocacy groups are so intent on vindicating their positions through confrontation rather than seeking a threshold level of agreement that consensus may prove a difficult if not impossible to achieve. As exemplified by peace-making and peace-keeping efforts from Beirut to Bosnia to Belfast, a great majority of people in the midst of these conflicts may be hoping for resolution of their conflict in a way that does no continuing harm to any interest. In such situations, however, there are sometimes actors whose intention is to do harm—to defeat and subjugate the other. Sometimes this approach is used for strategic purposes, to strengthen one's position for later negotiations, but in other instances conflict and defeat is itself the goal.

In both the Devils Tower and Bighorn Medicine Wheel cases, it was not parties to these negotiations who later chose to challenge them in court. It was commercial groups who enjoy private gain from the use of public lands and resources and who resent government agencies even taking into account the religious interests of indigenous peoples in making management decisions. For this reason, parties to an intercultural consultation and the land managers crafting a final plan all need to stay mindful of the possibility that whatever they do may eventually be challenged in court. Based on past experience in the field and federal case law, some of the following guidelines on designing a plan that will survive judicial review intact may prove helpful.

The first step for an agency contemplating the conduct of a multicultural consultation over sacred site management planning is to be as explicit as possible concerning the treaty-based, statutory, and regulatory authority under which the consultation is being conducted. If a recognized indigenous nation, tribe, or band has any sort of historical use relationship with the site in question, the trust responsibility doctrine is automatically implicated; it then becomes the starting point not only for process design but also for possible subsequent judicial review as well, at least insofar as a non-Indian establishment clause challenge to the resultant management plan is concerned.[5]

Also of relevance is the nature and duration of the historical relationship (including pre-Columbian) between the site in question and the tribes participating in the consultation, as well as the circumstances under which the tribes were originally divested of unregulated access to the site. Likewise, it can be helpful to ascertain whether there has been any effort since such divestiture to use the site for ceremonial purposes. All of these factors may eventually influence how determinative a role the trust relationship will play in sustaining a possible court challenge to a specific management plan.

Legal Pluralism and Judicial Duty in Sacred Site Cases: Contrasting Views

As the discussion of case law in several earlier chapters has demonstrated, when a court analyzes a sacred site case by viewing it only through the lens of First Amendment analysis or only through the lens of trust responsibility doctrine analysis, it is looking at only half the picture and doing only half its historical homework. Using either perspective alone is like viewing the situation through a spyglass, while to use both is like looking through binoculars. The latter provide both a wider angle view and a greater depth of field.

It is for this reason that Supreme Court opinions such as the five-member majorities' in *Lyng* in 1988 and *Employment Division v.*

Smith in 1990 do such a disservice to the evolution of constructive legally pluralistic public policy in this area. In these cases the Supreme Court refused to acknowledge that, once having evicted tribes from their traditional homelands and having taken measures throughout the late nineteenth and early twentieth centuries to destroy tribal religions and cultures, the U.S. government bears some responsibility for at least allowing them to maintain affiliation with their holiest sites and traditional religious practices. To find as these cases did is to deny our collective history and our mutual obligations arising out of it. Such decisions simply prolong the time it will take to heal from the deep self-inflicted wounds occasioned by Euro-American society's historical treatment of this country's indigenous peoples.

This is not to imply, however, that indigenous peoples are the only ones with rights and interests in these cases, or that theirs should always stand at the top of a hierarchical pyramid. That is why seeking to reframe the issues from a discourse of rights to a discourse of interests is such a crucial step in intercultural consultations over public lands management. For it is within this conceptual framework that everyone's rights can be accommodated at some threshold level—that lands and resources can be managed as a true intercultural commons.

The problem in the free exercise/sacred site cases is that instead of First Natives being accorded some form of elevated status, their rights have been assigned a status at or near the very bottom. And this is apparently due in part to the attitudes toward cultural and legal pluralism among Justices such as the five-member majorities in *Lyng* and *Smith*. A content analysis done on Supreme Court rhetoric in religion clause cases indicates that there does indeed seem to be a hierarchy of sorts within the court (especially the *Lyng* and *Smith* majorities) in terms of how much First Amendment freedom should be accorded a given religious group.[6]

This linguistic analysis shows that the high court has tended to view religious groups seeking First Amendment protections as falling into one of three categories: "Traditional" (basically the recognized religious denominations at the time the First Amendment was adopted and their progeny); "Modern" (the "civic religion" approach that looks for the commonalities across all forms of religious expression to identify a common secular moral basis for democratic governance that still respects individual religious rights; and "Postmodern" (new and recombinant forms of religious expression that, historically, have initially been seen as cults or cultural quirks [as was Mormonism in its early days]). Unfortunately for First Natives, the majorities in *Lyng* and *Smith* have so far chosen to assign their religious rights to the latter category:

> From the Court's perspective, the Native American religion cases are also examples of Postmodern religions. In each of these cases—concerning, respectively, social security payments, sacred burial grounds and the use of peyote in a Native American church—the majority of the Court treated Native American religions as postmodern. The Court's comments all relate to perceived Postmodern qualities: the religion's newness, the possibility for fraudulent representations to the government, the Court's difficulty in discerning a coherent basis for the religion or religious practice . . .
>
> While Native American religions are hardly new, inauthentic, provisional, or New Age in nature, when a Postmodern model of religion is applied, the Native American party loses.[7]

It is for this reason that mainstream religious denominations signing on as friends of the court in sacred site cases is such a significant event in American cultural evolution. It is an effort by these groups to educate the court—to change how the judges conceptually construct First Native religions. For at this point in time, the anti-pluralist majority in these cases regularly accords indigenous beliefs a constitutional status far inferior to that of established Euro-American religions.

The Supreme Court has not always taken so narrow and anti-pluralistic approach. At other times the Justices of the high court have seen their responsibilities in these matters in a very different light, as have judges in federal trial courts and courts of appeal. When the Fifth Circuit judges heard the 1991 *Peyote Way* case on appeal (see chapter 5), they quoted an earlier Supreme Court decision on the subject: "The course of constitutional neutrality in [First Amendment jurisprudence] cannot be an absolutely straight line; rigidity could well defeat the basic purpose of these provisions."[8] The Fifth Circuit judges asserted that the trust relationship precludes the degree of separation ordinarily required by the First Amendment, and then added: "The federal government cannot at once fulfill its constitutional role of protector of tribal Native Americans and apply conventional separatist understandings of the establishment clause to that same relationship."[9]

A year later, in a unanimous opinion joined by then-judge (now U.S. Supreme Court Justice) Stephen Breyer, the First Circuit quoted this same language as a basis for its holding in *Rupert*.[10] What these courts recognized was the same point made repeatedly in this book: that spiritual practices are not separable from other aspects of traditional indigenous cultures and that trying to vivisect them into component parts conforming to structural doctrines of the First Amendment religion clauses is an act that itself severely inhibits the ability of a tribe to preserve its culture within the context of a dominant nation-state.

The plaintiffs in the Devils Tower litigation understood this perspective but used it to opposite effect. They reasoned that if spiritual beliefs and practices are not structurally separable from other aspects of Indian culture, then agencies such as the National Park Service should be precluded from any activities the purpose of which is to aid in the preservation of spiritual aspects of tribal culture (including interpretive programs conducted by Native Americans), since to do will inevitably involve the impermissible "teaching" of religion.[11]

National Parks as National Classrooms; Public Lands as Sacred Commons

Were an argument such as the one put forth above to ultimately prevail, it would deny the Park Service its ability to fulfill one of the functions it has performed to some degree almost since its inception, which is to teach. It teaches visitors not just about the natural history of these sites but about their human history as well. Seen in one light, then, the Mountain States Legal Foundation's brief for the dissident commercial climbing guides may be regarded as an act of cultural warfare. It is an effort to deny visitors to national parks and monuments the opportunity to learn about the cultural pluralism that is so important an element of the human history of the United States.

It is an effort to suppress knowledge of the "other"—the minority culture groups who were the first to develop a relationship with the land and whose moral claims to the ability to honor their deities at the sites where they are believed to reside predate by hundreds or (in some cases) thousands of years the imposition of the legal system of the dominant culture that now controls the landscape. Suppression of knowledge of pre-Columbian and historic indigenous cultures therefore also entails suppressing knowledge of the moral basis for their undisturbed occasional use of sites they hold sacred in the present day.

A review of National Park Service interpretive programs will show that there is generally as much attention to similarities across culture groups in telling the story of human habitation of a park or monument as there is attention to differences. These programs explain how early peoples solved problems common to all humanity: how to survive, live, and prosper in the natural environment in a way that sustains culture by sustaining the ecological integrity of the environment on which cultural survival depends. These are teachings of inestimable value, and not just for the sake of preserving the ancient culture that originated them. The archaeological record shows that ancient peoples probably made some environmental mistakes along the way, in terms of overuse of the resource base; that they apparently learned from these mistakes; and that they incorporated that learning into their culture and spiritual practices in a way that survives to the present day. That learning can be as much a national treasure as the landscapes themselves.

Sometimes overlooked in our regard for national parks and monuments is the fact that they are also national classrooms. A quick survey of license plates in any major national park parking lot or careful listening to the accents and languages of visitors reveals that people from all over the nation and all over the world are visiting these sites. We come to learn about the natural wonders of these places, but we also come to learn about who we are by learning who we were. The parks are an intercultural crossroads in part because they are also crossroads in time. We encounter our collective past there as an important aspect of the ongoing task of charting our collective future as a culturally diverse society.

Some scholars claim that the United States has entered a somber

and frightening era characterized by what they call a "culture war"—
a period when the assertion of absolute and mutually incompatible
individual rights is crowding out and shouting down our concomitant
efforts to understand, appreciate, respect, and accommodate the cultural pluralism that has always been a defining feature of the American experience.[12] According to some of these same scholars, about
all that keeps this war of words from becoming a war of bombs
and bullets is the mitigating and moderating influences of our institutions (government, educational, commercial, and religious), for it is
through these institutions that the social values of tolerance, respect
for difference, and discernment of commonalities across differences
are taught.[13] Others assert that in isolated instances the shooting has
already started, as exemplified in the 1990s by acts of domestic political terrorism committed against family planning clinics, against
the field offices of western federal land management agencies, and
against federal employees and their families at sites such as Oklahoma
City's federal office building.[14]

Our national parks and monuments are surely among the mediat-
ing, moderating, and mitigating institutions that can teach us how
important it is to remember what value lies in ancient environmental
wisdom, as reflected in contemporary spiritual practice. In developing
a deeper knowledge and better appreciation for indigenous Earthen
spirituality, Euro-Americans may thereby develop a renewed appreciation for their own Earthen religious heritage as well, whether
expressed through the revival of pre-Christian traditions or through
the "greening of faith" most mainstream Western religions are now
undergoing.

In addition to teaching our pluralist history through its interpretive programs, intercultural consultations such as the one leading up
to the Devils Tower Climbing Management plan provide an opportunity for parties in the process to teach and learn about each other—
about who they are, what they value and why, and how it might be
possible to work together to achieve their respective ends. When
it works as expected, such a process can serve not only an educational
function but also a community building and healing one. It is a mode
of interaction on which the future of peaceable life in our pluralistic
society may well depend. This is one reason it is so important for

federal judges to uphold federal agency discretion—under both the trust doctrine *and* the First Amendment—to administer these processes and implement their outcomes, unless that outcome is deemed so egregious an infraction of the establishment clause that some mitigation seems called for.

From the standpoint of the culture wars hypothesis, it should come as no surprise that both the interpretive program and the climbing management plan at Devils Tower fell under attack in the Mountain States Legal Foundation's challenge. Its brief represents a fairly overt attempt at the assertion of cultural dominance—its effect if not its explicit intent being to suppress dissemination of knowledge of our pluralist heritage and to homogenize the present in the image of the dominant culture. In this case, resort to establishment clause jurisprudence to trump the trust responsibility doctrine can be seen as an effort by ideologically motivated plaintiffs to enlist federal judges in this cultural call to arms.

Further, some proponents of the culture wars perspective also point out that the drive for cultural hegemony on either side is often accompanied by an economic agenda as well: toward redistributive public policies on the part of "progressives" and toward privatization on the part of "traditionalists."[15] It is worth noting that every free exercise claim that the tribes have lost (and they have basically lost all of the land-based ones, at least in the published cases) has involved a tribal effort to halt or at least scale down privately remunerative uses of the public lands.

In the Devils Tower case, it was not recreational rock climbers who brought the establishment clause challenge subsequent to adoption of the climbing management plan. It was a small group of dissident commercial climbing guides who might suffer financial loss if even the voluntary climbing ban were successful; that is, if their would-be clients developed moral qualms about climbing the tower once they had been asked (but not ordered) by the Park Service not to. Although questions of cultural dominance are certainly at stake here, it isn't difficult to imagine that these plaintiffs may have been a little less concerned about perceived government coercion to honor the indigenous deities of Bear's Lodge than they were about a temporary impairment of their ability to use public lands for private gain.

This is not to imply that every litigant or federal jurist who perceives establishment clause implications in a federal agency management plan that limits the range of public activities at a public place in the interest of spiritual accommodation is an absolutist cultural warrior or an opportunistic privatizer cruising under First Amendment colors. As defendant interveners in the Devils Tower case demonstrated, there are plenty of examples of Park Service accommodation of religious practices at the sites they manage, from the weekly Christian worship services held in most national parks, to the several churches that are also national historical sites and monuments, to the national cemeteries. At all these sites, the behavior of visitors not associated with ritual observances is regulated in the interest of ceremonial participants. None of this behavioral regulation is seen as an establishment of religion but, rather, as equally important accommodation of it (which First Amendment jurisprudence also encourages).

The challenge for federal land managers is to find ways to accommodate tribal needs for autonomy and cultural preservation while simultaneously honoring the establishment clause principles discussed in this book. And the task for reviewing judges is to recognize that insofar as sacred site management planning is concerned, it is in the consensus-oriented mutual accommodation of intercultural differences by parties in conflict at sacred sites that the "integrity and unity of the larger body politic"[16] in as pluralistic a nation as ours is actually to be found.

Lost and Found

Euro-American society, especially its mainstream religious groups, is just now coming to appreciate the sanctity of our public lands and resources and to understand that, in addition to being natural resource supermarkets and outdoor playgrounds, they are also *sanctuaries*. These places have always been so regarded by indigenous peoples, even though—just like Euro-Americans—they may not always treat their own lands and resources with evident reverence (they also have more pressing economic justifications).

As we began to head back into the wilderness in large numbers during the second half of the twentieth century, this "corps of spiritual rediscovery" may not have been in search of material gain (as were the first European explorers), but there was still something of that same acquisitive approach. There was something "out there" that we had to go find: something to acquire, to take, to possess—even if it was only experience. Only by spending enough time there was it possible to realize that it is this very mindset, this sense of acquisitiveness, that makes for the sense of separateness, of disconnectedness, of being literally lost in the wilderness.

Curandera Diana Velasquez's Yaqui teacher, the Tiwan bison herd manager, the Tibetan lama, and Keresan Indian Larry Bird all taught basically the same thing: "You watch, and wait, and listen, and the answer *will come to you*. It's yours then, not like in school."[17] It is the essence of contemplative learning. A few years ago the poet David Wagoner put it this way:

Stand still. The trees ahead and bushes beside you
Are not lost. Wherever you are is called Here,
And you must treat it as a powerful stranger,
Must ask permission to know it and be known.

The forest breathes. Listen. It answers,
I have made this place around you.
If you leave it, you may come back again, saying Here.
No two trees are the same to Raven.
No two branches are the same to Wren.

If what a tree or a bush does is lost on you,
You are surely lost. Stand still. The forest knows
Where you are. You must let it find you.[18]

Notes
Index

Notes

Understanding Legal Citations

The references in this book were created in conformance with the *Chicago Manual of Style* (fourteenth edition) with the important exception of references to sources of legal information (primary source legislative, administrative, and judicial materials). Instead, these were created in keeping with *A Uniform System of [Legal] Citation* (sixteenth edition), a style manual published by a consortium of university law review editors. Summarized below are a few key features of this style, which will be helpful in deciphering the legal citations found among the references below.

Legal citations usually consist of a series of numbers, a series of letters, and another series of numbers. While the letters always represent an abbreviation of the title of the publication in which the cited document is located, what the numbers mean depends on what type of publication is being referenced, as the following examples illustrate.

A. *Legislative Materials*

With the exception of the state statutory references in Chapter 8, Table 1, all the legislative materials referenced are to actions taken by the U.S. Congress.

1. CONGRESSIONAL RECORD

Every day Congress is in session, a written record is kept of its proceedings. Member of both houses can also enter into the record various documents they wish both the Congress and the public to take notice of, in relation to matters before each house on a given day. The *Congressional Record* is bound into volumes and is cited by volume number, page number within that volume, and year of publication. For example, the citation "2 Cong. Rec. 2106–09 (1874)" indicates that the cited material can be found at pages 2106 through 2109 of volume 2 of the Congressional Record, published in 1874.

2. ACTS OF CONGRESS

Acts of Congress may be cited in three different forms: (1) public law number, (2) the *Statutes at Large,* and (3) the *United States Code.* The first two forms are simply chronological compilations of acts passed by Congress within any of its two-year terms; while the U.S. Code is a subject matter compilation of all the acts ever passed by Congress that are currently in effect.

Consider, for example, the citation *"American Indian Religious Freedom Act,* Public Law 95-341 (1978), 92 Stat. 469, 42 USC § 1996." The public law number citation means that AIRFA was the 341st law passed by the 95th Congress (and not vetoed by the president), and that it was passed in 1978. Once passed, the act was compiled into a bound set of volumes named the *Statutes at Large,* which annually publishes all such congressional enactments in public law number order. Thus the text of the act can be found at page 469 of vol. 92 of the *Statutes at Large.*

Congress eventually found it necessary to organize all the acts it has passed that are currently in effect by subject matter as well as order of passage, since it was otherwise very difficult to keep track of which previous acts of Congress were still good law, and which ones may have been amended or repealed. So early in the twentieth century Congress established the *U.S. Code,* which is organized into roughly fifty different subject headings, or *titles.* Within each title, the language of acts passed by Congress is organized into *sections,* represented in legal citations by the symbol §. Thus, in the example above, AIRFA may be found at Title 42 of the *U.S. Code,* beginning at section 1996. In several of the references below, the *U.S. Code* citation is followed by the notation *"et seq.,"* which is an abbreviation of the Latin term *et sequentia,* indicating that the law being cited *begins* at the section being cited, but appears in sections following the cited one as well. The *U.S. Code* is updated continuously, in an effort to ensure that all laws found there are as current as possible.

B. Administrative Materials

The citations to administrative materials in this book are either to Executive Orders or to rules and regulations promulgated by federal administrative agencies, all of which first appear in a legal notice publication issued each federal workday, the *Federal Register.* As an example, the citation "Executive Order No. 13,007, 61 Fed. Reg. 26,771–26,772 (1996)" indicates that this is the 13,007th executive order issued since the executive branch was established; and that it may be found at pages 26,771 through 26,772 of volume 61 of the *Federal Register,* this order having been published in 1996.

However, the same problem of keeping track of which congressional enactments were still in effect and which ones had been amended or appealed was just as true of agency rules and regulation, so a similar system of subject matter encoding—the *Code of Federal Regulations*—was adopted for the executive branch as well. For example, the citation "36 CFR § 2.1(c)(2)(d) (2001)" means that the cited rule or regulation may be found at section 2.1(c)(2)(d) of Title 36 of the *Code of Federal Regulations.* Like the *U.S. Code* (acts of Congress currently in effect), the *Code of Federal Regulations* (agency rules and regulations currently in effect) is updated continuously, in an effort to ensure that all laws found there are as current as possible.

C. Court Decisions

The two principal forms court decisions take are *unpublished* and *published.* The great majority of *trial court* decisions in both state and federal court systems remain unpublished; that is, they are simply issued as typewritten, photocopied documents issued to the parties to litigation and to anyone else willing to pay the reproduction costs. A published decision is one that appears in a bound set of books published by a private legal publishing house. For example, the citation "*Bear Lodge Multiple Use Ass'n. v. Babbitt,* Order, No. 96-CV-063-D, 2 F. Supp. 2d 1448 (D. Wyo.1998)" gives us the following information:

first, the names of the parties (plaintiffs first); second, the citation to the unpublished decision, indicating that it was an order of the court and that its docket number (an identification number the court clerk assigns to cases filed) was No. 96-CV-063-D.

However, this turned out to be such a significant decision that it was eventually published, in a set of legal volumes known as the *Federal Supplement* (now in its second series, abbreviated "F. Supp. 2d"), where all published decisions of the U.S. District Courts (the federal trial courts) are found. Thus, in the example above, the court's published decision in the *Bear Lodge* case is to be found beginning at page 1448 of volume 2 of the Federal Supplement, second series. This citation also indicates that the decision was handed down by the U.S. District Court for the District of Wyoming, and that it was issued in 1998.

This particular trial court decision was appealed by the plaintiffs, who lost at trial, to the U.S. Court of Appeals for the 10th Circuit (which has appellate jurisdiction over federal trial courts in states in the eastern Rocky Mountain region and western great plains); the published decisions of all federal circuit courts of appeal appear in a set of legal volumes named the *Federal Reporter,* which is now in its third series (abbreviated "F.3d") The citation to the appellate court's decision in this case is "*Bear Lodge Multiple Use Ass'n. v. Babbitt,* 175 F.3d 814 (10th Cir. 1999)." This citation indicates that the appellant (the party appealing the lower court decision) was the Bear Lodge Association, since its name is to the left of the "v" (an abbreviation for *versus*), and that the text of the decision begins at page 814 of volume 175 of the *Federal Reporter,* third series.

Again, the appellants lost, and so appealed their case to the U.S. Supreme Court, the officially published opinions of which appear in a set of legal volumes named the *U.S. Reports* (abbreviated "U.S."). Thus, the citation to the Supreme Court's ruling on this case, "*Bear Lodge Multiple Use Ass'n. v. Babbitt,* 529 U.S. 1037" (a one-sentence ruling declining to hear the appeal) tells us that it may be found at page 1037 of volume 529 of the *U.S. Reports.*

Chapter 1. Full Circle

1. Lloyd Burton and David Ruppert, "Bear's Lodge or Devils Tower: Intercultural Relations, Legal Pluralism, and the Management of Sacred Sites

on Public Lands," *Cornell Journal of Law and Public Policy* 8, no. 2 (1999), 201–247.

2. John Carroll, Paul Prockelman, and Mary Westfall, eds., *The Greening of Faith* (Hanover, N.H.: University Press of New England, 1997).

3. See Margot Adler, *Drawing down the Moon: Witches, Druids, Goddess Worshippers, and Other Pagans in America Today* (New York: Beacon Press, 1986).

4. See Carolyn Merchant, *Earthcare: Women and the Environment* (New York: Routledge, 1996).

5. Barry Lopez, "We Are Shaped by the Sound of Wind, the Slant of Sunlight," *High Country News* 30 (September 14, 1998), 1, at 11.

6. This story is from the Kiowa oral tradition. A variant of this is another Kiowa story, which involves two sisters, one a girl-bear who mistreated her sister. Seven brothers of these sisters came to the aid of the mistreated girl. In an attempt to help their sister and protect her from the bear-girl, the seven brothers called on a rock for help. The rock told the boys to encircle it four times and then come up on top. When they did this, the rock grew upward. The bear-girl made a lunge for the seven brothers and missed the top by inches, fell to the bottom, and scratched the rock's face. In this version, the seven brothers became seven stars. See *Notes on Kiowa Ethnography, Santa Fe Laboratory of Anthropology, Expedition of 1935.* n.d. From "Papers of Weston LaBarre, Typescript of Student Notes." Origin Story: The 10 Medicines and the Bear Society, Kiowa Tribal Environmental Program.

The Cheyenne version of the origin of the tower is quite different. The Cheyenne origin story tells of seven brothers, one of whom had the ill fortune of having his wife carried off by a bear to his cave. The youngest brother instructs the others to make four arrows while he transforms himself into a gopher and digs into the bear's cave. While the bear is asleep, the brother succeeds in escaping from the cave with his older brother's wife. The bear awakens and gathers other bears of his clan to give chase. The youngest brother, who had great power, always carried a small rock with him. He took the rock in his hand and sang to it four times. When he finished, the rock had grown to the size the tower is today. The bear attacked the tower, leaving the scratch marks that are visible today.

Other tribes have similar origin stories related to the tower. The Crow version of the story tells of two girls who were attacked by a bear while they played on a rock. The Great Spirit saved them by causing the rock to grow to its present size, carrying the girls aloft. See Jeffrey R. Hanson and Sally Chirinos, *Ethnographic Overview and Assessment of Devils Tower National Monument, Wyoming* (Intermountain Region Cultural Resource Selections No. 9) (Denver, Colo.: National Park Service, 1997), which also reviews additional stories collected by others from the Northern Cheyenne and the Arapaho. See also Dick Stone, *History of Devils Tower, 1804–1934*, microfilm on file at Wyoming State Archives, Museums and Historical

Department, Cheyenne, and Mary Alice Gunderson, *Devils Tower: Stories in Stone* (Glendo, Wy.: High Plains Press, 1988). Hanson and Chirinos also link Lakota stories regarding the tower to Lakota cosmology, and they review ethnographic accounts that point to the importance of the Black Hills, specifically to the tower as place where traditional Lakota religious activities took place in the past and continue to take place today.

7. Greg Beaumont, *Devils Tower* (Washington, D.C.: U.S. Department of the Interior, 1984), chap. 2.

8. In 1857, Lt. G. K. Warren and F. V. Hayden passed through the country and caught sight of "Bear's Lodge" to the north of their travels from Fort Laramie to explore the Black Hills. In 1875 Col. Richard Dodge, commander of a military escort for a U.S. Geological Survey party took special note of the tower; in his 1876 book, *The Black Hills,* he identifies the name of the tower as "Devils Tower," explaining that the Indian name for the tower was "The Bad God's Tower." See Ray H. Mattison, *Devils Tower National Monument: A History* (Washington, D.C.: U.S. Department of the Interior, National Park Service, 1956).

9. Dennis Tedlock and Barbara Tedlock, *Teachings from the American Earth* (New York: Liveright, 1975), preface.

10. See generally Clifford Geertz, *The Interpretation of Culture* (New York: Basic Books, 1973); James Spradley, "Ethnography and Culture," in James Spradley and David McCurdy, eds., *Conformity and Conflict,* 6th ed. (Boston: Little, Brown, 1987), 17–25; and John Bodley, *Cultural Anthropology: Tribes, States, and the Global System* (Mountain View, Calif.: Mayfield, 1994).

11. David H. Fischer, *Albion's Seed* (New York: Oxford University Press, 1989).

12. Elizabeth Cook-Lynn, *"Why I Can't Read Wallace Stegner" and Other Essays* (Madison: University of Wisconsin Press, 1996).

13. Wallace Stegner, *Wolf Willow* (NewYork: Penguin Books, 1961).

14. Alexis de Tocqueville, *Democracy in America,* 2 vols., trans. George Lawrence, ed. J. P Mayer (New York: Doubleday, 1969), 2:536.

Chapter 2. Contemplation and Connection

1. Keith Basso, *Wisdom Sits in Places* (Albuquerque: University of New Mexico Press, 1996), 32. The analogy between the Apache place-maker and my Puebloan host is not perfect since my host spoke in the past tense. But his way of evoking living history associated with a specific place while in that place did accomplish a similar objective.

2. Ibid.

3. Allison M. Dussias, "Ghost Dance and Holy Ghost: The Echoes of Nineteenth-Century Christianization Policy in Twentieth-Century Native American Free Exercise Cases," *Stanford Law Review* 49 (1997), 773–852.

4. The most notorious documented example of unauthorized gathering

and dissemination of information about religious practices of the Pueblo Indians is probably reflected in the activities of the early-twentieth-century ethnographer Ellie Clew Parsons. In the introductory essay to Bison Books's 1996 edition of Parsons's two-volume collection of purloined knowledge (*Pueblo Indian Religion,* first published in 1939), Pauline Strong recounts Parsons's use of bribery and subterfuge to obtain some of her research findings, along with the rationale Parsons offered (the cataloging of dying traditions in the name of science) in defense of her tactics.

Having published these findings, Ms. Parsons's legacy of moral compromise became not hers alone. The conundrum for a present-day scholar of Pueblo Indian religion is this: On the one hand, to ignore her historic, twelve-hundred-page body of published research is to ignore a significant—if dated—contribution to learning on this subject. On the other hand, to rely on her work is also to benefit from her dubiously obtained knowledge and therefore, by implication, to perpetuate the effects of this gesture of profound disrespect to Pueblo religious practice and belief and to Pueblo peoples. Whether to partially base one's own writing on this material then becomes a matter of ethical consideration for anyone working in the area, and different scholars equally concerned about the ethics of scholarship in this area have taken different positions on this issue.

5. See Robert Williams, "Large Binocular Telescopes, Red Squirrel Piñatas, and Apache Sacred Mountains: Decolonizing Environmental Law in a Multicultural World," West Virginia Law Review 96 (1994), 1133–1164; Armin Geertz, *The Invention of Prophecy: Continuity and Meaning in Hopi Indian Religion* (Berkeley: University of California Press, 1994), 257–322.

6. Joseph Epes Brown, *The Spiritual Legacy of the American Indian* (New York: Crossroad Publishing, 1982), xi.

7. Ibid., 4.

8. Alfonzo Ortiz, "The Tewa World View," in Dennis Tedlock and Barbara Tedlock, eds., *Teachings from the American Earth: Indian Religion and Philosophy* (New York: Liveright, 1975), 179–189, at 182.

9. In the view of at least one National Park Service anthropologist who has devoted much of his professional career to working with sacred site management issues, the next major development in this policy implementation area will probably be a shift from a preoccupation with the management of isolated, specific sacred sites within the public estate to a more inclusive examination of how surrounding areas are managed, as well. David Ruppert, regional anthropologist, Intermountain Region Support Office, National Park Service, and adjunct assistant professor of anthropology, University of Colorado at Denver, December 11, 2000, personal communication.

10. Frank Crosswhite, "The Annual Saguaro Harvest and Crop Cycle of the Papago, with Reference to Ecology and Symbolism," *Desert Plants* 2(1): 2–61, at 7 (Tuscon, Ariz,: Published by the University of Arizona for the Boyce Thompson Southwestern Arboretum, spring, 1980).

11. Dorothy Lee, *Freedom and Culture* (Englewood Cliffs, N.J.: Prentice Hall, 1959), 63. The internal quotations in this passage are from the earlier writings of a Dakota elder who was educated at the Carlisle School and was among the first to commit the teachings of his people to writing in their own words. Luther Standing Bear, *My People the Sioux* (Boston: Houghton-Mifflin, 1928).

12. David Suzuki and Peter Knudtson, *Wisdom of the Elders: Sacred Native Stories of Nature* (New York: Bantam Books, 1992), 212.

13. Basso, *Wisdom Sits in Places,* 34.

14. Interview with *curandera* Diana Velazquez, Denver, Colorado, July, 1993, as recounted in Ramon del Castillo, "Effective Management Strategies When Incorporating Curanderismo in a Mainstream Mental Health System," Ph.D. diss., University of Colorado at Denver, Graduate School of Public Affairs, 1999, 74.

15. Suzuki and Knudtson, *Wisdom of the Elders,* 122–123.

16. One example is Hopi and Navajo testimony in their doomed legal attempt to prevent ski resort development on the San Francisco peaks. See chapter 7 in this volume.

17. See Dussias, "Ghost Dance and the Holy Ghost." See generally Joseph Jorgensen, *The Sundance Religion* (Chicago: University of Chicago Press, 1972).

18. Jorgenson, *The Sundance Religion,* 7.

19. Ibid., 218.

20. Dennis Tedlock, "An American Indian View of Death," in Dennis Tedlock and Barbara Tedlock, eds., *Teachings from the American Earth: Indian Religion and Philosophy* (New York: Liveright, 1975), 248–271, at 266.

21. Ibid., 266.

22. See *Wilson v. Block,* 708 F. 2d. 735 (D.C. Cir. 1982).

23. Ibid., 740.

24. Vine Deloria, *God Is Red,* rev. ed. (Golden, Colo.: Fulcrum Publishing, 1994), 272–274.

Chapter 3. Nature as Haven, Nature as Hades

1. "Earthen" is used in this text to denote an Earth-based spiritual tradition, including the indigenous ones of the Americas and the pre-Christian spiritual traditions of Europe. The more common term with regard to the latter in this subject area is "pagan," a term coined by early Christians to describe worshipers of the pantheon of deities in Roman society.

2. William McNeill, *The Rise of the West* (Chicago: University of Chicago Press, 1963), 8.

3. Ibid., 19.

4. Riane Eisler, *The Chalice and the Blade* (New York: Harper and Row, 1988), 45.

5. Philip Davis, *Goddess Unmasked: The Rise of Neopagan Feminist Spirituality* (Dallas, Tex.: Spence Publishing, 1998).

6. Marija Gimbutas, *Gods and Goddesses of Old Europe* (Berkeley: University of California Press 1982), 237.

7. Miles Dillon, "Celtic Religion," *Encyclopedia Britannica*, 15th ed., vol. 3 (Chicago: University of Chicago, 1983), 1068.

8. A. H. M. Jones, "The Social Background of the Struggle between Paganism and Christianity," in Arnaldo Momigliano, ed., The Conflict between Paganism and Christianity in the Fourth Century (Oxford: Oxford University Press, 1963), 17–37.

9. A. A. Barb, "The Survival of the Magic Arts," in Arnaldo Momigliano, ed., *The Conflict between Paganism and Christianity in the Fourth Century* (Oxford: Oxford University Press, 1963), 100–125.

10. H. Bloch, "The Pagan Revival in the West at the End of the Fourth Century," in Arnaldo Momigliano, ed., *The Conflict between Paganism and Christianity in the Fourth Century* (Oxford: Oxford University Press, 1963), 193–217.

11. Quoted in Paul Santmire, *The Travail of Nature: The Ambiguous Ecological Promise of Christian Theology* (Philadelphia: Fortress Press, 1985), 50.

12. Gerald Messadié, *A History of the Devil*, trans. M. Romano (New York: Kodansha International Press, 1996).

13. Alexis de Tocqueville, *Democracy in America*, 2 vols., ed. J. P. Mayer; trans. George Lawrence,(New York: Doubleday, 1969), 1:33.

14. D. H. Fischer, *Albion's Seed: Four British Folkways in America* (New York: Oxford University Press, 1989), 18.

15. Roderick Nash, *Wilderness and the American Mind*, rev. ed. (New Haven, Conn.: Yale University Press, 1973), 2.

16. Ibid., 14.

17. Ibid., 17.

18. Fischer, *Albion's Seed*, 127.

19. Ibid., 341.

20. Ibid., 527.

21. Ibid., 708.

22. David Kinsley, *Ecology and Religion* (Englewood Cliffs, N.J.: Prentice Hall, 1994), 133–134.

23. Stephen Batchelor, *The Awakening of the West* (Berkeley, Calif.: Parallax Press, 1994), 242.

24. Rick Fields, *How the Swans Came to the Lake* (Boulder, Colo.: Shambhala, 1981), 61.

25. Qtd. in Kinsley, *Ecology and Religion*, 144.

26. Thoreau, *A Week on the Concord and Merrimac Rivers*: as quoted in Fields, *How the Swans Came to the Lake*, 63.

27. Henry David Thoreau, "Walking," in *Excursions, The Writings of Henry*

David Thoreau, Riverside edition (11 vols. Boston, 1893), 9: 275. Quoted in Nash, *Wilderness and the American Mind,* 84.

28. Qtd. in Fields, *How the Swans Came to the Lake,* 63.

29. Ibid., 74.

30. Nash, *Wilderness and the American Mind,* 125.

31. Lynn White Jr., "The Historical Roots of Our Environmental Crisis," *Science* 155 (1967), 1203–1207.

32. Ibid.

33. Ibid.

34. Margot Adler, *Drawing down the Moon,* 2d ed. (New York: Penguin, 1986).

Chapter 4. Culture and Justice

1. Bronislaw Malinowski, *Crime and Custom in Savage Society* (New York: Harcourt, Brace, 1926).

2. Karl Llewellyn and E. Adamson Hoebel, *The Cheyenne Way* (Norman: University of Oklahoma Press, 1941).

3. E. Adamson Hoebel, *The Law of Primitive Man* (Cambridge: Harvard University Press, 1954).

4. See generally James Clifford and George Marcus, eds., *Writing Culture* (Berkeley: University of California Press, 1986).

5. Quoted in Julian Boyd, "Dr. Franklin, Friend of the Indians," in Roy Lokken, ed., *Meet Dr. Franklin* (Philadelphia: Franklin Institute, 1981), 239; quoted in Donald Grinde, "Iroquois Political Theory and the Roots of American Democracy," in Oren Lyons, Donald Grinde, and John Mohawk, es., *Exiled in the Land of the Free* (Santa Fe, N.M.: Clear Light Publishers, 1992), 246.

6. Grinde, "Iroquois Political Theory," 237.

7. Benjamin Franklin, *Writings III,* 42; quoted in Carl Van Doren, *Benjamin Franklin* (New York: Viking Press, 1938), 209.

8. Van Doren, *Benjamin Franklin,* 209.

9. Ibid.

10. Oren Lyons, Donald Grinde, and John Mohawk, *Exiled in the Land of the Free* (Santa Fe, N.M.: Clear Light Publishers, 1992), 237.

11. Robert Williams, *Linking Arms Together: American Indian Treaty Visions of Law and Peace, 1600–1800* (New York: Oxford University Press, 1997), 120.

12. Ibid., 113–122.

13. Ibid.

14. Samuel Morison and Henry Steele Commager, *The Growth of the American Republic,* vol. 1 (New York: Oxford University Press, 1962).

15. Morton Horwitz, *The Transformation of American Law 1780–1860* (Cambridge: Harvard University Press, 1977).

16. For a critique of the Hardin analogy and several case studies of

common pool resources sustainably managed over hundreds of years, see Elinor Ostrom, *Governing the Commons* (Cambridge: Cambridge University Press, 1990).

17. David Fischer, *Albion's Seed: Four British Folkways in America* (New York: Oxford University Press, 1989), 578.

18. U.S. Constitution, art. 3.

19. Ibid.

20. Ibid., art. 1, sec. 8.

21. Ibid., art. 4, sec. 3.

22. Ibid., art. 2.

23. Ibid., art. 6, cl. 2.

24. Ibid., amend. 1.

25. Ibid., amend. 5.

26. *Marbury v. Madison,* 5 U.S. 137 (1803).

27. *McCullough v. Maryland,* 17 U.S. 316 (1819).

28. *Johnson v. McIntosh,* 21 U.S. (8 Wheat.) 543 (1823).

29. *Cherokee Nation v. Georgia,* 30 U.S. (5 Pet.) 1; 8 L.Ed. 25 (1831).

30. *Worcester v. Georgia,* 31 U.S. (6 Pet.) 515; 8 L.Ed. 483 (1832).

31. Quoted in Alexis de Tocqueville, *Democracy in America,* 2 vols., trans. George Lawrence, ed. J. P. Mayer (New York: Doubleday, 1969), 1:339.

32. Ibid., 1:331.

33. Ibid., 1:339.

34. *Dred Scott v. Sandford,* 60 U.S. 393 (1856).

35. The successive eras of removal, reservation, allotment, and self-determination in the evolution of federal policy toward American Indian tribes are carefully spelled out in S. Tyler, *A History of Indian Policy* (Washington, D.C.: Government Printing Office, 1973).

36. 2 Cong. Rec. 2106-09 (1874) 2d sess., 1874,: 2106–2109.

37. See Lloyd Burton, *American Indian Water Rights and the Limits of Law* (Lawrence: University Press of Kansas, 1991), 18.

38. Peter Nabakov and Lawrence Loendorf, *Restoring a Presence: A Documentary Overview of Yellowstone National Park* (Washington, D.C.: U.S. Department of the Interior Technical Report, 1999), 142.

39. Ibid., 143.

Chapter 5. Of Walls and Windows

1. Samuel Morison and Henry Steele Commager, *The Growth of the American Republic,* vol. 1 (New York: Oxford University Press, 1962).

2. David Fischer, *Albion's Seed: Four British Folkways in America* (New York: Oxford University Press, 1989), 578.

3. Roger Williams, "Letter to John Cotton (1643)," in *The Complete Writings of Roger Williams,* vol. 1 (1963), 392; cited in John Witte Jr., *Religion and the American Constitutional Experiment* (Boulder, Colo.: Westview Press, 2000), 29n. 21.

4. Laurence Tribe, *American Constitutional Law,* 2d ed. (Mineola, N.Y.: Foundation Press, 1988), 1159.

5. Ibid.

6. Richard Morris, *Witnesses at the Creation* (New York: Henry Holt, 1985), 102; Tribe, *American Constitutional Law.*

7. G. Hunt, ed., *The Writings of James Madison,* vol. 10 (1910), 487; quoted in Tribe, *American Constitutional Law,* 1159, n. 12.

8. James Madison, "Letter to Rev. Adams (1833)," in Daniel Dreisbach, *Religion and Politics in the Early Republic: Jasper Adams and the Church–State Debate* (Lexington: University Press of Kentucky, 1996), 120; quoted in John Witte Jr., *Religion and the American Constitutional Experiment* (Boulder, Colo.: Westview, 2000), 183.

9. U.S. Constitution, amend. 1.

10. Witte, *Religion and the American Constitutional Experiment,* 125–136.

11. *Cantwell v. Connecticut,* 310 U.S. 296, at 303–304, 310 (1940).

12. U.S. Constitution, art. 2, sec. 2, cl. 2.; art. 6, cl. 2.

13. *Johnson v. McIntosh,* 21 U.S. (8 Wheat.) 543; 5 L.Ed. 681 (1823).

14. Ibid., 587.

15. *Cherokee Nation v. Georgia,* 30 U.S. (5 Pet.) 1; 8 L.Ed. 25 (1831), 17.

16. Although slightly dated, one of the more thoughtful in-depth overviews of the trust relationship is Reid Chambers, "Judicial Enforcement of the Trust Responsibility to Indians," *Stanford Law Review* 27 (1975), 1218. As Chambers demonstrates, a reading of Marshall's decisions in historical context does allow for a more charitable interpretation than their language on its own might suggest. During the time these cases were being decided, Euro-Americans were illegally entering and settling on tribal lands throughout the western frontier, and the federal government was doing little to stop it, in part because it had also failed to keep its promise to states to eject indigenous peoples from within state borders. Thus the "Marshall trilogy" of decisions—*M'Intosh, Cherokee Nation, and Worcester v. Georgia*—achieved the dual objectives of subordinating tribal rights to federal authority on the one hand while shielding tribes from land predation by hostile state governments and settlers on the other. For additional discussion of these decisions in historical context, see Charles Wilkinson, *American Indians, Time, and the Law* (New Haven, Conn.: Yale University Press, 1987).

17. See S. Lyman Tyler, *A History of Indian Policy* (Washington, D.C.: U.S. Department of the Interior, Bureau of Indian Affairs, 1973).

18. Anastasia Winslow, "Sacred Standards: Honoring the Establishment Clause in Protecting Native American Sacred Sites," *Arizona Law Review* 38 (1996), 1291–1343.

19. *Indian Reorganization Act of 1934,* 48 Stat. 904, 25 USC § 461 et seq.

20. See Tyler, *History of Indian Policy,* 151–188.

21. *Indian Civil Rights Act of 1968,* 82 Stat. 77, 25 USC 1301; *Indian Self-Determination and Assistance Act of 1975,* 25 USC § 450a–450n.

22. *American Indian Religious Freedom Act* [AIRFA], Public Law 95-341 (1978), 92 Stat. 469, 42 USC § 1996; *Native American Grave Protection and Repatriation Act,* 25 USC § 3001–3013 (1990), 16 USC § 470a.; *Religious Freedom Restoration Act,* Public Law 103-141, 107 Stat. 1488, 5 USC § 504; *American Indian Religious Freedom Act Amendments,* Public Law 103-344 (1994), 108 Stat. 3125, 42 USC § 1996a.

23. *Morton v. Mancari,* 417 U.S. 535 (1974).

24. Ibid., 555.

25. 124 Cong. Rec. 21, 444–445 (1978).

26. *Sequoyah v. TVA,* 620 F. 2d 1159 (6th Cir. 1980); cert. den. 449 U.S. 953 (1980); *Badoni v. Higginson,* 638 F. 2d 172 (10th Cir. 1980); *Wilson v. Block,* 708 F. 2d. 735 (D.C. Cir. 1982).

27. "Congress shall make no law respecting an establishment of religion, or prohibiting the free exercise thereof." U.S. Constitution, amend. 1.

28. See Winslow, "Sacred Standards," 1291–1292.

29. *Lyng v. Northwest Cemetery Protective Association,* 485 U.S. 439 (1988).

30. *Northwest Indian Cemetery Protective Association v. Peterson,* 764 F. 2d 581 (9th Cir. 1985).

31. Here the court was distinguishing *Sherbert v. Verner,* 374 U.S. 398 (1963), a decision in which it had voided enforcement of a state employment law requiring the plaintiff to work on her Sabbath.

32. *Lyng,* 454.

33. *Employment Division, Oregon Department of Human Resources v. Smith,* 494 U.S. 872 (1990).

34. Ibid., 879.

35. Ibid., 888–890.

36. Ibid., 891–907.

37. Ibid., 920–921, citing H.R. Rep. No. 95–1308, p. 2 (1978).

38. *Peyote Way Church of God v. Thornburgh,* 922 F. 2d 1210 (5th Cir. 1991).

39. Ibid., 1217.

40. *Rupert v. Director, U.S. Fish and Wildlife Service,* 957 F. 2d 32 (1st Cir. 1992).

41. Ibid., 35. For a discussion of *Peyote Way* and *Rupert* as exemplifying an appropriate path of judicial analysis in support of agency discretion in the accommodation of tribal religion, see Craig Alexander, "Protection of Indian Sacred Places and the Religious Accommodation Doctrine," Proceedings of the Tenth Sovereignty Symposium, June 9–11, 1997, Tulsa, Oklahoma (Washington, D.C.: Office of Tribal Justice, U.S. Department of Justice), unbound. On file with the author.

42. The Supreme Court has since ruled that the compelling interest test does not apply to judicial review of local government land use regulation of church property. *City of Boerne v. Flores,* 521 U.S. 507 (1997).

43. Sally Engle Merry, "Legal Pluralism," Law and Society Review 22 (1988), 869–896.

44. Ibid., 872–873.

45. Stephen Griffin, "Pluralism in Constitutional Interpretation," *Texas Law Review* 72 (1994), 1753–1769.

46. This is precisely the approach encouraged by observers who see in federal statutes such as the National Historic Preservation Act the potential for rich, community-building intercultural education and cultural cohabitation on which the potential for peaceable existence in a pluralistic society depends. See chapter 7 regarding the Bighorn Medicine Wheel case.

47. Griffin, "Pluralism in Constitutional Interpretation;" Richard Fallon, "A Constructivist Coherence Theory of Constitutional Interpretation," *Harvard Law Review* 100 (1987), 1194; Robert Post, "Theories of Constitutional Interpretation," *Representations* 30 (1990), 13–19; Philip Bobbitt, *Constitutional Interpretation* (Oxford, UK: Basil Blackwell, 1991), 13–21.

48. *Lemon v. Kurtzman,* 403 U.S. 602 (1971).

49. *Marsh v. Chambers,* 463 U.S. 783 (1983).

50. Post, "Theories of Constitutional Interpretation," 17.

51. *Lynch v. Donnelly,* 465 U.S. 668 (1984).

52. Post, "Theories of Constitutional Interpretation," 23.

53. *Brown v. Board of Education,* 346 U.S. 483 (1954); *Plessy v. Ferguson,* 163 U.S. 537 (1896).

54. Raymond Cross and Elizabeth Brenneman, "Devils Tower at the Crossroads: The National Park Service and the Preservation of Native American Cultural Resources in the 21st Century," *Public Land and Resources Law Review* 18 (1997), 5–45.

55. Alexander, "Protection of Indian Sacred Places."

56. See Winslow, "Sacred Standards."

57. Timothy Egan, "Senate Bills Would Reduce Rights of Indian Tribes," *New York Times,* August 27, 1997.

58. Fisher v. District Court, 424 U.S. 382 (1976).

59. *Sta. Clara Pueblo v. Martinez,* 436 U.S. 49 (1978); *U.S. v. Antelope,* 430 U.S. 641 (1977).

60. Winslow, "Sacred Standards," 1342.

61. Ibid.

Chapter 6. Rising to Heaven or Risen from Hell?

1. Early sociologists, such as Emile Durkheim, *The Elementary Forms of Religious Life,* Joseph Swain, trans. (1915; rpt., New York: Free Press, 1965), viewed religion as a reification of society itself. This view has been echoed to some extent in the comparative anthropological literature, which shows statistical relationships between a cultural group's political economy or its socialization practices and the form its religious beliefs and practices

exhibit. See, for example, Guy Swanson, *The Birth of the Gods: The Origin of Primitive Beliefs* (Ann Arbor: University of Michigan Press, 1960); Anthony Wallace, *Religion: An Anthropological View* (New York: Random House, 1960); Marvin Harris, *Cultural Anthropology* (New York: Harper and Row, 1983); and Robert LaVine, "Witchcraft and Co-Wife Proximity in Southwestern Kenya," *Ethnology* 1 (1962), 39. In a general sense, one can say that among American Indian traditionalists the line distinguishing the "sacred" from the "profane" is not as sharply drawn as it is in the dominant non-Indian society with a Western or European origin. This general difference in how these groups express the distinctions between the religious and the secular may have some relationship to differences in the historic aspects of their respective social organizations.

2. Lloyd Burton and David Ruppert, "Bear's Lodge or Devils Tower: Intercultural Relations, Legal Pluralism, and the Management of Sacred Sites on Public Lands," *Cornell Journal of Law and Public Policy* 8, no. 2 (1999), 201–247, esp. 206.

3. Jeffrey Hanson, "Ethnohistoric Problems in the Crow–Hidatsa Separation," *Archaeology in Montana* (1979), 20.

4. Ibid.

5. Jeffrey Hanson and Sally Chirinos, *Ethnographic Overview and Assessment of Devils Tower National Monument, Wyoming* (Denver: National Park Service, Intermountain Region Cultural Resource Selections No. 9, 1997).

6. Thomas Odell, *Mato Paha: The Story of Bear Butte, Black Hills Landmark and Indian Shrine—Its Scenic, Historic, and Scientific Uniqueness* (Spearfish, S.D.: Thomas E. Odell, 1942); G. H. Smith, *The Explorations of the La Verendyres in the Northern Plains, 1738–1743* (Lincoln: University of Nebraska Press, 1980); and Ralph Ehrenberg, "Exploratory Mapping of the Great Plains before 1800," in F. C. Luebke, F. W. Kaye, and G. E. Moulton, eds., *Mapping the North American Plains* (Norman: University of Oklahoma Press, 1987), 3.

7. R. G. Thaites, ed., *The Original Journals of the Lewis and Clark Expeditions*, 8 vols. (New York: Antiquarian Press, 1959).

8. Personal communications with Dr. David White, Applied Cultural Dynamics, Santa Fe, N.M., November 11, 1997, with reference to a draft manuscript prepared by Linda R. Zellmer "Close Encounters: Mapping Devils Tower." This map was retrieved from the National Archives by Ms. Zellmer: Records of the Office of the Quartermaster General, Record Group 92, Post and Reservation File, Map 281. Map inscriptions await handwriting analysis as it is speculated that notes on the map may be from the hand of William Clark of the Lewis and Clark Expedition.

9. G. W. Colton and C. B. Colton, *Coulton's Montana, Idaho, and Wyoming* (New York: G. W. & C. B. Colton, 1876). Entered according to Act of Congress in the year 1876 in the office of the Librarian of Congress at

Washington. In Coulton's *General Atlas of the World* (New York: G. W. & C. B. Colton, 1881).

10. Map of Yellowstone and Missouri Rivers and Their Tributaries, explored by Capt. W. F. Raynolds and First Lieutenant H. E. Maynadier, 1859–1860. Revised and enlarged by Major G. L. Gillespie, U.S.A. Chief Engr. Military Division of the Missouri, 1876. (Washington, D.C.: U.S. War Department. Published by authority of the Secretary of War Office of the Chief of Engineers, U.S. Army, 1876); D. N. Smith, "Black Hills Map Including Nebraska and Part of Dakota, Wyoming, Colorado, and Kansas" (1876), National Park Service archives; V. L. Pirsson, "Description of the Character of the Igneous Rocks Making up Mateo Teepee and the Little Missouri Buttes," *American Journal of Science* 47 (1894), 341–346; I. C. Russell, "Igneous Intrusions in the Neighborhood of the Black Hills of Dakota," *Journal of Geology* 4 (1896); Thomas Jagger, *Laccoliths of the Black Hills.* Twenty-first Annual Report of the U.S. Geological Survey to the Secretary of the Interior (Washington, D.C.: U.S. Geological Survey, 1901) 3:163–303.

11. Memorandum, Directive to All Regional Directors (Washington, D.C.: U.S. Department of the Interior, National Park Service, 1991). This memorandum stated that "each park area with climbing activities should develop a climbing management plan based on Chapter 8.3 of the NPS Management Policies."

12. A presidential proclamation (no. 658; September 24, 1906–34 Stat. 3236) established the monument under authority of the newly passed Antiquities Act. The proclamation focuses on preserving the tower for its value to geologic science. No mention is made of preserving the tower for cultural reasons.

13. Hanson and Chirinos, *Ethnographic Overview and Assessment.*

14. Two groups were formed to protect sacred Indian sites. The first of these was the Medicine Wheel Alliance, which was spearheaded by a highly respected Northern Cheyenne elder, the late Bill Tall Bull. Another organization with a similar purpose was formed later and named the Medicine Wheel Coalition. The coalition differed from the alliance in that its members were sanctioned by the tribal councils of each tribe that joined the group. This factor was of some importance when it came time for the National Park Service to form the planning work group that would help design the climbing management plan for Devils Tower.

15. See Duane Suagee, "Tribal Voices in Historic Preservation: Sacred Landscapes, Cross-Cultural Bridges, and Common Ground," *Vermont Law Review* 21, no. 1 (1996), 164.

16. In so doing, the Park Service actions were in keeping with the most widely accepted principles of effective contemporary environmental conflict management practice. See generally Barbara Gray, "Framing and Re-Framing of Intractable Environmental Disputes," *Research on Negotiations in Organizations* 6 (1997), 163.

17. Hanson and Chirinos, *Ethnographic Overview and Assessment.* The Access Fund, a national organization representing the interests of rock climbers, was invited to sit at the work group table, as were the local chapter of the Sierra Club and the local county commissioner. All three of these groups agreed to become members of the work group for the climbing management plan. Agency officials were concerned that such a work group would be in violation of the Federal Advisory Committee Act, which was designed to prevent special interest groups from having too great an influence on government management decisions. Consequently, the work group was designed to ensure that members were reacting to agency proposals and not constructing alternative actions themselves. However, throughout the lengthy meetings during the planning process, the work group provided many important ideas that were seriously taken into consideration when the agency constructed the draft and final plan.

18. The superintendent at that time, Debbie Bird, traveled to offices of other tribes and organizations who were not themselves invited to become members of this work group although they were known to have a real interest in the issues. She sought concurrence from affiliated tribes with her decision to have the coalition represent tribal interest on the planning work group.

Deb Liggett, who succeeded Bird as superintendent, shepherded the climbing plan to its final form and eventually implemented it in the park. The first year of implementation of the voluntary climbing closure in 1996 resulted in an 85 percent compliance rate. Simply, this means that 85 percent of those climbers who normally would have climbed the tower in June did not.

19. American Indian work group members felt strongly that it was wrong to drill for bolts or in any way use intrusive equipment on the tower since it is viewed as damaging a sacred site. The climbers in the work group demonstrated newer equipment such as "friends"—a ridged, tapered piece of metal that is secured by wedging it within rock cracks without removing rock. Equipment like this is normally removed after each use.

20. The time taken to hold a number of meetings over a relatively long period of time anticipated the need for work group members to return to their constituents to discuss what they had heard and to get advice on how to proceed. Of course, all tribes are different, but as a general rule consultation with American Indian groups often involves the need for those representing tribes to "take the issues home" to discuss with other appropriate tribal members, including elders and chiefs. A consultation process that does not allow time for this may often be viewed as incomplete.

21. The final plan did call for mandatory closure of selected climbing routes during the nesting season of predatory birds that nest at the tower. This closure for natural resource reasons led one Indian work group member to comment that the National Park Service gave more weight to the protection of birds than it did to the protection of Indian heritage.

22. U.S. Department of the Interior, National Park Service, *Final Climbing*

Management Plan: Finding of No Significant Impact for Devils Tower National Monument ([Denver, Colo.] : U.S. Dept. of the Interior, National Park Service, Rocky Mountain Region, [1995]). For a recounting of administrative action on this matter and the contents of the plan, see *Bear Lodge Multiple Use Ass'n. v. Babbitt*, No. 96-CV-063-D (D. Wyo. June 8, 1996), Order Granting in Part and Denying in Part Plaintiffs' Motion for Preliminary Injunction, 1–3.

23. Ibid., 2.

24. Executive Order No. 13,007, 61 Fed. Reg. 26,771–26,772 (1996).

25. *Bear Lodge v. Babbitt*, 14.

26. U.S. Department of the Interior, National Park Service, *Devils Tower National Monument: Reconsideration of Certain Climbing Limitations in the Final Climbing Management Plan* (Wyo.: Office of the Superintendent, Devils Tower National Monument, November 26, 1996).

27. *Bear Lodge v. Babbitt*, 8.

28. *Badoni v. Higginson*, 638 F. 2d 172 (10th Cir. 1980).

29. *Bear Lodge v. Babbitt*; Transcript of Hearing on the Merits (hearing held April 18, 1997; transcript certified September 2, 1997).

30. Transcript of Hearing, 28–29.

31. *Lee v. Weisman*, 505 U.S. 577 (1992). In this decision, the Court found that the establishment clause was offended by the recitation of a Christian prayer at a high school graduation ceremony since it compelled non-Christian students to involuntarily engage in a sectarian ritual if they wished to participate in their own graduation.

32. Transcript of Hearing, 44–45.

33. Ibid., 78.

34. Ibid., 61–69. The case is *City of Albuquerque v. Browner*, Civ. No. 93–2315 (10th Cir. October 7, 1996).

35. Transcript of Hearing, 97.

36. Ibid., 100.

37. *Bear Lodge v. Babbitt*, Order No. 96-CV-063-D 2 F. Supp. 2d 1448 (D. Wyo. April 2, 1998).

38. Order at 17, 19; 2 F. Supp. 2d, at 1454–1457.

39. Corporation of the Presiding Bishop of the Church of Jesus Christ of Latter Day Saints v. Amos, 483 U.S. 327 (1987).

40. *Bear Lodge v. Babbitt*, 14.

41. *Bear Lodge Multiple Use Ass'n. v. Babbitt*, 175 F. 3d 814 (10th Cir. 1999).

42. Ibid., 818n. 6.

Chapter 7. Other Spaces, Other Cases

1. This history of U.S. public land law history is summarized in George Coggins, Charles Wilkinson, and John Leshy, *Federal Public Land and Resources Law*, 3d ed. (Westbury, N.Y.: Foundation Press, 1993), 45.

2. *Multiple Use and Sustained Yield Act of 1960,* U.S. Code, vol. 16, sec. 528 (2000).

3. *Federal Lands Policy and Management Act, U.S. Code,* vol. 43, sec. 1701 (8, 12) (2000).

4. Comments of U.S. Rep. Morris K. Udall (2d Dist. Ariz), advocating passage of the *American Indian Religious Freedom* Act [of which he was the author and chief sponsor], 124 Cong. Rec., 21,444,–21,445 (1978).

5. *Sequoyah v. Tennessee Valley Authority,* 620 F. 2d 1159 (6th Cir. 1980); *Badoni v. Higginson,* 638 F. 2d 172 (10th Cir. 1980).

6. *Wilson v. Block,* 708 F. 2d 735, 738 (D.C. Cir. 1982).

7. Ibid.

8. *California Wilderness Act of 1984,* Public Law 98-425, 98 Stat. 1619 (1984).

9. *Lyng v. Northwest Cemetery Protective Ass'n.,* 485 U.S. 439 (1988).

10. Ibid., 453.

11. *Mt. Graham Red Squirrel v. Madigan,* 954 F. 2d. 1441, 1446 (9th Cir. 1992).

12. Robert Williams, "Large Binocular Telescopes, Red Squirrel Piñatas, and Apache Sacred Mountains: Decolonizing Environmental Law in a Multicultural World," *West Virginia Law Review* 96 (1994), 1133–1164.

13. Ibid., 1161, 1163.

14. Ibid., 1163.

15. Ibid., 1164.

16. James Boggs and Fred Chapman, Medicine Mountain Cultural Landscape, Draft National Register Nomination (U.S. Forest Service, 1999). Report on file at the Bighorn National Forest Supervisor's Office, Sheridan, Wyoming.

17. Ibid.

18. See John Eddy, "Astronomical Alignment at the Bighorn Medicine Wheel," Science 184 (1974), 1035–1043.

19. Ibid.

20. Michael Milstein, "Medicine Wheel Remains Unprotected," *High Country News* 25, no. 9 (May 3, 1993). Online: http://www.hcn.org/1993/may03/dir/wr3.html.

21. *National Historic Preservation Act Amendments of 1992,* 16 USC § 470a, 470f.

22. Historic Preservation Plan for the Bighorn National Forest, 1999. Document on file in the Office of the Supervisor, Bighorn National Forest. This quotation from the plan may also be found on page 1 of *Wyoming Sawmills v. U.S. Forest Service,* Civil No. 99CV 031J (D. Wyo.), Defendants' Response to Plaintiff's Opening Brief, filed September 24, 1999.

23. Executive Order No. 13,007, 61 Fed. Reg. 26,771–26,772 (1996).

24. Ibid., 5.

25. *Wyoming Sawmills v. U.S. Forest Service,* Civ. No. 99 CV 031J (D. Wyo. 1999), "Complaint."

26. Ibid., "Defendant's Response to Plaintiff's Opening Brief."

27. Michael Milstein, "Medicine Wheel Debate Goes to Court," *Billings Gazette* (March 19, 1999).

28. As this book was going to press, the U.S. District Court for the District of Wyoming ruled for the Forest Service and against Wyoming Sawmills/Mountain State's Legal Foundation's claim that the management plan for the Bighorn Medicine Wheel site violated the establishment clause. In the words of Northern Arapaho tribal chairman Al Addison, "it is especially heartening to have a federal court give the Forest Service's careful planning process a seal of approval." Associated Press, "Ruling Favors Plan to Preserve Wheel," *Billings Gazette* [online], Dec. 21, 2001." http://www.billings gazette.com/index.php?display=/rednews//2001/12/21/build/wyoming/40-wheel.inc

29. Tom Graff, class lecture in environmental law, School of Law (Boalt Hall), University of California, Berkeley, spring 1981.

Chapter 8. Birthing the Woolly Cow

1. For a recounting of this context, see *Intertribal Bison Coop. [ITBC] v. Babbitt*, 25 F. Supp. 2d 1135, 1137 (D. Mt. 1998).

2. See *Fund for Animals v. Clark*, 27 F. Supp. 2d 8, 14 (D.D.C. 1998).

3. Riane Eisler, *The Chalice and the Blade* (New York: Harper and Row, 1988), 22.

4. David Kinsley, *Ecology and Religion: A Cross-Cultural Perspective* (Englewood Cliffs, N.J.: Prentice Hall, 1994), 119.

5. Peter Nabakov and Lawrence Loendorf, *Restoring a Presence: A Documentary Overview of Yellowstone National Park* (Washington, D.C.: U.S. Department of the Interior Technical Report, 1999).

6. lvin Josephy, *The Indian Heritage of America* (New York: Knopf, 1968), 58.

7. Joseph Brown, *The Sacred Pipe* (Norman: University of Oklahoma Press, 1953), 3.

8. 2 Cong. Rec. 2106–2109 (1874).

9. Tina Boradiansky, "Comment—Conflicting Values: The Religious Killing of Federally Protected Wildlife," *Natural Resources Journal* 30 (1990), 709–754.

10. Nabakov and Loendorf, *Restoring a Presence*.

11. Lawrence Friedman, *A History of American Law* (New York: Simon and Schuster, 1985), 107–115.

12. This traditional position is clearly explicated in the U.S. Supreme Court's 1896 decision in *Geer v. Connecticut*, 161 U.S. 519 (1896).

13. *Missouri v. Holland*, 252 U.S. 416 (1920).

14. *Bald Eagle Protection Act of 1940*, 54 Stat. 250 (1940), 16 USC § 668.

15. *Wild Free-Roaming Horses and Burros Act of 1971*, Public Law 92-195

(1971), 85 Stat. 649, 16 USC § 1331 et seq.; *Endangered Species Act of 1973,* Public Law 93-205 (1973), 87 Stat. 884, 16 USC § 1531 et seq.

16. *Kleppe v. New Mexico,* 426 U.S. 529 (1976).

17. *Endangered Species Act of 1973,* sec. 1331.

18. For example, *American Horse Protection Ass'n. v. Watt,* 694 F. 2d 1310 (D.C. Cir. 1982).

19. *Intertribal Bison Coop. v. Babbitt,* 25 F. Supp. 2d 1135, 1137 (D. Mt. 1998).

20. *Fund for Animals v. Lujan,* 794 F. Supp. 1015 (D. Mont. 1991).

21. *ITBC v. Babbitt,* 1137.

22. Ibid., 1136.

23. *Fund for Animals v. Lujan,* 1018.

24. Norman Cheville, Dale McCullough, and Lee Paulson, *Brucellosis in the Greater Yellowstone Area* (Washington, D.C.: National Research Council, 1998).

25. *Fund for Animals v. Clark,* 27 F. Supp. 2d 8 (D.D.C. 1998).

26. Renato Rosaldo, *Culture and Truth* (Boston: Beacon Press, 1989), 26.

27. See, for instance, Brown, Sacred Pipe, and Michael Steltenkamp, *Black Elk, Holy Man of the Oglala* (Norman: University of Oklahoma Press, 1993).

28. Nurit Bird-David, "Animism Revisited: Personhood, Environment, and Relational Epistemology," *Current Anthropology* 40 (1999), S67–S91.

29. Ibid., S89.

30. Joan Lowy, "Concern for Environment Gains Religious Significance," *Denver Rocky Mountain News,* February 7, 2000, 2A.

31. *Fund for Animals v. Clark,* 8.

32. Webster's Ninth New Collegiate Dictionary (Springfield, Mass.: Merriam-Webster, 1991), 265.

33. *Fund for Animals v. Clark,* 14.

34. Steven Torbit and Mark Heckert, "Challenges to Maintaining Wildlife in the Public Trust as a Free-Roaming Species: The Yellowstone Experience" (1999). Unpublished paper on file with the author.

35. *Greater Yellowstone Coalition et al. v. Babbitt,* 952 F. Supp. 1435, 1445 (D. Mont. 1996).

36. *ITBC v. Babbitt,* 1140.

37. Comments of Fred DuBray, Herd Manager, Cheyenne River Sioux Tribe, Convocation of the Inter-Tribal Bison Cooperative, Denver, Colorado, February, 1999.

Chapter 9. Conservation and Cultural Renewal

1. Joanna Macy, *World as Lover, World as Self* (Berkeley, Calif.: Parallax Press, 1991), 198–205.

2. Ibid., 202.

3. Dennis Tedlock and Barbara Tedlock, eds., *Teachings from the American Earth: Indian Religion and Philosophy* (New York: Liveright, 1975), xv.

4. See generally Roderick Nash, *The Rights of Nature: A History of Environmental Ethics* (Madison: University of Wisconsin Press, 1989).

5. See Joseph Des Jardins, *Environmental Ethics* (Belmont, Calif.: Wadsworth, 1993), 21.

6. Peter Wenz, *Environmental Ethics Today* (New York: Oxford University Press, 2001), 126.

7. David Suzuki and Peter Knudtson, *Wisdom of the Elders: Sacred Native Stories of Nature* (New York: Bantam Books, 1992), 120–123.

8. *Missouri v. Holland,* 252 U.S. 416 (1920).

9. *Bald Eagle Protection Act,* 54 Stat. 250 (1940), 16 USC § 668.

10. *Free-Roaming Horses and Burros Act,* Public Law 92-195 (1971), 85 Stat. 649, 16 USC § 1331 et seq.

11. "(a) Findings. The Congress finds and declares that (1) various species of fish, wildlife, and plants in the United States have been rendered extinct as a consequence of economic growth and development untempered by adequate concern and conservation; (2) other species of fish, wildlife, and plants have been so depleted in numbers that they are in danger of or threatened with extinction; (3) these species of fish, wildlife, and plants are of esthetic, ecological, educational, historical, recreational, and scientific value to the Nation and its people; (4) the United States has pledged itself as a sovereign state in the international community to conserve to the extent practicable the various species of fish or wildlife and plants facing extinction." *Endangered Species Act,* Public Law 93-205 (1973), 87 Stat. 884, 16 USC § 1531 et seq.

12. *TVA v. Hill,* 437 U.S. 153, 178 (1978).

13. Aldo Leopold, *A Sand County Almanac* (New York: Oxford University Press, 1949), 230–231.

14. *United States v. Dion,* 476 U.S. 734, 745–746 (1986).

15. *U.S. v. Billie,* 667 F. Supp. 1485 (D-Fla. 1987).

16. See Charles Wilkinson, "Symposium: Indian Law into the Twenty-first Century: The Role of Bilateralism in Fulfilling the Federal–Tribal Relationship—The Tribal Rights–Endangered Species Secretarial Order," *Washington Law Review* 72 (1997), 1063–1107.

17. Remarks of Bruce Babbitt, Washington, D.C. (June 5, 1997); quoted and cited in ibid., 1086.

18. *Dion,* 741–742.

19. Anthony Ramirez, "Die Like an Eagle: Indian Rights vs. a National Sanctuary," *New York Times,* November 19, 2000, P-16.

20. The Hopi Tribe, "Press Release: Hopi Denied Access to Religious Sites by Wupatki National Monument Officials" (Flagstaff, Ariz. Initial Date of Release: June 29, 1999). Accessed online January 31, 2002 (http://www. nau.edu/~hcpo-p/current/pressreleases/archive/eagles.htm); interview with Sam Henderson, superintendent, Wupatki National Monument, Flagstaff, Arizona, January 10, 2001; Hopi Tribe, "Press Release."

21. 36 CFR § 2.1 (c)(2)(d) (2001).

22. Henderson iterview.

23. Ibid.

24. Ibid.

25. *Metcalf v. Daley,* 214 F.3d 1135 (9th Cir. 2000).

26. Ibid., 1137.

27. Ibid., 1138.

28, Ibid., 1139.

29. Courtenay Thompson, "Renewed Tradition Heads into the Unknown," *Portland Oregonian,* October 1, 1998.

30. Ibid.

31. Deborah Wang, "Tribe Harpoons Gray Whale," *ABCNEWS.com.* Story dated May 17, 1999; site accessed 1/5/01.

32. Peggy Anderson, "Makah Hunt Draws Attention," *[Portland] Oregonian,* August 28, 1998.

33. *Metcalf v. Daley,* 214 F.3d 1135 (9th Cir. 2000).

34. Keith Johnson, "An Open Letter to the Public from the President of the Makah Whaling Commission." Excerpts appeared in the *Seattle Times* op-ed page on August 23, 1998. Text of the letter in its entirety accessed via the *Native Americans and the Environment* Web site, 1/5/01.

35. Frank Crosswhite, "The Annual Saguaro Harvest and Crop Cycle of the Papago, with Reference to Ecology and Symbolism," *Desert Plants* 2(1): 2–61, at 7 (Tucson, AZ: Published by the University of Arizona for the Boyce Thompson Southwestern Arboretum, spring, 1980).

36. Ibid.

37. *Saguaro National Park Establishment Act of 1994,* Public Law 103-364 (1994), 108 Stat. 367 16 USC § 410zz–1.

38. Interview with Stanley "Steamer" Lawhead, resource manager, Western Unit, Saguaro National Park, March 2000.

39. Dean Suagee, "The Cultural Heritage of American Indian Tribes and the Preservation of Biological Diversity," *Arizona State Law Journal* 31 (1999), 483, 517–518.

40. Ibid. 517–518.

41. *Wyoming Farm Bureau Federation v. Babbitt,* 987 F. Supp. 1349, 1372–1376 (D. Wyo. 1997).

42. *Wyoming Farm Bureau Federation et al. v. Babbitt,* 199 F. 3d 1224 (10th Cir. 2000).

43. *City of Albuquerque v. Browner,* 97 F. 3d 415, 419–420 (10th Cir. 1996).

44. Ibid., 428.

45. Ibid., 429.

Chapter 10. Pacific Rim Variations

1. *Calder v. Attorney General of British Columbia,* [1973] S.C.R. 313 (Canada).

2. *Guerin et al. v. R.* [1984] 2 C.S.R. 335 (Canada).

3. *Constitution Act of 1982,* sec. 35.

4. Quoted in Charles Marecic, "Nunavut Territory: Aboriginal Govern-ing in the Canadian Regime of Governance," *American Indian Law Review* 24 (1999/2000) 275-295, 279.

5. Ibid., 278.

6. Ibid.

7. Ibid., 282.

8. Royal Commission on Aboriginal Peoples, *Report of the Royal Com-mission on Aboriginal Peoples: Perspectives and Realities,* vol. 2 (Ottawa: The Commission, 1996), 430.

9. Marecic, "Nunavut Territory," 278 n. 21.

10. Ibid.

11. Lloyd Burton, "Indigenous Peoples and Environmental Policy in the Common Law Nation-States of the Pacific Rim: Sovereignty, Survival, and Sustainability," *Colorado Journal of International Environmental Law and Policy* (1998 Yearbook), 136, 142.

12. *Mabo v. Queensland (Mabo II)* [1992] 107 A.L.R. 1 (Austl.).

13. Ibid., 28–29.

14. *Racial Discrimination Act (Mabo I)* [1988] 83 A.L.R. 14 (Austl.).

15. Australian Cultural Network, "Uluru and Bald Rock: Australian Monoliths," www.acn.net.au/articles/1999/06, accessed January 15, 2001.

16. Greg Roberts, "Whose Land Rights Rank Highest?" *Bulletin,* November 15, 1994, 15.

17. Ibid.

18. Australian Minister for the Environment, "Uluru-Kata Tjuta National Park Finalist in National Reconciliation Award" (Press release, May 27, 1997), www.environment.gov.au/minister/env/97, accessed January 15, 2001.

19. Australian National Commission for UNESCO, "Aboriginal People Recognised in World Heritage Award" (News Bulletin, July 1995), www.dfat.gov.au:80/intorgs/unesco, accessed January 15, 2001.

20. Claudia Orange, *The Treaty of Waitangi* (Wellington, N.Z.: Bridget Williams Books, 1987), 32–91.

21. Ibid.

22. Christopher Milne, *Handbook of Environmental Law* (Wellington, NZ: Royal Forest and Bird Society, 1992), 38.

23. *Huakina Development Trust v. Waikato Valley Authority,* [1987] 2 N.Z.L.R. 188 (N.Z.).

24. *New Zealand Maori Council v. Attorney General,* [1992] 2. N.Z.L.R. 576 (N.Z.).

25. Resource Management Act, part 2, sec. 5.

26. Milne, *Handbook of Environmental Law,* 38.

27. See Lloyd Burton and Chris Cocklin, "Water Resource Management

and Environmental Policy Reform in New Zealand: Regionalism, Alloca-
tion, and Indigenous Relations—Part II," *Colorado Journal of International
Environmental Law and Policy* 7, no. 2 (1996), 331–372.

28. Hugh Barr, "DOC Advocates Treaty Land Grab," *Federated Moun-
tain Clubs Bulletin* 15 (1994), 15; Symposium: "The Treaty and the Estate,"
Royal Forest and Bird (Wellington, New Zealand: Royal Forest and Bird
Society, 1994).

29. New Zealand Ministry for the Environment, "Draft: Towards a Set
of Principles for Effective Collaborative Management Strategies" (2000).
Unpublished report on file with the author.

30. Burton and Cocklin, "Water Resource Management," Part 2, 363–373.

31. L. Fuchs, *Hawaii Pono: An Ethnic and Political History,* cited in *Rice
v. Cayetano,* 528 U.S. 495 (2000), at 500.

32. *Rice v. Cayetano,* 500.

33. 30 Stat. 750 (1898).

34. Hawaiian Organic Act of April 30, 1900, 31 Stat. 159 (1900).

35. *Rice v.Cayetano,* 1051.

36. *Hawaiian Homes Commission Act,* Act of July 9, 1921, chap. 42, 42
Stat. 108 (1921).

37. Hawaiian Constitution, art. 12, sec. 5.

38. See chapter 4

39. *Rice v. Cayetano,* p. 1058.

40. 107 Stat. 1510 (1993); cited in *Rice v. Cayetano* at 533.

41. Interview with Jim Martin, superintendent, Hawaii Volcanoes
National Park, July 20, 2000.

42. Paul Chaat Smith, "How Do You Define Sacred?" *High Country
News* [online] 29, no. 10 (May 26, 1997), http://www.hcn.org/servlets/
hcn.Article?article_id=3427.

43. Group 70 International, *Mauna Kea Science Reserve Master Plan
Draft #4—Prepared for the University of Hawaii* (November, 1999), p. VI-2.

44. Ibid., IX-44.

45. Ibid., VIII-7.

46. Ibid., VIII–1.

47. Ibid., VIII-11–VIII-23.

48. Nelson Ho, "Mauna Kea Plan's Defects Mean Long Battles Ahead,"
Hawaii Island Journal (July 16–31, 2000), 5. Mr. Ho is conservation chair of
the Sierra Club's Hawaii Chapter.

49. *Master Plan,* V-5.

50. Only those rituals and experiences are described here that seem
appropriate to telling this story in this context and that my friend and host
also agreed were fitting to share. As I had learned from conversations with
other native Hawaiian cultural interpreters, there are both strong similarities
and some divergences in the understandings that various cultural interpreters
have been taught. Rather than get into doctrinal disputes, however, most of

those with whom I spoke simply acknowledge that variations exist and focus instead on the similarities.

Chapter 11. Coming Home

1. *Journal of Meriwether Lewis,* Monday, August 12, 1805. Accessed via Public Broadcasting Web site, http://www.pbs.org/cgi-registry/lewisand clark/journals.cgi. Accessed February 28, 2002.

2. Aldo Leopold, *A Sand County Almanac* (New York: Oxford University Press, 1949), 131–132.

3. Jack Kerouac, *The Dharma Bums* (New York: Viking, 1958), 78.

4. Ibid., 191.

5. See Rick Fields, *How the Swans Came to the Lake: A Narrative History of Buddhism in America* (Boulder, Colo.: Shambala Press, 1981), 70–82.

6. Robert Aitken, *The Mind of Clover* (San Francisco: North Point Press, 1984), 136–139.

7. "Sattipatthana Sutta (The Foundations of Mindfulness)," in Bhikku Nanamoli and Bhikku Bodhi, trans., *The Middle Length Discourses of the Buddha—A New Translation of the Majjhima Nikaya* (Boston: Wisdom Publications, 1995), 145.

8. "Culasunnata Sutta (Shorter Discourse on Voidness)," in Bhikku Nanamoli and Bhikku Bodhi, trans., *The Middle Length Discourses of the Buddha—A New Translation of the Majjhima Nikaya* (Boston: Wisdom Publications, 1995), 965–966.

9. Stephen Mitchell, trans., *Tao Te Ching* (New York: Harper and Row, 1988), 15.

10. J. Baird Callicott, *Earth's Insights: A Multicultural Survey of Ecological Ethics from the Mediterranean Basin to the Australian Outback* (Berkeley: University of California Press, 1994).

11. Ibid., 19.

12. Peter Wenz, *Environmental Ethics Today* (New York: Oxford University Press, 2001) 228.

13. Ibid. These quotes from church policy statements given in Wenz are drawn from another secondary source: Roger Gottlieb, ed., *This Sacred Earth: Religion, Nature, Environment* (New York: Routledge, 1996).

14. *Coalition on Environment and Jewish Life* Web site, http://www.coejl. org/about/, accessed February 28, 2002.

15. *Midrash Ecclesiastes Rabbah,* 7:13. Cited in ibid.

16. *Lyng v. Northwest Cemetery Protective Association,* 485 U.S. 439 (1988).

17. *Employment Division, Oregon Dept. of Human Resources v. Smith,* 494 U.S. 872 (1990).

18. Ibid., 879–890.

19. *Religious Freedom Restoration Act,* Public Law 103-141 (1993), 107 Stat. 1488, 5 USC § 504.

20. *City of Boerne v. Flores,* 521 U.S. 507; 117 S. Ct. 2157; 138 L. Ed. 2d 624 (1997).

21. *American Indian Religious Freedom Act Amendments of 1994,* Public Law 103-344 (1994), 108 Stat. 3125, 42 USC § 1996a.

22. *Bear Lodge Multiple Use Ass'n. v. Babbitt,* 175 F. 3d 814 (10th Cir. 1999).

23. Cathy Robbins, "Monumental Chaos: An Urban Explosion Splinters a Sacred Landscape," *High Country News* 31 no. 20 (October 25, 1999), 1.

24. Ibid.

25. "Open Letter to the American Religious Community," cited at the Web site for the National Religious Partnership for the Environment (NRPE), http://www.nrpe.org, accessed May 15, 2000. In part, the letter reads, "Many of us have had profound experiences of awe and reverence before the universe. We recognize that what is regarded as sacred is most likely to be treated with respect. Efforts to safeguard planetary environment need to be infused with a vision of the sacred and as a universal moral priority."

26. Ibid.

27. "The Center for Biological Diversity and Christians Caring for Creation have filed a formal notice of intent to sue the U.S. Fish & Wildlife Service for refusing to designate and protect 'critical habitat' for 12 species ranging from Minnesota to Puerto Rico to Guam " *Enviros, Christians to Sue for Habitat Protection from Minnesota to Micronesia: 12 Species at Risk,* Center for Biological Diversity, Bio-Diversity Alert #221, http://www.endangeredearth.org/alerts/result-m.asp?index=715, accessed January 22, 2000. "Several dozen Christian and Jewish religious leaders converged upon Capitol Hill this week to call for an end to the timber sales program in national forests, and a 'halt to logging in ancient forests throughout Creation.' Their visit climaxed Wednesday with a meeting at the White House, during which they urged that President Bill Clinton issue an Executive Order to end logging on federal public lands. The coalition, known as the Religious Campaign for Forest Conservation, represents nearly every Protestant denomination, Catholic and Jewish leaders. On Monday, they held a prayer breakfast with Interior Secretary Bruce Babbitt, and have since visited over 100 Congressional offices, and met with Forest Service chief Mike Dombeck and staff." Lycos Environmental News Service, February 4, 1999: *Christian Forest Conservationists Go to Washington.* http://ens.lycos.com/ens/feb99/1999L-02-04-09.html, accessed February 28, 2002.

28. Joan Lowy, "Concern for Environment Gains Religious Significance," *Denver Rocky Mountain News,* February 7, 2000, 2A.

29. Bruce Barcott, "For God So Loved the World," *Outside Magazine* (March 2001).

30. Leslie Wirpsa, "Culture Complements Faith in Chiapas: A 'Pioneer' Church Celebrates Indigenous History and Values," *National Catholic Reporter* 30 no. 15 (February 11, 1994), 9.

31. National Conference of Catholic Bishops/U.S. Catholic Conference, *Renewing the Earth,* http://www.nccbuscc.org/sdwp/ejp/bishopsstatement. htm. Accessed February 28, 2002.

32. Wirpsa, "Culture Complements Faith," 9.

33. Lawrence Iliff, "Church of the Indians: Many in Chiapas Fear That Commitment to the Dispossessed Is Threatened," Religion [section], *Dallas Morning News,* January 29, 2000.

34. "Mexican Bishop Responds to Attacks against the Church and the Holy Father and Clears up Pope's Remarks on 'Indian Theology'," *Daily Catholic* 10 no. 25 (February 5–7, 1999).

35. Correspondence attached to deposition filed in Civ. no. 91–1350-PHX-WPC (D. Ariz. April 6, 1992). For more background on this case, see Robert Williams, "Environmental Justice: Large Binocular Telescopes, Red Squirrel Piñatas, and Apache Sacred Mountains: Decolonizing Environmental Law In A Multicultural World," *West Virginia Law Review* 96 (1994) 1133.

36. Jim Robbins, "Holy Water: The Catholic Church Seeks to Restore the Columbia River and the Church's Relevance to the Natural World," *High Country News* [online] 32, no. 17 (September 11, 2000), http://www. endangeredearth.org/alerts/result-m.asp?index=715 .

37. Ibid.

38. Ibid.

39. Margot Adler, *Drawing Down the Moon,* rev. ed. (New York: Penguin, 1986), 45.

40. Ibid., 42.

41. Ibid., 416.

42. *Congressional Record—Senate,* September 26, 1985, p. S12174; quoted in Adler, *Drawing down the Moon,* 45.

43. For instance, in *Van Koten v. Family Health Management Inc.,* 955 F. Supp. 898 (N.D. Ill. 1997), the court upheld the Equal Employment Opportunity Commission's interpretation of Title VII of the Civil Rights Act to encompass "sincerely held beliefs and practices" as applying to Wicca. Most federal court cases ruling on Wicca's religious validity have actually been in the context of the (more limited) free exercise rights of prisoners; they have all ruled Wicca to be a religion and acknowledged plaintiff prisoners' rights to practice it, but have also upheld prison officials' authority to limit modes of practice and possession of ritual objects in the interests of maintaining prison order and security. One case dealt extensively with the definitional question in the criminal context (i.e., whether the Euro-American defendant could escape prosecution by claiming an illegally possessed drug to be a sacrament); that is *U.S. v. Meyers,* 906 F. Supp. 1494 (D-Wyo. 1995).

44. Adler, *Drawing Down the Moon,* 421–426.

45. Ibid., 162.

46. Armin Geertz, *The Invention of Prophecy: Continuity and Meaning*

in Hopi Indian Religion (Berkeley, Calif.: University of California Press, 1994), 307.

47. Marilyn Ferguson, *The Aquarian Conspiracy: Personal and Social Transformation in the 1980s* (Los Angeles: Tarcher, 1980), 29.

48. David Toolan, "Harmonic Convergences and All That: New Age Spirituality," *Cross Currents* 46, no. 3 (1996), 369.

49. Ibid.

50. Elizabeth Manning, "There's a Notion That Indians Practicing Their Religions Are Less Than Religious," *High Country News* 29, no. 10 (May 26, 1997), quoting Charlotte Black Elk.

51. Geertz, *Invention of Prophecy,* 222.

52. See Philip Deloria, *Playing Indian* (New Haven, Conn.: Yale University Press, 1998).

53. Smith, "How Do You Define Sacred?"

54. Ibid.

55. The quote is from a Forest Service regulation: 64 *Fed. Reg.* 48,959 (1999), as upheld in *U.S. v. Linick,* 195 F. 3d 538 (9th Cir. 1999).

56. U.S. Department of the Interior, *The National Parks: Index 1997–1999* (Washington, D.C.: Government Printing Office, 2000)

Chapter 12. The National Commons as Sacred Space

1. Edward. Wilson, *Biophilia* (Cambridge: Harvard University Press, 1984), as quoted in David Suzuki and Peter Knudtson, *Wisdom of the Elders: Sacred Native Stories of Nature* (New York: Bantam Books, 1992), 102, 115.

2. *Guidelines for Evaluating and Documenting Traditional Cultural Properties* (Bulletin 38) (Washington, D.C.: National Park Service, Interagency Resources Division); *National Historic Preservation Act Amendments of 1992,* 16 USC § 470a, 470f.s A critical element of this bulletin is the set of guidelines to provide a measure of protection for sites that are of contemporary importance to living communities. Bulletin 38 was the first serious attempt to deal with properties like Devils Tower, which are seen as having cultural importance to existing ethnic groups — beyond its value to the earth sciences.

3. Executive Order No. 13,007, 61 *Fed. Reg.* 26,771–26,772 (1996).

4. See William Ury, Jeanne Brett, and Stephen Goldberg, *Getting Disputes Resolved: Designing Systems to Cut the Costs of Conflict* (San Francisco: Jossey-Bass, 1988).

5. Of course, this is not to imply that other federal land management planning statutes do not also apply, including public participation processes either mandated or recommended in their implementation.

6. Rebecca French, "From Yoder to Yoda: Models of Traditional, Modern, and Postmodern Religion in U.S. Constitutional Law," *Arizona Law Review* 41 (1999), 49.

7. Ibid., 82.

8. *Walsh v. Tax Com of City of New York*, 397 U.S. 664, 669 (1970), quoted in Peyote Way, 922 F. 2d 1210 (5th Cir. 1991), 1217.

9. Ibid.

10. *Rupert v. Director, U.S. Fish and Wildlife Service*, 957 F. 2d 32 (1st Cir. 1992), at 35.

11. *Bear Lodge Multiple Use Ass'n. v. Babbitt*, No. 96-CV-063-D, Opening Brief of Plaintiffs, 25.

12. James Hunter, *Culture Wars: The Struggle to Define America* (New York: Basic Books, 1991). For a treatise dealing exclusively with the assertion of rights aspect of this phenomenon, see Mary Ann Glendon, *Rights Talk* (New York: Free Press, 1991).

13. Rhys Willliams, *Cultural Wars in American Politics* (New York: Aldine de Gruyter, 1997), 284–293.

14. James Hunter, "Reflections on the Culture Wars Hypothesis," in James Nolan, ed., *American Culture Wars: Current Contests and Future Prospects* (Charlottesville: University Press of Virginia, 1996), 249.

15. William Hoynes, "Public Television and the Culture Wars," in James Nolan, ed., *American Culture Wars: Current Contests and Future Prospects* (Charlottesville: University Press of Virginia, 1996), 61.

16. Jill Norgren and Serena Nanda, *American Cultural Pluralism and Law*, 2d ed.(Westport, Conn.: Praeger, 1996), 7.

17. Dennis Tedlock and Barbara Tedlock, Teaching From the American Earth (New York: Liveright, 1975), preface.

18. David Wagoner, "Lost," *Traveling Light: Collected and New Poems* (Champaign, Illinois: University of Illinois Press, 1999).

Index